SCAM-PROOF YOUR ASSETS

GUARDING AGAINST WIDESPREAD DECEPTION

GARRETT SUTTON, ESQ.

FOREWORD BY ROBERT KIYOSAKI

RDA PRESS

Published by RDA Press

Rich Dad Advisors, B-I Triangle, CASHFLOW Quadrant and other Rich Dad marks are registered trademarks of CASHFLOW Technologies, Inc.

RDA Press LLC
15170 N. Hayden Road
Scottsdale, AZ 85260
480-998-5400

Printed in the United States of America

First Edition: October 2020

ISBN: 978-1-947588-14-1

Visit RichDad.com and CorporateDirect.com

102020

Contents

Foreword

In a post-COVID-19 world, people are uncertain, unsettled, and desperate for money. Many have gotten a lot smarter when it comes to lies, cheating, and stealing.

If high-profile Twitter accounts can be massively hacked, then who is safe?

Garrett Sutton is my personal asset protection attorney. He has saved me tens of millions by protecting me and my companies from financial predators... *very smart* financial predators.

In this post-COVID-19 world, no one is safe.

Locking your doors and windows will not keep predators out. Our lives are porous. Predators have millions of schemes to worm their way into your wallet—and your life.

Here are a few scams that I almost fell for:

Scam #1: Computer Virus

"You have been infected! Download antivirus X right now to protect your computer!"

I am old. I know little to nothing about computers, so I panicked when I received this one. Fortunately, my staff is younger and more tech-savvy than I am. They just laughed and told me to ignore it.

Scam #2: Presidential Election Scam

*During the 2016 Presidential election, **Cambridge Analytica Ltd (CA)** was a British political consulting firm that combined misappropriation of* *digital assets, data mining, data brokerage and data analysis with strategic communication during the electoral processes.*

This was big news, but (as I've mentioned...) I am an old guy, and I had no idea what they were talking about.

Scam #3: Nigerian Damsel in Distress

The offer went like this:

Dear Beloved Friend:

I know this letter will come as a surprise to you but permit me of my desire to go into business relationship with you. I have heard you are an honorable and trustworthy person...

She then tells me that her father was murdered and that $4.2 million is tied up in some bank. Her offer is 20% of that $4.2 million, *if* she can transfer the $4.2 million into my bank account.

I may be old, but I am not that stupid.

Scam #4: Free Motorboat

I almost fell for this one. The guy was really good. He should get a real job. The problem was, I did not need a motorboat. Otherwise I might have become another sucker falling prey to his scheme.

Why do I recommend this book by Garrett Sutton? There are a few reasons, actually. Garrett is a smart guy who brings his expertise and "A student" research and writing skills to every project he undertakes. Equally important: The crooks today are getting smarter. So we need to get smarter, too. And Garrett's book *Scam-Proof Your Assets* can help us all do that.

Be safe. Get smarter.

Robert Kiyosaki

Introduction

I am glad you are reading this book. The world is now awash with massive amounts of misinformation. Who and what can you believe? Especially when the deceptions are so deviously crafted. You ask yourself: "How do they know me so well?" You have to stand back and realize that much of this deception is for the express purpose of stealing your assets.

Is your life improved by technology when constant vigilance is now required to benefit from it? Everyone will have their own answer. But, as everyone now knows, you must forever keep your guard up to stay protected. This book is intended to help you in that effort.

In my other books, I have used mainly fictional case studies to illustrate and flesh out the legal principles being discussed. *Scam Proof Your Assets* is different in this regard. All of the stories you will encounter ahead are true. All of the resulting wreckage – lost savings, shame and embarrassment, suicidal feelings – are the very real consequences of falling prey to the scam artists in our midst.

While a popular term, let's be clear that scam artists are not "artists" in any positive way. In truth, they are among the worst criminals we face. Invisible in many cases and, unfortunately, with impunity, they prey upon millions of us and reek both financial and personal destruction throughout society.

Let's get your guard up...

Chapter One

Three Magic Latin Words

What if I could provide you with three magic Latin words that would scam proof your life forever? Would you dare risk losing out on such a simple means for gaining a powerful edge over a cruel world populated by evil, black hatted cyber criminals?

Now, of course, there is a small cost to this. Nothing so supreme is ever free. But in paying the money you are going to be released from this surge of harmful, heinous frauds that now exist everywhere in our daily lives and will only continue to proliferate. You are going to affirmatively protect your assets. You are going to be dominant for this.

You are certain to be impressed with the testimonials I will provide from real people whose lives have been immeasurably improved by the scam proofing techniques available only to a select few who act right now. You are certain to feel keenly positive that these techniques will work because I have given you every impressive reason through a long litany of positive and empowering declarations to feel confident in the process and in the highly preeminent and credentialed people who have carefully and with great effort created this unique and select system.

Fearful that if you don't pay the $497 right now the offer may be taken from you, leaving you to suffer a dangerous life of hateful hoaxes, you get out your credit card. The call center operator says you are making a very wise choice.

It seems like forever but in less than a week, the scam proof package arrives. The three magic Latin words are found inside a double sealed envelope. The words are so powerfully and obtusely Latin that you don't recognize even one root variation. These are serious words. You are warned not to share this mighty mantra of magic words with anyone.

A link to a song is provided. At the exact midpoint of Bachman-Turner Overdrive's "Takin' Care of Business" you will snap your fingers and loudly chant the three magic Latin words.

Miraculously, your life is now free of scams!

Except it is not.

While two negatives may equal a positive in multiplication and division, you can't rid yourself of scams with another scam.

Instead, you need to constantly work at it.

Work? I have to work?

Of course you do. You work to create assets. Why shouldn't you have to work to protect them?

Consider the landscape of Europe. There are castles everywhere. These fortifications were built to defend and protect assets. In the grand scheme of things, you've got it relatively easy. You don't have to cut and lift giant stones into place. You just need to think clearly.

Critical Thinking

Access to information is now incredibly easy, and increasing all the time. This is beneficial, but with the good, always comes the bad. And when the good involves technologies that dramatically shift societal norms, the bad can be big and bad. A big bad we face is the amount of misinformation flowing into every corner of our lives. This pervasive deception has hurt millions of people in various ways. This book will illustrate not only the financial loss – billions and billions every year – but the emotional, and even spiritual hardship resulting from massive misinformation campaigns.

As misinformation spreads, truth retreats. As people only believe in the talking points of their own narrative, truth retreats. People on both sides will challenge you for even considering any other narrative but their virtuous own. Without free discussion, truth retreats.

And so, in this new world it is even harder to know what is true. Again, you must work at it. You must be critical in your thinking.

The average person makes 35,000 conscious decisions every day. Clearly, each of us is doing a lot of thinking.

But what if you could improve your decision making? All sorts of benefits would flow to you. Here are some of them:

1. Better relationships – You would be more open minded and able to understand others' point of view. You would also be better able to avoid those bad choices in certain people who are just trying to take advantage of you.

2. Happier Life – With better decision making you can avoid the negative thinking and limiting beliefs that hold you back. The quality of both your thoughts and decisions leads to a happier life.

3. Better Career – Critical thinking is one of the most sought-after skills in our new and evolving work place. Employers want those who are problem solvers, information analyzers and creative thinkers.

4. Scam-Proof – You're reading this book to avoid the widespread effort by criminals to get at your assets. Critical thinking will bar the bad guys from your domain.

So what is critical thinking? It's hard to improve on something if you can't define it. The Foundation for Critical Thinking defines it as:

"Critical thinking is the intellectually disciplined process of actively and skillfully conceptualizing, applying, analyzing, synthesizing, and/ or evaluating information gathered from, or generated by, observation, experience, reflection, reasoning, or communication, as a guide to belief and action."

I don't mean to be critical, but that is too much thinking. Let's use a more popular and easier definition:

"Deciding what's true and what you should do."

In deciding what is true, you've got to do more than let the information into your most important real estate, that space between your ears. You've got to question it at the welcome mat. You've got to think about it and decide whether or not to even let it in.

As humans, we are primitively wired to be protective of our property. As humans now living with hand held sorcerer's stones (aka smart phones), we must rely even more on this ancient human instinct. We have to pull the welcome mat back before allowing any information in. You must learn to screen it.

If you can do that right now, you are halfway there. Deciding what is true, and only letting that information in which you believe to be true, is the most important component for scam proofing your assets. This takes some effort, but if you start doing that right now, you will be ahead of the game. Don't wait until you finish this book. Do it now.

The next step is analyzing and considering the information you initially accept, and doing your own investigation (due diligence) into the matter. Often, information appears to be credible, but upon investigation you will find out that it is not. To quote a former president for the umpteenth time: "Trust but verify".

Know that sometimes you will do the due diligence and still get it wrong. Warren Buffet's Berkshire Hathaway, Inc. is widely considered one of the greatest investment houses of all time. They are immaculate in their due diligence. And yet they lost $340 million in a California company called DC Solar. In a massive Ponzi scheme (we'll meet Mr. Ponzi ahead) over $1 billion was lost by otherwise sophisticated investors, including Warren Buffet.

There are many scams competing for your assets. Don't be embarrassed if you get it wrong. It happens to everyone. Still, by engaging in critical thinking in all facets of your life, most of the time you will get it right. When it comes to scams, critical thinking will protect your assets. You will have your guard up and that is a good posture to take in this devious world.

In this book, I'll discuss the wide range of rip-offs that exist, from those silly bait-and-hook emails, to long cons calculated to decimate financial portfolios and shatter lives. I'll share stories of real-life scams, from health care hoaxes promising miracle cures and dramatic weight loss to email phishing scams, imposter schemes that turn you into a sucker with one phone call, real estate rip-offs, and complex Wall Street pyramid schemes cleverly constructed to make millions with your money. I'll show you how these schemes have been practiced on educated, rational people—and examine what made those victims susceptible to trickery. Plus, I'll offer practical advice for protecting yourself from falling prey to scam artists.

Critical thinking involves seeing patterns. In this book, by reading the case studies, you will see the patterns of the scam – greed and fear, confidence and trust, "expert" positioning and charm as manipulation. Remembering these patterns will become your red flags for future dealings. The scams will change and evolve but the patterns are constant. Starting now, the flags go up and so does your antennae. You will react with skepticism – a healthy skepticism. And you will protect your assets.

We have talked about Critical Thinking, sometimes referred to as CT. Scholarly articles have argued that CT should be introduced into the school system at an early age. Many educators argue for important changes and discussion ensues.

In this context CT sounds uninspiring. Institutions and scholarly articles and debates about how to do it. Yawn.

So to bring this into the real, we need to take it down a notch. We need every person who cares about their and our collective future to understand it in these brief, bold and non-political terms:

People are actively deceiving us at an unprecedented rate.

People are taking advantage of the dumbing down of America to take our assets.

Which is why all these scams are working. Too many are too unprepared to think clearly. Our education system is partly at fault for this surge in scams. Teaching to the test does not lead to critical thought. And yet, as we will see in this book, many highly educated people are also scammed. The school system can't be blamed for not addressing a key factor in such cases: Very Large Egos. CT loses in that matchup.

But no matter the cause, the bigger issue is that it is not right for all these criminals to get away with such widespread financial mayhem. It is not natural for so many to be swindled by so few. Our current shadow crime wave is unparalleled in human history. Could a barbarian scam a Roman from across the frontier? Could Spain have scammed the Aztecs without invading? Can an anonymous hacker from anywhere now scam anyone on earth with just three clicks of a mouse?

And yet the government does next to nothing about it. Little effort is put into going after the criminals who steal billions of dollars from average, hardworking Americans every year. The same is true for entrepreneurs. If a business owner gets hacked, the government penalizes the business owner. The business is at fault for not properly defending against the criminal. The business gets penalized and the criminal goes free.

This is not healthy. The longer the government allows these black hats (more on them later) to roam free, the more time they have to develop skills to take down the government. As we will learn in Chapter 13, these threats are extremely serious, even existential, and must be fought back against.

But we need to frame our response properly. To get away from the academics of CT, we need to take it down a full letter. C becomes B and T becomes S. And that is what we focus on: BS.

You need to cry BS now and then. When that information comes in, and you have analyzed it and it doesn't make sense, you need to cry "Bullshit!" (Pardon my French, but we really are fighting on the beaches of Normandy here.)

We need to go back to what many cherish as the BS Detector. Those are your three magic words: Bull Shit Detector. If it doesn't make sense, it doesn't feel right and it's too good to be true, the BS Detector kicks in. You cry BS on it and walk away.

We humans, whether you clearly recognize it or not, have relied on BS Detectors for eons. From primordial swamps to concrete jungles, the innate skill to recognize that something just isn't right has served us well. Don't forget that this ability is right there within you, right now, hard wired into your being. You possess it at this second. Your ancestors had it and if they didn't, you wouldn't be here. And while we remember and honor our ancestors, we need to recognize that they never faced anything like we're up against now. For the last 50 years we have been barraged with a head spinning array of technological improvements and "advancements," along with an addictive parade of images and archetypes, manufactured celebrity and success, that leaves us diminished and wanting. We feel small up against what they want us to see. But thanks to our evolution, you still have the power – if you are willing to use it – to see through it all. You still have the power to protect yourself against this onslaught.

To start sharpening your detection skills, let's meet the King of the Scam...

Chapter Two

Meet Mr. Ponzi

CASE #1: Ponzi, the King of the Scam

If there's a lesson to be learned from some of the world's most notorious con artists, it might be this: If it seems too good to be true, it probably is.

Nowhere is this lesson clearer than in the case of Charles Ponzi, who, in 1920, made his own name synonymous with the word *scheme* by turning the "rob Peter to pay Paul" scam into an art.

By all accounts, the 38-year-old entrepreneur who measured only five feet two inches tall and 130 pounds, was quite a likable fellow. His charming Italian accent and smooth-talking demeanor made him a delight to listen to, particularly when he was fired up about an idea. He had a way of carrying the listener along on the current of his excitement—even if they didn't really understand what he was saying.

In fact, Ponzi was a university dropout who came to the U.S. from Italy in 1903 with $2.50 in his pocket (significantly less than he'd boarded the ship with, thanks to some gambling on board that left him with almost nothing). Upon his arrival in the U.S., he worked at a restaurant, but he was fired soon after for swindling customers. It turned out that Ponzi had an irresistible urge to plan get-rich-quick schemes. Perhaps it was a case of like attracting like when he went to work in a bank where his boss also turned out to be a fraudster who had been shortchanging customers. When the manager, fearing arrest, disappeared, Ponzi was left jobless, once again scrambling for dough. A stint writing fraudulent checks, transporting illegal aliens across the border and other criminal activity eventually landed him in prison, albeit not for long.

It was after his release, as he scrambled for money and repeatedly came up empty-handed, that the seed of an idea began to germinate in his mind.

It was 1920, a time when a radium drug called Radithor was hailed as a miracle cure for anything from gout to arthritis and even cancer, making the drug company money hand over fist. The American dream became equated with fast, easy cash. Anyone could hit it big... and they often did. That is, until it all came crashing down around them, like the makers of Radithor whose empire crumbled when its users began developing jaw necrosis and bone cancer, eventually dying painful deaths.

Rather than saving hard-earned pennies, people wanted to get rich quickly, and they were willing to go to extremes to do so. Ponzi made a living by seizing the national zeitgeist, and wound up making the term "get rich quick" a part of our vernacular.

His plan? Too simple, really. It involved International Reply Coupons, which were slips of paper that could be redeemed for postage stamps. Available for purchase in every country, it was enclosed by users in their correspondences abroad, much like a self-addressed, stamped envelope. The recipient could then write a reply, take it and the IRC to his or her nearest postal office, and receive stamps for the proper postage amount in that nation's currency (regardless of the differing values between nations) in order to post the response letter.

In this Ponzi saw an opportunity to capitalize on countries' differing postal rates. A mechanism for receiving proper postage, sanctioned and blessed by a trusted arm of the U.S. government, appeared to Ponzi as an excellent money-making scheme—never mind that he wasn't sure how he'd convert that postage into cash. He'd deal with that later.

The Italian lira had been greatly devalued in recent years, Ponzi knew, and rationalized that IRCs purchased there were worth about double in the United States. Though it was a difference of pennies—certainly not enough to lead to profits in the millions—he calculated that if that math were multiplied by hundreds of thousands, it could mean serious money. How had no one thought of this before?

His first matter of business, after christening his enterprise the Securities Exchange Company (no relation to the SEC of today) in December 1919, was getting enough money to purchase the IRCs, and finding a way to get hold of enough of them to make the scheme worth the effort. Before long, a tiny pool of investors got wind of his outrageous promise: A return of fifty percent within forty-five days. A friend in Italy began sending stacks of IRCs, and the plot was under way.

Those first investors, who'd given small amounts to begin with, received their payments as promised, and they became the greatest salespeople Ponzi could have asked for. It wasn't just him selling the idea, it was trusted friends evangelizing Ponzi's miracle method for doubling profits. Within seven months, he had turned pennies into millions.

People believed they could watch their money multiply before their eyes, and many did. They were so astounded that they salivated over the profits that could be made and threw caution to the wind. Many turned around and reinvested their money, doubling their initial investments within three months. The IRS says the average net income in Massachusetts in 1920 was about $3,400, so watching a hundred dollars become two hundred in three months was nothing to sneeze at.

"He was enormously charismatic, he was charming, he was this sort of dapper figure. I call him a banty rooster of a man," said Mitchell Zuckoff, a journalist and author of the biography *Ponzi's Scheme: The True Story of a Financial Legend*, in an interview with *The Washington Post*.

Zuckoff points to the root of Ponzi's success: His charm, but also his keen understanding of the American sensibility. After all, he'd lived in the country long enough, scrambling for cash, to know that everyone, from the poorest to the richest, wanted to believe they could have it all with very little effort. That, at heart, was the American Dream, wasn't it?

The Washington Post said it was panache that Ponzi had in great measure, and such an entrepreneurial spirit and innovative vision could, ironically, have taken the man far had he put it toward legitimate dealings.

And the man had a talent for schmoozing. He always knew how to say the things people wanted to hear. When a *Boston Post* reporter interviewed him at the zenith of his success in July 1920, he said, "I get no pleasure out of spending money on myself, but a great deal in doing some good with it. Always I have said to myself, if I can get one million dollars, I can live with all the comfort I want for the rest of my life. If I get more than one million dollars, I will spend all over and above the one million trying to do good in the world. Now I have the million. That I have put aside. If my business closed tomorrow, I am sure that I will have that amount on which to make myself and family comfortable for the rest of our days."

At the time, his estimated wealth exceeded $8.5 million. His behavior proclaimed that, now that he was all set, he didn't *need* investors, but he would take them to be generous and kindhearted.

"With a maestro's touch," Zuckoff wrote in his book, "Ponzi had struck a perfect balance among the forces competing to control the new American identity: altruism and avarice."

Ponzi sought small amounts from large numbers of investors, so that no one would really lose much or demand much. The problem was that the number of IRCs was limited, and he never had figured out how to take those stamps and use them to secure cold cash.

But after he returned the first investors' money, he realized he needn't bother with the stamps. He could simply hold investors' money in the bank; he would just keep new investors' money and give back returns with it to old investors. As long as people saw it working, they'd keep investing. Satellite offices were set up across the country to take investments.

Few understood his investment model—even his wife, Rose, couldn't figure it out—but he was splashy and exciting enough to get investors carried away, and when their friends and colleagues began bringing home returns in their hands, the benefits could no longer be denied. Before long, lines formed outside Ponzi's office, full of people desperate to give him their hard-earned dollars. Within seven months, by July 1920, he was making $250,000 a day.

But this was a pyramid scheme that was no longer built on anything but air.

Employees of the postal service noticed his excessive wealth—everyone had, as his claims were highly publicized—and they starting doing the math, checking registered IRCs against those in actual circulation, and the numbers didn't line up. The reporters at the *Boston Post* started doing their own poking around. Word got out that Ponzi was under suspicion, and investments dwindled as people started demanding their money. Before long, the whole thing imploded. Ponzi owed more than $15 million to about 40,000 investors. Federal agents raided his office, found no magical stock of stamps to support the investment model, and shut him down. Ponzi was arrested in August 1920, one year after discovering his first IRC and conceiving of his plan. He was tried in October, and after a meteoric rise that lasted only nine months, he was convicted and wound up in prison for eleven years. Following his release, he was deported back to Italy, and he eventually died, destitute and alone, at age 66 in a charity hospital in Rio de Janeiro.

It is a true testament to Ponzi's magnetism and charm that even after he was busted and his victims were found to have been defrauded, they defended him, so convinced were they still by his proclaimed Midas touch (or, more likely, too ashamed by their own gullibility to do otherwise).

Modern day scammers learned this lesson from Ponzi: Many victims will never go to friends, family or the authorities because they are too embarrassed.

Falling for this next one would be embarrassing:

-----Original Message-----
From: Nilofar Bhatkar
Sent: Wednesday, August 8, 2020 8:35AM
To: Recipients
Subject: Please reply back...

I'm Captain Karen Nana of the US Army, presently in Afghanistan for a peace keeping mission. Please I need your Kind assistance in regards safe keeping some important items for me. For more details, reply back at the following email...

This email arrived in my inbox a few days ago, and I barely gave it a second glance. Like most people, this sort of obvious hoax email is a daily occurrence for me, and, like most people, I chuckled, thought in reply, "Sure you do," then clicked delete.

We've all received invitations to outlandish scams (*The prince of Nigeria wants to give me his bars of gold? Wow, sign me up!*) and have even gotten some entertainment value out of them. Also like most people, I learned early on to recognize this kind of thing for what it is. Most of us know to immediately delete these things... to throw that junk mail in the garbage, maintain our spam filters and purge the files, to hang up the phone as soon as we hear that robotic voice (or not answer a number we don't recognize in the first place).

A colleague of mine, also an attorney, received this message just the other day:

From: Magne Haga
Sent: Tuesday, July 31, 2020 9:39 AM
Subject: Do you handle P/S agreement?

Hello: Do you have the capacity to draft us a purchase and sale agreement? If yes, your service will be needed for the sale of a Vessel to a buyer from your state?

Thanks,
Magne Haga
General Manager
CHL Shipping B.V.
Schiedamsedijk 200,3011 EP
Rotterdam, The Netherlands

As if the sketchy "From" address weren't enough of a tip-off, the email is full of red flags: bad English, enough vagueness to send an attorney running, and an international return address. He deleted the message within a second and didn't give it another thought (until I asked him to share it with me as an example for this book!).

In many situations, like the emails above, you can spot the scam a mile away. (*Yeah, right, a U.S. Army captain needs MY help with keeping her items safe.*) Bad grammar, random capital letters, outlandish propositions, the bait-and-switch "Do this for me and I'll reward you handsomely" call to action... all obvious and well-worn tactics.

But, unfortunately, some scams aren't so easy to spot. Some victims aren't so lucky or savvy. Some don't get the opportunity to delete, opt out, or report suspicious activity before they're taken. And as research repeatedly tells us, *anyone* can be conned — young and old, rich and poor, high school dropouts and those with Ph.D.'s. No one is off limits. We've *all* been ripped off at some point in our lives and made to feel foolish.

The more consumers learn about today's scams, the more criminals are developing increasingly sophisticated cons to try on you tomorrow. Learn the defenses. It used to be that con artists cheated you face to face, hawking snake oils and selling you fake Rolexes. You could look that person in the eye, watching how he stores those "Rolexes" in cardboard boxes or examine the faked Gucci logos on that table full of handbags.

But nowadays, those are the mild rip-offs, mere child's play. These days, technology makes it easier to reach you and millions of others within seconds, while simultaneously also making these criminals harder to see, recognize, or catch. Many of their scams are difficult or even impossible to recognize as frauds at first glance. And they're usually done by transnational teams from as far away as India, Costa Rica, or Nigeria, using cloaking technology that makes it seem as if their messages are coming from just the next town over, so the scammers are difficult to find or prosecute. As discussed in Chapter 13, a bounty system could change that.

There have been high-profile cases in which the folks you'd least expect to fall prey to con artists — doctors, physics professors, financial experts, even psychotherapists who actually treat scam artists for a living — became susceptible to tricksters who capitalized on certain characteristics, some aspect of gullibility, and took them for everything they had. Many of these stories are too strange to be believed, but they're all true, and I'll share many of them with you in this book.

We've all heard outrageous stories about scam artists, and they reveal a very real threat. The Rich Dad team recently polled members of its community about their greatest fears, and fear of being ripped off was one of the most common fears reported.

And it's no wonder. The financial, mental, emotional, and even physical tolls that scams take on victims, their families, their friends, and even their business associates, can be utterly devastating.

Paying the Price

According to the Federal Trade Commission's annual report of top U.S. consumer complaints, over 3.2 million fraud reports are filed by consumers each year with the FTC. The two most common complaints of fraud pertained to identity theft and imposter scams.

What are the results of all this fraudulent activity?

The Insurance Information Institute reports that in recent years, there were 16.7 million victims of identity fraud, in which a person's identification information was stolen and used for the scammer's personal or financial gain. And know that not everyone reports their problems to the FTC.

Even those of us who weren't directly victims of identity theft were put at great risk for it; 30 percent of consumers in the U.S. were notified of data breaches in 2017, which was up considerably from the previous year's 12 percent. The exponential costs of such breaches are easy to see when you realize that those criminals made off with a record $16.8 billion that year.

The second most commonly reported complaint, imposter scams, by far tops the list in terms of costs to their victims. These schemes, in which a criminal pretends to be someone a victim can trust in order to steal that person's money (a government official, a loved one in trouble, a representative from a well-known business or agency, a tech support representative), cost the average victim nearly $450 each.

In total, Americans were swindled out of $1.9 billion in 2019, a number that continues to grow each year, revealing a worrisome trend. The Better Business Bureau reported nearly 500,000 complaints related just to sweepstakes and lottery scams over the last three years, with those resulting losses totaling nearly $350 million.

Stacey Wood, a professor of psychology at Scripps College in Claremont, California, has given quite a lot of thought to the issue of scams, even conducting psychological experiments on people's responses to scams. In her article for the academic journal *The Conversation* in July, 2018, she adequately sums up the scope of danger that scams present to us as a society: "Scams cost individuals, organizations and governments trillions of dollars each year in estimated losses, and many victims endure depression and ill health. There is no other crime, in fact, that affects so many people from almost all ages, backgrounds and geographical locations."

And why are we doing nothing? The very real impacts of losing your shirt to a scammer can range from minor (but nonetheless aggravating) losses to very severe. They can include bounced checks (and the resulting fees), maxed-out credit cards, late fees, legal fees, loss of credit standing, outrageous debt, bankruptcy, and complete destitution. But without minimizing those very serious outcomes, let's put the financial costs aside for a moment.

Even after you've been swindled financially, one of the worst outcomes is the emotional cost, the toll on one's sense of well-being. Victims have, understandably, reported high rates of shame, guilt, embarrassment, grief, difficulty sleeping, anxiety, and depression. Many actually don't report that they were victimized by scammers because of the overwhelming shame, which compounds the problem. In some cases, victims even have committed suicide. Please see the article, *Suicide and Cyber Criminality,* by Ted Sutton and Will Boyden in Appendix B.

Such bitter experiences often lead to a general lack of trust and personal confidence, and, combined with the blame and persecution inflicted by others, can have long-lasting effects on victims' relationships, and even their spirituality.

Fear of the overwhelming and terrifying costs of scams is coupled with the knowledge that there's simply no way to know them all. Take a look at the average IT department message warning recipients not to click on attachments, not to open messages, not to answer calls from that particular phone number, or not to fall for imposters claiming to be Microsoft, and you'll quickly realize that even if you knew all of today's trending hoaxes, brand-new ones are in the works this very minute, ready to be rolled out tomorrow.

There is good news: Education is power. Understanding the scams at work, the techniques their perpetrators use, the character traits that make you vulnerable, and the tricks that can help you to be less of a victim may help minimize the effects of scams over time.

"...I hit the American people where it hurts—in the pocketbook. Those were confused, money-mad days. Everybody wanted to make a killing. I was in it plenty deep, rolling in other people's money."

— Charles Ponzi, 1948

Chapter Three

Charming Man

CASE #2: Frank Abagnale, the Great Imposter

It's likely you know about Frank Abagnale from Hollywood, thanks to the 2002 Steven Spielberg Academy Award nominated film, *Catch Me If You Can*, starring Tom Hanks as an FBI agent and Leonardo DiCaprio as fast Frankie himself.

Abagnale is not only one of the most notorious con artists of our time, but he also perpetrated his crimes while he was, for the most part, a teenager. He began pulling scams at age 16, and by 21 he was being hunted (and was eventually captured) by the FBI.

Abagnale was the classic con artist, utterly charming and delightful in every way. His good looks, which seemed much more mature than his actual age would suggest, helped him to get away with a lot. He discovered he had a gift for charm and impersonation at age 16. A runaway who looked like a full-grown adult, he had a penchant for passing bad checks (what was called "paper-hanging" at the time) and cashing them at hotels in New York City, and thanks to a fake ID that stated he was ten years older than his actual age, he was mostly successful. People had no trouble believing he was in his mid-twenties, and he was vastly likable.

One day, he spotted something that changed his life: A pilot and his flight crew leaving one of those upscale New York hotels where he typically cashed his rubber checks. He'd had no trouble convincing people he was a professional in his mid-twenties, so he clearly was talented at impersonation. It struck him that the uniform the pilot wore—a dark suit with the regal yellow piping—instilled confidence in its wearer, and clearly the lovely stewardesses were impressed. Still young enough to be willing to take risks and still confident enough that he believed looks, not talent, would get him what he wanted, he decided then and there that he would impersonate a pilot and receive instant respect, admiration, and trust, which would enable him to cash checks anywhere in the world.

He called Pan Am Airlines and pretended to be a pilot whose uniform had been stolen—could he get a temporary replacement? When asked to fill out a request form with his employee ID number, the five-digit blank made it easy for him to make up a few numbers off the top of his head. He researched facts about airline pilots, even going so far as to call Pan Am pretending to be a high school journalist, then asking questions about the work so he could learn about the job and the lingo of the profession. He'd already made a fake ID that had worked; it wasn't hard to make a Pan Am ID and pilot's license. He used these to "deadhead," or fly for free in empty seats, and to stay in posh hotels at no charge. He even opened a bank account in his new pilot's name, Frank Williams, and charged expenses to Pan Am.

Hoaxes became an addiction for Abagnale. His outrageous success at Pan Am gave him the confidence to take an even bigger risk: Posing as a pediatrician at a local hospital in Atlanta, Georgia. When he wasn't being asked to supervise the pediatric ward—allowing real doctors to actually diagnose and treat patients and simply agreeing with what they said—he was hiding in the closet to avoid being called to attend to patients. Later, he posed as Robert E. Conrad, a Harvard law graduate who worked for the attorney general, and a sociology professor at Brigham Young University in Provo, Utah. Always, with his calm, confident demeanor and his ability to tell people what they wanted to hear, he found it surprisingly easy to impersonate anybody.

His check-forging skills, in the meantime, had become increasingly sophisticated as well. His knowledge of how banks handle checks—utilizing a series of numbers along the bottom that indicated the state, city, and bank in which the check could be processed—meant that he could create checks that would take days, even weeks to be processed, by which time he would be far away and long gone. Within a few short years, Abagnale had accumulated wealth, in real money, totaling nearly $75,000. But he'd also fallen in love with a girl in San Francisco, even confessing to her, in a moment of vulnerability, his true identity. This was the beginning of the end of Abagnale's string of crimes as she related these facts to the authorities.

When he'd realized that he'd been ratted out, he fled to Las Vegas, where he had a brief fling with a graphic designer who told him everything he wanted to know about printing authentic-looking checks. He bought a camera and an offset press, rented a small warehouse, and began printing authentic-looking Pan Am checks. By age nineteen, Abagnale's personal cash assets totaled half a million dollars.

Emboldened by his string of unlikely successes, Abagnale took more risks, opening bank accounts all over the country under the name Frank Adams; jetting off to Mexico and Paris, where he convinced a local printer to duplicate his Pan Am check; purchasing a million-dollar Heidelberg printing press to create the most realistic-looking checks available; and even posing as a bank security guard in Boston to avoid prosecution by the FBI, who'd been tracking him for nearly a year. He escaped police custody twice, but he was eventually captured in Southern France and arrested, facing extradition warrants from 26 countries. He was convicted in the U.S. and sentenced to prison.

Five years into his prison sentence, the U.S. government offered him a deal. He would be released on the condition that he would use what he knew about perpetrating fraud to help the authorities, and without pay, find and capture scam artists. Once he had met the conditions for release, he went on to offer those same services to banks; he explained how he had perpetrated his phony check scheme and indicated that he had suggestions for how to prevent such scams in the future. Before long Abagnale was making a legitimate living as a security consultant. Today his business, Abagnale and Associates, advises businesses and the FBI on security and fraud issues.

You've heard the term "con man" or "con artist," but do you know what it means? Some people think the "con" is short for "convince," "convey," or "conversation"—after all, a con artist has a way of convincing you to do things against your better judgment, conveying false information to you, or drawing you into conversation so he (or she!) can charm the pants off you. Some think of the shortened version of the word "convict" as in a criminal. But while the activities are criminal, convict is not the right word. You might even think of the word in its other sense: pro and con. A con is a negative, something contrary to your needs and desires, that conflicts with what's right.

All of these make sense, but the term actually is derived from the phrase "confidence trick," which is pretty much just what it sounds like: A trick in which the perpetrator earns your confidence or trust in order to pull a fast one on you. A confidence man is someone who is able to win you over with a smile, smooth talk, a convincing argument, the promise of a "can't-lose" proposition, and, yes, absolute confidence in himself and his ability to succeed. You couldn't help but fall for him and anything he has to say... right up until he rips you off.

Beware the Charming Man

Kurt Vonnegut once said, "Charm was a scheme for making strangers like and trust a person immediately, no matter what the charmer had in mind."

We have a tendency to think of charm as something a person is born with, a natural gift, but scammers have honed charm into a razor-sharp tool specifically designed to cut deeply and painfully. While we may assume we can spot con artists right away—get a negative gut feeling and instinctively know not to trust them—the opposite is usually the case. Con artists rarely look like lowlife criminals. They are geniuses at using their practiced charm—their confident postures, good looks, magnetic personalities, ease at conversation, and seemingly intuitive understanding of others' needs and desires—to get what they want, often without even needing to ask for it. They know how to say the right thing, the thing you really need to hear, and are so good at persuading you to do what they want that you'd almost believe it was your idea. You might even think of charm as another word for the gift for manipulation.

As Dr. Jeremy Dean, British psychologist and founder of PsyBlog, points out, "Good hustlers are excellent intuitive psychologists. Just like magicians they understand enough about how the mind works to exploit its vulnerabilities."

Numerous studies have been performed to pin down the profile of your typical scammer. While every one of these people is, of course, unique certain traits repeatedly show up:

- **They're well dressed.** Why would you trust someone with your money who didn't appear to know how to make any of it himself? Charles Ponzi's excellent taste in clothing gave him the appearance of being made of money—tremendously successful at attracting wealth easily. He had a large home, bought hastily with others' money and furnished with the finest items; his flashy Locomobile, the most expensive car made in America at the time, custom-built and purchased in cash, appointed with sterling silver trim, crystal bud vases, and a chauffeur; and his attire, which included a new Palm Beach suit, a silk handkerchief, polished shoes, a starched white collar, and a diamond pin. Potential investors, upon seeing from his appearance that he clearly could work magic with money, were convinced to give him theirs.

- **They rely on sleights of hand and distraction.** Often, a con artist's talk will be well dressed, too. He'll use impressive language, an air of arrogance and superiority, and, if his first contact with you is by mail, prestigious addresses and affiliations. He may even drop impressive names casually—prominent people he's worked with or major companies who were his clients. But like a magician performing sleights of hand, the lovely smoke and mirrors are distractions that belie the truths hidden from view.

The classic example of this distraction principle is Three-card Monte, the infamous card trick performed in city streets before crowds of onlookers. "Find the lady," the dealer calls to the delight of the crowd, and peals of laughter and the sounds of active conversation are designed to present the appearance that the "mark" (in other words, you) has stumbled upon a game that, until moments ago, was being played by others like you—others who appear to be on a winning streak. In truth, though, every one of them is in on it, but you're too distracted by the excitement of the scene to notice the game is rigged.

- **They are clever at disguising themselves.** As Edwin Piers points out in his book *Con Artistry*, "Con artists understand that standing out is a great disadvantage to successful scamming. So, they always blend in, by looking and sounding like a normal everyday Joe or Jane." Numerous household repair scams have been pulled off by normal, safe-looking people in professional-looking work clothes. They don't look creepy or shifty; they look completely above board. They have the right tools, the right kinds of truck, and they're saying the right things. They blend in—often so well that they aren't memorable. But scammers are masters at disguising their true motives. They'll use the right lingo and terminology to sound the way you think they ought to sound. They'll say the words they know you want to hear, knowledgeable-sounding words that imply trustworthiness and relatability.

- **They'll capitalize on your ignorance.** Charles Ponzi never did figure out how to turn those International Reply Coupons into cash. It was a good idea in theory, but in practice it made no sense. Even his own wife couldn't figure it out. Yet for nine months, he managed to convince them all that it would work. The evidence of its success was right in front of them, in the wads of cash clutched in their friends' and colleagues' hands. Why argue? He was the financial wizard, they reasoned, so he must understand something they didn't.

Look, we've all practiced a bit of B.S. in our lifetimes. I can recall dashing off a few late-night, coffee-fueled papers in college that managed to meet the required lengths thanks to some artfully constructed sentences that sounded intelligent and meant almost nothing, all in order to distract from the fact that I didn't really understand the material. If the teachers are good, they can see through it—they're trained to spot the B.S., to see that ignorance, and to ensure that students can demonstrate their knowledge by pointing to facts and evidence. They can teach critical thinking.

But the average person doesn't want that lovely thing he or she is being promised to be wrong. We really want it to be true. And a good con artist knows this little human trait well. We humans are optimists at heart, and we're often willing to overlook the things that don't quite make sense (especially because that would expose our own ignorance) if it means we get what we want in the end.

Rather than risk sounding foolish by saying, "I'm sorry, that doesn't quite make sense, can you explain that again?" we say, "Oh, yeah, sure, I get it. So all this means I'll get rich, you say?"

A hustler will even try to make you feel incompetent by asking you questions you don't know the answers to, to expose you as ignorant and make you feel that you need the product or service being offered, even if you don't really understand it. Scammers like to use legal or technical jargon that they know you don't understand, even if they're using it incorrectly. You'll never know, and it sounds impressive, right? As a result, victims decide it's best to avoid asking questions and seeming stupid. We'll do anything to avoid looking stupid, even if by *not* asking questions we prove how foolish we really are.

But as any good, qualified, respectable real estate agent, financial advisor, mortgage broker, or accountant will tell you: It's crucial that you understand exactly what you're signing your name to, what plan you're agreeing to, and if you don't understand the deal, keep asking questions until you do. There are no stupid questions. You're stupid if you don't ask.

- **They're hard to pin down.** He's often on the road so you can never reach him. He moves a lot—in fact, he's only in town for six weeks, so you're lucky to have this rare opportunity. He just happened to be in the neighborhood with extra supplies and saw you needed a new roof, but tomorrow he's headed out of town for the next job, so this is your only chance. His address is a post office box, and the number you've called to follow up is no longer in service. After all, a scammer can only stay in one place so long before you catch on, so he has to keep moving. He comes to you, never the other way around. The name of his business sounds pretty generic, not at all like what he's peddling. He might even ask you to write a blank check because he has a stamp in the office with the proper name. A con artist is a master at disappearing in a cloud of smoke, but take a clue: If there's no brick-and-mortar office, no permanence, no phone number, no record of a business name, no Better Business Bureau listing, there's probably nothing but smoke behind his promises.

- **They blow a lot of hot air.** Even as children, we innately know that flattery will get us everywhere ("You are the best daddy in the whole world. I love you *sooooo* much. Can I have some candy?"). In fact, my wife even used it on our kids on occasion ("You're the only one in this house who knows how to do the dishes the right way. Would you mind doing them again so your sister can learn by watching you?") We've all gotten our way at one time or another by buttering up a spouse, a friend, a teacher, a boss, or a coworker, and it's usually harmless. But con artists know the power of flattery, and they love to offer it in the hopes of getting something from you in return. They'll generously lob compliments about your lovely hairstyle, your fine clothes, your fascinating job or upbringing, your excellent taste, your generous nature, or your superior intellect, hoping to put you at ease and warm you up to whatever scheme they're offering. And when you start to doubt them, they might even put on a show of being wounded.

One time, a gentleman came knocking at my door selling "magazine subscriptions," and actually showed a certificate and official-looking order form for this company that offered at-risk young people opportunities to take educational trips by raising money selling exorbitantly priced subscriptions, some of them up to $150 each. Each one sold would earn this bright, smiling, friendly young man a number of points toward his goal: A trip to Washington, D.C. He poured on the flattery, telling me how delicious our dinner smelled or how smart or intuitive I was to ask certain questions. He cracked jokes, trying to win me over by buttering me up. I had to tell him that, unfortunately, I had absolutely no belief that the "company" calling itself CSA had any intention of either providing the magazines he was selling or of sending this enthusiastic young man to D.C. His crestfallen face actually had me wondering whether this was all part of the act—if so, he missed his calling in Hollywood—or if even he had been suckered into believing the scam. A 2015 report in *The Atlantic* says that tens of thousands of young people are lured into doing this work, and many such magazine subscription rackets will even abandon these young people in strange towns as they move on to their next target destinations. I felt sorry for the eager, polite young man, even as I closed the door in his face.

- **They drive the bandwagon.** It's an unfortunate fact that people are a lot like sheep: We love to follow the herd. If everyone else is doing it, we want to do it too. We hate to miss out. Marketers know this and have built entire marketing campaigns relying on it: "Discover what millions of people around the world already know!" "Get it now before it's gone!" "It's America's favorite brand!" Con artists are master manipulators, and they employ this technique to the fullest. They might tell you how they just left your neighbor's house, where they just completed a job (*"Gosh, the Joneses are doing it? Maybe I should, too!"*), or that they only have a few items left because they've been so popular (*"Well, I don't want to be the only person who doesn't have one."*).

On another occasion, an attractive young co-ed rang the doorbell to sell, again, "magazine subscriptions". She actually showed me a check, purportedly written by someone who lived down the street who had purchased three subscriptions—I assume it was her way of not only trying to convince me that she was legit, but also to believe that anything short of three subscriptions would make me stingy by comparison. I didn't take the bait. (Of course, the publishing industry is now scrambling to figure out how to sell any subscriptions.)

In other cases, they assume the bandwagon will do the talking for them. Charles Ponzi, Bernie Madoff, and other famed con artists utilized two very important techniques to get people to buy in to their schemes: First, they let former customers evangelize their schemes to their families and friends, who in turn would want to jump on board. Second, they behaved as if getting to invest was a special privilege, only open to a select few in a secret club of in-the-know investors. Aspiring to be part of the exclusive club, investors dove in head first. Con artists love to tell you about hot tips from inside sources, how only a select few are being offered this deal, how this is the only chance to get in on the ground floor, and how everyone else who participated was successful. Everyone loves an exclusive club when we actually get to be part of it.

It's like that game of Three-card Monte: Everyone else looks like they're having fun and winning money. So why shouldn't you play?

- **They like to tell you how the clock is ticking.** Here's another technique employed heavily in advertising: "Time's running out, so act quickly!" Con artists know that the more time you have to think about their proposals, the more your reasoning capabilities have the chance to win out. Think about it: How often do we really make good, effective split-second decisions?

They're banking on your impulses and your fear of missing out. Why else do you think grocery stores put the tabloids and candy at the register? Because if you have more time than it takes to stand in line at the register, you'll either stand in the aisle reading that intriguing article, thereby eliminating your need to buy the magazine, or you'll walk past them in search of the other items on your shopping list. Or you'll realize that neither the tabloid nor the candy has any real nutritional value and you'll walk away. Telemarketers don't want to mail you literature so you can read more information; they want you to commit now, because if given the time, you'll turn them down. Charity organizations will even tell you how much you'll be donating while they have you on the phone, to save you time: "So we can put your twenty-five-dollar donation on a Visa or Mastercard, which will it be?" Creating a sense of urgency is a scammer's go-to tool. Multiple scientific studies have proven that when people are forced to make decisions under duress or time pressure, they will take shortcuts and make decisions based on emotions—usually insecurity or a fear of missing out. When someone is pushing you to give answers right away or act quickly, consider that a huge red flag, a warning to step back.

- **They prey on your greed and fear.** Two of humans' basest instincts are also the most powerful ones. Fear, in particular, is primal, hard-wired into our DNA, signaled by the brain's amygdala with the release of hormones that course through our veins, causing our hearts to pump faster and our breathing to speed up. Fear sets off our fight-or-flight responses, which causes cortisol to tear through our bodies, eliminating our ability to use reason or exercise caution. While the majority of people will say that they are afraid of being scammed, con artists are good at turning that fear to their advantage. Instead, they'll give you something more urgent to fear (a computer virus, a hard drive crash, a faulty roof, or a summons by the IRS) and then promise to solve your problem and remove the thing you're afraid of—just install this spyware on your computer, let this tech support guy have access to your account, hire this contractor who has the supplies in his truck outside, or wire the necessary funds quickly. Scammers love to prey on your fear, and they'll serve it up in large doses, creating in you a fear of missing out, of not fitting in, or of impending disaster.

They also know we have a natural fear of authority figures, and they'll even pretend to have authority over you in order to take advantage of this. Much like we'll hand over our credit cards to servers or our keys to valets, we'll often use the excuse "I'm not tech-savvy," then give over access to our computers, so someone claiming to be tech support can protect us from unknown threats, or we'll pay to make a problem with the IRS go away.

Con artists typically use a greed-fear setup. They play on your fear, but they also play on your innate greediness. Say what you will about your honest motives (*"I'm NOT greedy!"*), but everyone in a capitalistic society harbors an inner desire to make a buck. In a 2018 article for *The Atlantic*, Rene Chun reports on a new breed of shoplifter that has sprung up in the age of self-checkout—people who certainly can afford to purchase items at the grocery store and have no need to commit such petty crimes, yet they do it anyway simply because they can. For instance, many pull what's called "the banana trick," in which something that's normally pretty expensive—for example, a T-bone that normally goes for $13.99 a pound—is placed on the scale, and the customer types in the code for something a lot less expensive by weight—like bananas, which go for $0.49 a pound. Another increasingly popular trick is "the switcheroo," in which pricing stickers on similar-weight items are swapped so customers can get cheaper pricing. People who normally wouldn't even consider stuffing food under our shirts and walking out of the store are now trying to beat the system by ripping stores off at self-checkout lines, more often than not just for the pure fact that it's easy to do without being caught.

And more people than you'd think are doing this. A survey by Voucher Codes Pro found that nearly 20 percent of people surveyed had stolen at self-checkout in the past. And a study by the University of Leicester, in which a million self-checkout transactions over the course of a year were audited, found that about $850,000 worth of goods had left the store without being paid for.

Maybe we rationalize doing it by convincing ourselves that we're owed something—for a hard day, for our hard work, for the fact that *we're* now doing the labor at the store instead of the people paid to work there, that the prices keep going up, that the store employees are rude, or that the machines are so frustrating to work with—but clearly a good many of us don't have qualms with this sort of theft, the kind in which it's hard to get caught.

The bottom line is that when there's very little chance of being caught, we humans simply can't resist a little larceny. Inside every one of us is a hope that we'll win the lottery, find a hundred-dollar bill on the ground, get too much change back at the register, or wind up getting something for nothing. Greed is as powerful as a drug, and con artists know this. They might even act as if you're in it together, this plan to win the game and play the system, taking you into their confidence and promising a win-win scenario. Trust me, the only one who wins is the con man.

- **They like secrets.** Scammers know there are businesses out there devoted to teaching people how to avoid rip-offs, and to helping consumers protect themselves. The more people you have whispering in your ear and giving you advice, the less chance that con artist has of separating you from your money. That's why they rely on secrecy to get away with their plans. They'll tell you not to call the bank but instead to wire money secretly (and untraceably) through Western Union. They'll argue that the sweepstakes money will only be sent if you don't tell anyone. Like domestic abusers who make threats that they'll inflict more pain if their victims tell the police, con artists want to isolate you from your loved ones and keep you from talking to anyone who could possibly talk some sense into you. Consider this: Anyone who's legitimately trying to do business with you wants you talking about their products and services to anyone who'll listen.

- **They have every reason to be confident.** The sad truth is that he'll probably get away with whatever scam he's pulling. Many scams go unreported because people are either too ashamed to admit they were taken advantage of or because they don't believe it's even possible to catch them. It's time-consuming to pursue legal action. And the truth is that many law enforcement agencies and lawyers won't even touch instances of fraud below a certain dollar amount. Getting proof that a certain person was connected to a crime is nearly impossible—after all, we can't trace those calls that interrupt our workdays—and so many of these calls and emails associated with imposter scams are generated in faraway countries. These people make outrageous requests and do so with an aura of confidence. That's usually for a reason: They'll probably get away with it. But as we'll discuss, we all need to fight back.

Every criminal, every motive or method is unique, of course, but chances are that you've encountered a few attempted scams, and these traits should seem familiar. Let's list the scam signs list again:

1. They're well dressed.
2. They rely on sleights of hand and distraction.
3. They are clever at disguising themselves.
4. They'll capitalize on your ignorance.
5. They're hard to pin down.
6. They blow a lot of hot air.
7. They drive the bandwagon.
8. They like to tell you how the clock is ticking.
9. They prey on your greed and fear.
10. They like secrets.
11. They have every reason to be confident.

As the cases are presented in this book, consider these signs. Let them become your red flags from now on.

Of course, it takes two to play a confidence game: The con artist and the mark. Are you a mark?

Chapter Four

On Your... Mark

"That would never happen to me."

"How stupid can you get?"

"Jeez, what an idiot!"

Admit it, you have said these things to yourself or to friends after hearing stories about people who fell for scams. It's easy to say, "Oh, man, I can't believe they fell for that, I would *never* be so stupid!" then judge others for falling victim, but over 3.2 million Americans report incidents of fraud each year, and that's only the people who actually said anything—a great many don't. (Remember, shame is a powerful thing). They can't *all* be idiots. Any one of us can be a mark. Any one of us can be vulnerable to rip-offs, because the scammers behind them have just gotten that good.

The term "mark" actually comes from the world of traveling carnivals. Those masters of clever tricks were the epitome of con artists, selling something that didn't exist (bearded women who were really just delicate-voiced men, for instance). When a carney believed he had found someone gullible who would fall for their tricks, they would put chalk in the palms of their hands and, as they pretended to cozy up with the patron, give them a jovial clap on the back that marked the patrons as suckers.

In fact, while anyone can be victimized by fraudsters, there are some classic character attributes that these criminals look for, things that make for a good mark.

- **Once a sucker, always a sucker.** You might think that a person who has been scammed in the past would be more apt to recognize it for what it is, and successfully avoid it the next time. But as it turns out, that old adage, "Fool me once, shame on you, fool me twice, shame on me" directly applies to too many of us. A study by the AARP actually found that the most likely targets of scams are those who have already been scammed. Doug Shadel with AARP told *Psychology Today*, "It's pretty well known in the fraud world that the best list to get is the list of people who have already been taken."

Why is this? It's not completely clear. Maybe those people have a natural predisposition to fall for flattery. Maybe it's a desire to overcome shame, to deny what happened before and finally be the one to be proven right. Maybe it's a constant need to be needed, or an inner loneliness that causes the victim to enjoy what he or she believes is a special relationship with the con artist. But the fact remains, victims who have lost before are the ones most likely to lose again.

- **They're elderly.** Elderly Americans lose over $37 billion a year to fraud. Seniors age seventy and up lose more money, by far, to scam artists and fraudsters than any other generation. And that figure is probably too conservative: A North American Securities Administrators Association (NASAA) survey of securities regulators found that almost all of them—97 percent—believed elder fraud cases go overwhelmingly unreported, while 30 percent had seen an increase in reports.

And you think it's only the senile seniors who get taken? Think again. A study reported in the *American Journal of Public Health* reveals that one out of every 18 "cognitively intact" seniors is a victim of financial scams, fraud, or abuse. We can't blame the schools for this generation. They went to good schools back then.

The FBI attributes this problem to other reasons. First, scammers go where the money is, and as a generation, seniors control trillions of dollars. These are the folks most likely to have pensions, IRAs, and nest eggs, and their credit, on the whole, tends to be good. People of this generation were raised in a time when it was important to respect and trust authority and to be polite to strangers, so they're more likely to listen to a scammer's spiel on the phone or on the front step rather than hanging up or slamming the door. This makes them susceptible to claims of miracle cures or can't miss investments. They tend to know less about technology than younger people, and are even fearful of it, so they aren't as savvy about the tricks that can be played on them online. These people often have health issues that make them easily confused, and they're often lonely to boot, so they often mistake scammers' overtures to engage them in conversation as genuine human connection.

Only 18 percent of those seventy and older reported being victims of these crimes, though experts know it happens more frequently than they would admit. But older people are simply less likely to report fraud because of fear and shame. After all, their children may suggest the need to relocate to assisted living or hand over control of their finances once they learn how easily their parents were victimized. And when they do report fraud, they often make lousy witnesses, thanks to the effects of aging on memory and cognition.

- **They're young.** Adults in their twenties comprise the single largest group of fraud victims, with scam prevalence among twenty-somethings far outstripping that of even seniors.

But wait... didn't I just say it's the elderly who lose the most? Well, yes, in total losses, that's true. The average fraud victim age eighty-plus loses $1,092 per incidence, whereas the average victim aged 20 to 29 loses something like $400.

But it might surprise you to learn that while the elderly lose the most money to scams, Millennials are victimized more often—they just don't have as much money to lose. In fact, a whopping forty percent of young adults ages 20 to 29 reported losing money to fraud.

But how can that be? The young are tech savvy, jaded, cynical. They grew up in an age when scam and spam are everyday occurrences. How can they be taken so often?

According to a Better Business Bureau study of 18- to 24-year-olds cited in *Consumer Reports*, Millennials "are afflicted with a so-called "optimism bias" that makes them feel invulnerable and causes them not to take safety precautions." Young people feel emboldened to take risks, confident that things will work out in the end. They engage in riskier online behaviors, and they live dangerously, often without health insurance, taking chances those older adults often wouldn't. Many even believe they can outsmart scam artists and welcome the opportunity to engage them in conversations that they can later transcribe and make viral on social media.

Yet they're more than three times as likely as seniors *not* to recognize a scam. Their lack of life experience simply makes them gullible; they don't know what they don't know. And they don't like being told what to do—especially by parents or other authority figures.

- **They're uneducated.** Just as young people fall prey to scams due to life experience, it is often the case that people with lower levels of education simply fall prey more often than those who possess lots of it. Not that the more highly educated among us don't—they certainly do, in great numbers—but statistically it happens less frequently.

Psychology professor Stacey Wood and her colleagues set out to conduct an experiment to determine what type of people are most likely to fall victim to scams. They culled 25 solicitation letters for what they considered "successful" mass-marketing scams to determine what similarities they share that might have contributed to their success in convincing people to go along with them. They included the factors I've touched on here: A reliance on urgency and the need to act immediately, the use of names that are associated with credibility (Marriott or Costco, for example), the use of persuasive techniques like the bandwagon method, and other impressive-sounding language that provided an illusion of legitimacy.

Drawing upon these tactics, Wood and her colleagues drafted their own solicitation letter, for the purposes of the experiment. The letter indicated that the recipient was "already a winner" and that the reader only needed to call with an activation number to claim the prize. Some were told that it was free to claim the prize, and some were told they needed to pay a fee to activate the prize, ranging from $5 to $100. The participants were told they were part of an experiment and were asked to rate their willingness to give their activation numbers, with or without the fees, as well as what they saw as the potential risks versus benefits of responding. Demographic information was collected on respondents to determine common traits among potential victims.

The results were fascinating. Even knowing this was an experiment, and regardless which letters they received—whether the "prize" could be activated for free or with an initial payment of $100— a full 48 percent indicated they had some willingness to call the number, seeing a relatively low perceived risk in doing so. And who were these people, by and large? "The consumers who indicated they would have responded to this solicitation tended to have fewer years of education and be younger," wrote Wood in her report for *The Conversation*. But it turns out, the appeal of high benefit versus low risk is a big factor here as well, which leads me to my next characteristic...

- **They have an insatiable craving for a good deal.** Of course we all want a good deal. We all want to save money or get more for less. In and of itself, there's nothing wrong with that. What I'm talking about here is an *insatiable craving* for it. These are people who will seize the "buy one, get three free" opportunities without question, even though the item is something they normally wouldn't even want and they're now stuck with four of them. There's a deep, abnormal desire in these people to save a buck, to feel they're getting away with something, when the truth is that the only one who's winning is the person or company offering the deal. (They wouldn't offer it otherwise, right?)

A client once told me the story of how someone pretending to be with the tech support department at Dell Computers called her from an 800-number and explained that the extended warranty she had purchased for her computer was now being offered to every customer at no additional charge. The company, this person told her, would be refunding her the money she had paid for the warranty. All they needed to do was wire the money directly to her. Now, let me just say that this is a smart, talented woman who had been approached many times by scammers and thought she was too smart to be swindled. But she was also a young woman with a new family who was struggling to make ends meet, and she wanted desperately to believe that she had finally gotten a good deal, a lucky break. This person had all her computer's identification numbers, the date on which she had purchased the computer, everything, so maybe she had hit the jackpot, she thought. And when this person asked her to check her bank account balance to ensure the transfer was complete, low and behold, there was an extra $2,000 in her account—not the $200 he had promised. She got excited. After all, what kind of scammer would *give* her money, right? This *had* to be the real deal, didn't it?

"Oh no!" the scammer said to her on the phone. "That amount is incorrect! I need you to wire us that extra $1,800!"

This is when she realized she was caught up in a trick. She'd been too blinded by dollar signs, by seeing that much-needed extra money in her checking account to realize that her savings account had been depleted by $2,000. She hadn't received any money; this person had just transferred funds between her accounts as part of the trick, thanks to the identifying information he already had from her. And it had almost worked until she realized that legitimate tech support workers with Dell don't ask people to go to the Western Union on the corner and wire back the money they mistakenly gave her. She promptly hung up the phone, called her bank, and immediately changed bank accounts, vowing never to fall for such scams again. But a lot of people take longer to catch on, or the "deal" they're getting is even more seductive, more blinding.

If it seems too good to be true, it usually is. But for some, the lure of the deal is too strong to pass up.

- **They're dreamers.** Like the folks who are seduced by a good deal, many people become marks because they have a tendency toward big, impossible dreams. Gamblers tend to fall into this category, always dreaming they're going to strike it rich, beat the house, get out of debt, and live lives of luxury. Having lived and worked in Nevada for many years, this is something I'm pretty familiar with. But like a lot of other locals, I know that those casino resorts wouldn't be nearly so large and opulent, or their CEOs nearly so wealthy if the chances of beating the house were that high. Gamblers and other dreamers often suffer from illusions of superiority and control— this time they're going to hit it big, they've figured out a way to beat the system, they're smarter than the rest, they've studied and figured it out, they have control over the situation. These people might as well have "SUCKER" written across their backs in chalk. They make perfect marks.

- **They are trusting and not cynical.** Numerous studies point to a constellation of characteristics that seem common among fraud victims. These include an interest in, and susceptibility to, persuasion; a lack of defensive measures against frauds and scams (being optimists who believe it's unlikely to happen anyway); and a generally trusting nature. Tactics that the AARP see working include such comments as, "From one ex-Marine to another," or "My clients are earning at least thirty percent on this deal..." While comments like this are likely to have positive effects on all of us at one time or another, victims seem particularly influenced by these tactics, which exploit a person's trusting nature and general positive, rosy outlook. It's an unfortunate reality that being a cynic can be a good thing. Victims also tend to overestimate their ability to back out of deals that prove to be scams. The facts, however, prove otherwise. These people are often relentlessly pursued by phone, mail, or email due to their generally trusting natures.

- **They're often lonely.** This is why many elderly people fall victim to scams. The AARP report says that 66 percent of fraud victims reported that they "often or sometimes feel isolated." This group of people in particular are vulnerable to romance scams, in which culprits use online dating sites to exploit victims—to take their money or get them to engage in risky behaviors like drug smuggling, for instance. Desperate for human interaction, these people often grasp at any opportunity for conversation and relationship development, to the point of engaging in con games that a more socially secure person might not fall for.

- **They're coping with difficulties in life.** People who are sick, depressed, anxious, or reeling from personal traumas aren't thinking clearly. They often aren't able to make rational decisions. I know when I have even a bad cold, any challenge or provocation seems overwhelming to me, my brain simply isn't able to process it effectively. The AARP says recent job loss was a common trait shared by many fraud victims surveyed in its study. And according to a recent FTC study, if you've lost a loved one, gone through a divorce, been laid off from a job, or had some other time of life trauma in the last two years, your chances of being scammed more than doubles—likely because you simply don't have the mental and emotional bandwidth to make better decisions.

- **They engage in risky behaviors.** Plenty of research shows that those who engage in riskier behaviors are also more likely to fall prey to con artists. This is particularly true among investment fraud victims, as these are people who in the past have invested in riskier deals, like penny stocks or oil-and-gas options. In actual fact, many legitimate-but-risky investments look a lot like scams, with their need to act fast and better-than-average returns, so people who are drawn to one often may be drawn to the other.

- **They lack self-control.** Impulse control is a common trait seen among victims—and criminals too, as a matter of fact. Studies show that people who seem to have lower amounts of self-control seem to also have higher rates of being scammed, which seems obvious. If you're the type of person who struggles to eat right or stick to an exercise plan, who is easily swayed by friends or family to do things you initially didn't want to do, you might also lack the self-control necessary to keep yourself from being a mark.

- **They live in economically depressed areas.** According to the Federal Trade Commission, the states with the highest reported incidents of fraud in 2017 were Florida, Georgia, and Nevada—coincidentally, Florida and Nevada had the highest foreclosure rates in the nation, and Georgia's student loan debt is the second-highest in the U.S. All three states saw significant losses in housing values. (Florida's high population of seniors may also have something to do with this.)

- **They're white men.** A recent AARP report on victims of fraud says the typical investment fraud victim is a white, middle-aged man who's making good money, financially literate, and under some financial pressure—maybe struggling to pay the mortgage or married to a nonworking spouse. These people are the ones most likely to find themselves in sales situations, more susceptible to persuasion tactics, and more likely to take a financial risk if there's a potential for reward.

If you've spotted yourself in any of these character traits, I'm not surprised. I see plenty of myself in them as well. As you can see, any one of us can become victims at any time, depending on our personal or financial circumstances. The "artist" part of the term *con artist* is not a positive description. These people see inside us certain vulnerabilities, and they are malevolently artful in their tactics. As you'll see in the stories I share in this book, many are so skilled at identifying their marks and manipulating them that it's frightening. You must protect your assets by avoiding the scam.

Let's list the 13 Signs of a Mark again:

1. Once a sucker, always a sucker
2. They're elderly.
3. They're young.
4. They're uneducated.
5. They have an insatiable craving for a good deal.
6. They're dreamers.
7. They are trusting and not cynical.
8. They're often lonely.
9. They're coping with difficulties in life.
10. They engage in risky behaviors.
11. They lack self-control.
12. They live in economically depressed areas.
13. They're white men.

Understand where you are in this collection of attributes. The list is unfortunately very broad and you may fit into two or more categories. Work on being resilient and skeptical within every grouping and tier. Don't let misinformation, deceit and cunning challenge your assets. You worked hard to earn them. In these times you must work hard to protect them.

"A con artist gains your confidence... If you look at any successful professional, a salesperson, a marketer, a real estate agent, a trader, they all have the same qualities as the con man. The only difference is that one side uses their talents in the right direction and the con man is taking the easy way out." — Frank Abagnale, 2016

Chapter Five

Sharing Your Life

Understanding Identity Theft

CASE #3: The Original Internet Godfather

Brett Shannon Johnson has thinning hair, a salt-and-pepper beard, and the kind of rounded belly that speaks to middle age and plenty of good living. He's average looking, not threatening but not oozing charm either. In fact, on sight, there's little that's scary about him. You wouldn't consider for a moment that he might be one of today's most notorious scam artists, a man who once appeared on the Most Wanted list maintained by the U.S. Secret Service, who called Johnson "the Original Internet Godfather."

He began his life of crime when he was ten years old and started shoplifting. He came by it honest: His family conducted a fraud ring led by none other than Johnson's mother. Even his grandmother joined in. "It was almost written in stone that I was going to end up in some sort of fraud," he told Dionysios Demetis, who wrote an article about Johnson for *The Conversation* in 2018.

By the time he was old enough to marry, Johnson had graduated to insurance fraud, staging a phony car accident in 1994 and using the payout to finance his wedding. His first foray into internet fraud involved selling nonexistent merchandise on eBay—collecting the money and never mailing anything. He sold transmission cards for pirated satellite dishes to Canadian customers, and when he realized he could no longer keep up with demand, in true Ponzi fashion, he decided he could just take the money without providing them with anything. "Who would they complain to, anyway?" he reasoned.

In an interview with Herb Weisbaum from NBC News, Johnson claimed to be "the idiot" who figured out how to use the internet to commit tax refund fraud—he simply filed quick returns (a process he claims took him all of six minutes) under the names of dead people that he culled from the California Death Index, collecting refunds for people who had yet to be reported as dead to the IRS. He managed to earn $6,000 a week this way, opening scores of bank accounts online in order to house the money.

In 2002, after engaging in a series of chats with two other disreputable online buddies, Johnson began operating the website ShadowCrew.com, a cybercrime message board where he appeared under the name Gollumfun. The site was an underground forum and marketplace for cybercriminals to exchange information—including stolen personal information or credit card numbers—as well as tips on hacking as well as developing computer viruses, scams, or phishing schemes. The site also sold fraudulent bank accounts and prepaid debit cards. Johnson went on to take over CounterfeitLibrary.com in 2004, a site that used hijacked identification information to provide fake identities to cybercriminals.

"I didn't care who the victim was," Johnson told NBC's Weisbaum. "I always tried to justify it. I told myself, I'm not ripping off the person, I'm ripping off the store or the government or the bank... and they could afford it."

ShadowCrew.com operated until Nov. 2, 2004, when the U.S. Secret Service shut it down and arrested some of its members—though Johnson managed to avoid arrest during the raids. By this time, the site had about four thousand members who together were estimated to have taken roughly $4 million from victims. Site moderator Albert Gonzalez was sentenced to twenty years in prison for his masterminding the theft of 170 million credit card numbers, according to Demetis.

Eventually, Johnson's connections in the dark web caught up to him, and in 2005 he was arrested, at which point he followed in Abagnale's footsteps. He turned informant for the Secret Service. Like Abagnale, he dabbled simultaneously in good and evil for a while, working both as an informant and a part-time hacker at night, and he spent some time on and off in jails and prisons for a few years before finally managing to stay on the straight and narrow.

Today, Johnson is in his late forties, lives in Alabama, and owns Anglerfish Security, a consulting firm that advises Fortune 500 companies on how to protect themselves from cybercrime.

In the Middle Ages castles protected your assets. Today, people trick us into giving up the keys to the castle. I got a letter the other day from my bank. The letter stated that one of my credit cards had possibly been compromised, so the bank had issued me a new card. I was instructed to stop using the old card, to keep an eye on my account for suspicious activity, and to activate the new card immediately once I received it.

We've all had this happen, usually more than once, and I'll admit, my immediate thought was, "Ugh, what a pain."

After all, every time that happens, we now have work to do, right? We have to think about all the places where our card numbers are on file for automatic payments, and then either wait for notifications that the payments couldn't be processed (*"What?! I was dropped from car insurance for nonpayment?!!"*) or take time out of our day to call all those people and update their records. And then, of course, there's the matter of waiting for the new card to arrive and (yes, a total first-world problem) experiencing an unfamiliar fear associated with not having immediate, convenient access to our own money.

It's a frustrating fact of modern life that we must constantly live with the specter of identity theft hanging over our heads. And if we don't arm ourselves and take these exasperating and time-consuming steps to protect ourselves, we'll be forced to sorely regret it.

Each year, there are over 17 million victims of identity fraud, and it keeps growing. These consumers lose a staggering amount of money – over $17 billion dollars every year.

Just try to get your head around those numbers for a second: 17 million people. To illustrate, here's a frame of reference. Based on U.S. Census state population estimates, that's the same amount of people as the total populations of Oklahoma and Pennsylvania combined.

And that's just the people who reported it and know about it. "[A] startling number of people don't even know their identities have been stolen," says one of the most notorious con artists in history, Frank Abagnale.

How does this crime happen with such astounding frequency? According to Abagnale himself, it's surprisingly, frighteningly easy.

"First of all," he writes in his 2007 book *Stealing Your Life*, "it is elementary to pull off. If you have my name, my date of birth, and my Social Security number, that's pretty much all you need in order to become me. It takes very little investment capital. A phone and a cheap computer will get you started. If you want to write phony checks, you'll need a few vital tools like a blow-dryer, cake pans, and a common household chemical. You can pick them up at your nearest discount drugstore, and no one will be the wiser.

Plus, the chances of being caught are next to none. The government doesn't pay enough attention to it."

While in his heyday, Abagnale had to purchase a million-dollar printing press and make a fake ID to cash his fake checks. Today's identity thieves can do all this from their home computers, in their own living rooms, often from faraway countries. Law enforcement officials have no jurisdiction and no idea how to even begin tracking down these armchair criminals, so addressing identity theft has become more a matter of protecting ourselves than it is about what they see as an entirely futile effort of trying to catch the bad guys. Of course, that attitude has to change. Governments must go after these criminals.

Interestingly, although we've just spent the last chapter identifying the tricks of the visible, problematically charming con artist, I'm now talking about a crime in which the criminal never makes him or herself known at all.

There's an old episode of the comedy series *Friends* in which one of the main characters, Monica, realizes she has been the victim of credit card theft. When she gets a list of the fraudulent charges made on the card and discovers that the thief used it to charge a series of dance classes, Monica signs herself up for the dance class, then goes out of her way to confront the thief. Not only does Monica end up admiring the woman's adventuresome spirit and willingness to try new things, but the woman turns out to be a lovely, charming person who ultimately owns up to her crime and goes to jail.

It's a nice thought, but in reality, there's almost nothing about this scenario that mimics real life. In nearly all cases, the identity thief is absent, a phantom somewhere on the other side of the world who hacked into a computer and found your numbers. All you, the victim, ever knows is that your money and your feeling of security are gone. The perpetrator rarely goes to jail.

All the advantages and convenience technology offers us—the ability to pay and pump gas in one spot, the option to store credit card information online and buy things at the click of a button—also makes us supremely susceptible to fraud. And they may be our undoing. Javelin Strategy & Research, a third-party research firm whose work primarily focuses on finance and technology, recently conducted a study to examine fraud trends. Researchers found that of all the techniques identity thieves were using, account takeover was growing faster than any other method, with a rate that tripled from the previous year to reach a four-year high.

What is account takeover? If you've ever received a call from your bank indicating that someone tried using your credit card numbers to make a purchase in another state, you may have been the victim of an attempted account takeover—a crime in which someone uses a person's account information to get access to that person's money. According to Brian Innes' book *Fakes & Forgeries*, the increasing use of digital storage and transmission of personal data has made identity theft more and more appealing. Scotland Yard reports that it's "replacing drug trafficking as the crime of choice for underworld operators and terrorist cells," Innes writes.

The problem is that we have account numbers everywhere we turn—in our computers, in mailboxes, in our garbage and recycling bins, in our wallets or purses, and on our phones. Whether you're using a credit card, paying a utility bill, even getting blood drawn at your doctor's office, you have to provide account and personal information that gives a hacker the opportunity to pilfer your information. Because our creditors are more reliant on technology to conduct business, it's getting harder and harder to distinguish the real transactions from the fake ones. An email to consumers from a source pretending to be a credit card company might state that a refund will be deposited in the recipient's bank account, if only the consumer enters some personal data in the link to "verify his identity." Another solicitation might claim that the recipient has won a lottery or some kind of award, but the recipient must provide some personal details to claim it. This is all a thief needs to do in order to get hold of crucial information, pillage your bank accounts, and steal your identity.

And the result is that account takeover losses are now over $5 billion a year. The average victim paid at least $290 out of pocket and spent 15 hours just to resolve the issue and get back to their life.

As we increasingly move toward making purchases online rather than in stores, online credit card fraud looms as the biggest threat. Card-not-present fraud is now 81 percent more prevalent than point-of-sale fraud.

This leads me to point to the one part of that *Friends* episode that actually rings true: The perpetrator of the crime was a woman. As it turns out, identity theft is particularly appealing to women. Michigan State professor Judith Collins conducted a study of more than 1,000 identity theft arrests in the United States, and she found some interesting results. Among them is the fact that about half of the crimes were committed by women—a significant departure from most other types of crime.

"This crime is much different than any other crime," Collins told NBC News. "Men tend to be more risk-takers, and committing crime is high risk. But ID theft is low risk. For example, credit card fraud can be committed online... So we're probably going to continue to see as many women as men commit the crime."

In fact, identity thieves are people of all ages, races, cultures, religions, education levels, and professions. And their victims aren't all wealthy either. Having money often means knowing about and having greater security measures. More than half of victims make less than $50,000 a year, says the Identity Theft Resource Center.

Collins' study also found that about 70 percent of identity theft starts with an employee stealing personal data from his or her own company. We often think of these people as tech geniuses running major international hacking operations out of seedy basements, or unsavory characters digging through people's trash. But the truth is that, most of the time, it's an inside job—someone who works for the company entrusted with your personal data, who has easy access to it. It's a crime of opportunity. And here's something you'll probably find surprising: It's not always the broke, entry-level employees stealing this information. It's the employers themselves. Six out of ten American companies and government agencies have been hacked.

Even Frank Abagnale, a man so learned in the ways of criminals, says he's always watching his back. Whereas in Abagnale's day you had to go down to the county records office and wade through bureaucracy knee-deep, filled with paperwork in triplicate and layers of personnel in order to find personal information, now you don't even have to be particularly good at deception or sleight of hand. Identity theft doesn't depend on you being a sucker or falling for a convoluted story. You're just a series of numbers who got picked for the lottery, and all it took for you to wind up at risk was having a credit card, a Social Security number, a driver's license, a job, phone service, or health insurance, or being someone who uses the internet. That is pretty much all of us.

This leads me to point to another sad reality: Even our most innocent citizens, those who aren't even conducting transactions, carrying credit cards, applying for jobs, or driving are victims. Children are increasingly becoming targets for identity theft, because their Social Security numbers may sit gathering dust for years before being put to use. Until the child is old enough to start obtaining credit, a thief may have been operating under that number for years, thanks to the child's squeaky-clean credit report, so that by the time that child finally reaches adulthood, he or she already is in financial trouble.

Types of Identity Theft

The ways in which identity thieves work to commit fraud are as varied as the people who become their victims. However, the FTC's Sentinel Network Data Book, which tracks consumer reports of fraud each year, has categorized them into the following basic types:

- **Credit card fraud:** This type of identity fraud is far and away the most common, with the number of occurrences being more than double the second type on the list, employment or tax-related fraud. In credit card fraud cases, the thief has either grabbed your card and used it to make purchases, either online or in person, or he or she has stolen your credit card number, PIN, and security code to conduct transactions without your card even being present. Meanwhile, having access to the card provides the thief with access to other personal information, including your birth date, address, and Social Security number, so he or she may even go open new credit accounts in your name.

- **Employment or tax-related fraud:** In this type of fraud, which was reported nearly 84,000 times in recent years, the perpetrator has used your Social Security number to either get the tax refund you are owed or a job he or she isn't qualified for. In some cases, illegal immigrants desperate to remain in the country and find jobs have stolen other people's identities in order to appear to be legal residents. Interestingly, while reports of tax fraud were down quite a bit from the previous year (46 percent), employment and wage-related fraud was up by 23 percent. In a case like this, the employer reports your income to the IRS using your Social Security information, but the thief has been receiving that income, so the IRS will show that you've received income you never received, and guess who ends up owing taxes on them? Yep—you.

- **Phone or utilities fraud:** Your good credit and payment record could be used by identity thieves to skate along on free power, gas, phone service, or cable or satellite TV service. Once the culprit has your account information (often snagged by reading your mail or sorting through your trash), all that person has to do is offer up bogus addresses on a change of address form. They never pay the bills, and by the time they've tracked you down—the rightful owner of the payment information—you're in collections over a service you never used and the thief has moved on to someplace else. The FTC reports that this type of fraud is reported over 55,000 times every year, with percentages of landline phone fraud in particular skyrocketing.

- **Bank fraud:** Even more sinister are the 50,000-plus cases of bank fraud reported annually, in which the fraudsters gained access—through a variety of means, including telephone solicitations, interceptions of wire transfers, spying on ATM transactions, check fraud, raiding employer records, or plain old going through the trash to find bank statements or receipts—to the victims' bank account information. Using this information, the identity thieves then had access to the victims' money. Instead of holding tellers up at gunpoint and demanding money out of the vault, these sly perpetrators take account holders' money quietly and nonviolently, and often without being noticed.

- **Loan or lease fraud:** In this type of identity theft, which is reported more than 30,000 times per year, the identity thief utilizes personal information to secure bank loans, mortgages, auto loans, student loans, apartment leases or other types of financing, getting free money by pretending they're you. Or they falsify information on an application to get loans approved or to increase the size of the loan. And it isn't just borrowers who do it—it's brokers and appraisers too, pushing applications through to get sales that wouldn't pass muster otherwise. In some cases, the perpetrators have set up entire households in victims' names, damaging the victims' credit and putting them, if the bills aren't paid, into considerable financial and legal trouble.

- **Government documents or benefits fraud:** In recent years, many politicians have argued that too many people are taking advantage of welfare and other government benefits. While many folks legitimately need and deserve these important benefits, it is indeed correct: Too many people—to the tune of 25,849 of them in 2017 alone—use fraudulent information on government documents or benefits paperwork. The amount of reports of government benefits applied for or received fraudulently went up 34 percent over the previous year, though this is certainly not the only way this type of identity theft is committed. Unfortunately, many government programs require only that applicants provide names and Social Security numbers, so with only the most basic information in hand, a thief can steal from taxpayers. And victims may never find out until they go to apply for these benefits and find themselves denied. Fraudsters may also use your information to get drivers' licenses, passports, or other government-issued identification, paving the way for future fraudulent activity.

- **Miscellaneous other types:** More than 70,000 reports a year go to the FTC for what it deems "Other Types," which include medical services fraud, in which the theft uses a victim's identification information to secure prescriptions, medical care, or medical insurance; stealing someone's identity to evade the law (even, in some cases, damaging your reputation and forcing the courts to issue warrants in your name); falsifying identification information to secure insurance; fraudulently using information to create online shopping or payment accounts, for instance through PayPal or retailers; creating email or social media accounts under someone else's identity, and more.

And here's something important to keep in mind: It isn't always strangers who steal your identity. In fact, because your family members and friends often have carte blanche to your personal information—from knowing where you keep important documents and your date of birth to having access to your Social Security number, PIN numbers, bank account numbers, and even the passwords to your computers and online accounts—it stands to reason that the people we know are not only capable of committing identity theft and fraud, but they frequently do. Javelin recently reported that 550,000 fraud and identity theft victims reported that their information had been compromised by someone they knew.

How Identity Thieves Can Take Your Life

Identity theft is a crime of opportunity. By simply being out in the world, we open ourselves up to identity fraud all the time. Even folks who are careful—myself included—not to share our personal information indiscriminately and have good systems in place aren't one hundred percent impervious to the occasional slip-up, and this is where identity thieves take full advantage. All it takes is having access to a couple important numbers for a whole house of cards to come tumbling down.

How to do identity thieves get these numbers? Here are few tried-and-true techniques:

- **Credit card co-opting:** A friend of mine told me a story about when he used to wait tables in the early 90s, when he was fresh out of college. One of his fellow servers was arrested while she was working a busy lunch shift. It turned out that she had committed credit card fraud. On the lines where customers wrote in their tip amounts on their credit card receipts, this server had been using some clever penmanship to make adjustments to her tip amounts—for instance, changing a 4 to a 9. Since the restaurant managers reconciled those receipts by adding tip amounts to the computerized totals at the end of the night, rather than relying on the totals arrived at through customer math (a mistake they've surely rectified by now), the server was clearing far more cash at the end of the night than her customers had intended. She was caught when, finally, an attentive customer returned with her receipt to ask why her total was so different from the one that had been charged. The resulting investigation revealed dozens of differing receipts that had been handled in this manner, over a period of months. It's ironic that for what probably amounted to maybe $50 extra in her pocket, this woman's reputation, employability, and credibility were forever wrecked by the scheme. And it's telling that over several months' time, the victims hadn't bothered to compare their receipts with their card statements to check on the totals.

This type of credit card fraud is fairly mild compared to the way many identity thieves operate. They don't simply write in a few extra dollars on your transaction; they take your account information and charge thousands of dollars without a trace of it being on paper.

Anyone who has seen your card or watched you punching in the numbers—think nosy customers behind you at ATMs, grocery store checkout lines, or gas station attendants—can grab your card information and use it against you. Eater.com points out that the restaurant industry in particular is a dangerous place for this type of theft because it's one of the only places where your card is in a stranger's hands and out of your sight for minutes at a time, and you rarely watch where it goes or what's done with it.

With the help of a small, palm-sized card reader called a skimmer, anyone (including a server who can hide the device in a sleeve) can scan the magnetic strip on your card and record all your credit card information. Recently, 28 servers were indicted as part of an organized crime ring that involved lipstick-sized skimmers used to capture credit card information and charge thousands of dollars' worth of high-priced luxury items for resale.

And some devices never even need to be near your card—they need only come into proximity of your wallet in order to capture your pertinent information. This means that your chip card isn't so foolproof as you may have believed.

Companies entrusted with your data, or with whom you have credit accounts, are often hacked, and the data breaches provide thieves with hundreds, or even thousands, of people's personal information.

- **Clever calling:** If someone has the right information on you, they need only call one of the three credit-reporting agencies (TransUnion, Experian, or Equifax) pretending to be a prospective creditor in order to receive a detailed credit report on you. Or they might call the bank, pretending to be you, and ask to change your mailing address. A new card is issued to the thief.

- **Manipulating with authority:** In Frank Abagnale's book *Stealing Your Life*, he writes of a college professor in the Midwest who, in 2004-2005, instructed his freshman and sophomore students to write at the tops of their test papers, in addition to their names, their Social Security numbers and dates of birth. Unquestioningly abiding by the request from an authority figure, students did as they were instructed. In fact, many colleges have for years gotten away with posting student grades by Social Security numbers, instead of names (laughably, to safeguard "privacy"). This professor was respected and well liked, right up until he began charging more than $200,000 to their credit cards.

Elsewhere, an elementary school held a poster contest and asked students to write their Social Security numbers down on the backs of the posters as identification.

At doctors' and dentists' offices and hospitals around the country, health care professionals ask patients for their Social Security numbers and other crucial personal information as a matter of course. Retailers ask for it upon granting credit accounts at the register. Drugstores may ask for it in the process of creating patient pharmacy records. Heck, if you want to buy a new dishwasher, the store will ask you to fill out a questionnaire that eventually asks for nearly every piece of demographic information about you, even your Social Security number.

And because these are people we perceive as having authority over us, we hand the information over. The problem is, these situations rarely require this essential information, and handing it over exposes you to identity theft.

Just because someone asks for this information doesn't necessarily require that you offer it. Only a handful of places actually have a valid need for it: Credit applications, anything involving large cash transactions, government benefit applications, military paperwork, and the DMV.

In fact, it isn't just Social Security numbers we hand over indiscriminately. In *Stealing Your Life*, Abagnale describes a scheme in which identity thieves call pretending to be long-lost friends: "Hey, remember me? It's Bob! I was just thinking how your birthday is coming up... Oh, it's not your birthday? Gosh, I must have you confused with someone else. When's yours again? Hey, I want to put a card in the mail to you, but I don't have a current address. Can you give me that?" Voila, you've just handed over vital information to a total stranger, all because you didn't want to be rude and say no.

Stepping around the whole "I need this information" conversation can be awkward, particularly in places such as the doctor's office, but a few moments of awkwardness are worth it to avoid months or even years of financial troubles as a result of identity theft.

- **Online databases:** In his book *The Complete Idiot's Guide to Frauds, Scams, and Cons*, author Duane Swierczynski tells of schemes some crooks use to sell your personal information to the highest bidder. He shares how one bold thief actually posted an ad on eBay that read, "100 (one hundred) Social Security # Numbers Obtain False Credit Cards Identity Theft I Don't Care Bid Starts at a Dollar a Piece USPS Money Orders only all Different."

In January 2018, a 27-year-old Ontario, Canada, man was arrested for selling billions of stolen passwords online through a now-defunct website called LeakedSource.com. Many sources believe the site's administrator also ran AbuseWith.us, a site boasting that it helps people hack emails and online gaming accounts.

In July of 2018, the Better Business Bureau announced it had received reports from victims of a vehicle history scam. In the scam, a person looking to sell a car posts an ad online. Someone calls claiming to be interested in the vehicle and asks the seller to go to an unfamiliar website and input the Vehicle Identification Number (VIN) in order to run a vehicle history report. The site not only charged for this "report," but it captured personal information such as address, driver's license number, and/or credit card information.

Digital databases such as these make it far too easy for crooks to get hold of your personal information. Some — yes, completely legal — websites exist purely for the sake of allowing users to find personal details that ought to be private. The Church of Jesus Christ of Latter-Day Saints operates a site called FamilySearch.org, the third-largest database in the world, which enables users to search family histories, including death records and even Social Security numbers of the dearly departed. Another site, DocuSearch.com, which not only offers the ability to find people or look up phone numbers, but also allows you to search public records, find Social Security numbers ("for any legal reason," it says, but let's face it, criminals lie), or discover hidden assets — all for the low low price of $49. NetDetective.com touts the following at the top of its home page: "Net Detective Lets You Search for People on Our Enormous Database Find Information on Anyone." This frightening website claims that you can do searches on anyone in total privacy and that it's "100% legal." Touted benefits include cloaking your email so you can't be found, allowing you to make phone calls through a third-party so you aren't traceable, providing lists of speed traps in the U.S., identifying locations for where you can purchase security equipment such as listening devices, and a lot more.

Today, a Social Security number is available on the dark web— the areas of the internet hidden by network overlays that require anonymizing software to access—and only for a couple of dollars. And your number might come up next. Ironically, many boast that what they're doing is American, making information accessible and transparent to all. Criminals know about these sources and plenty more, and they aren't afraid to use them.

- **Data breaches:** *Business Insider* reported that between January 2017 and August 2018, sixteen retailers were hacked, causing consumer information to be leaked. And Shape Security, a cybersecurity firm, issued a report showing that as much as 90 percent of login attempts to online retailers are done by hackers using pilfered data.

  When you give any personal or financial information to a company, that information becomes at risk for being hacked and used against you. This information might include credit card numbers, Social Security numbers, home address, date of birth, medical history, or even purchase histories. Corporate information, such as consumer lists, may be leaked as well. Typically, this is because of flawed payment systems, both online and in stores. Some may be the result of malware; for instance, hackers implant malware into computer systems, and then data entered into the computer is captured and retrieved by the thief. And it's not shady or half-rate companies either—we're talking about the likes of Macy's, Bloomingdales, Target, Sears, Delta Airlines, Best Buy, Whole Foods Market, Saks Fifth Avenue, and even (gulp) Equifax, one of the big three credit-reporting agencies. So even if you're carefully guarding the information in your possession, the information entrusted to certain million-dollar, otherwise-credible sources may not be so safe.

- **The good-old-fashioned grab-and-run:** Not every identity thief is a hacker pilfering your numbers online. Some do it the old-fashioned way. If you're still throwing your receipts, statements, and mail in the garbage without shredding it, or putting mail in the mailbox with the flag up, shame on you. These moves precipitate the oldest moves in the book. All a would-be thief needs to do is watch you leave your trashcan or recycling bin at the curb, or raid your unlocked mailbox for mail, then grab what he needs and run. Every "Congratulations! You're approved!" solicitation, every bill you mail a check for can become a means by which a thief can take you for a ride. And even if you don't do these things, clever pickpockets and purse thieves prey on victims all the time, bashing in car windows or using distraction in order to grab your money and run.

- **Hastily disposed-of electronics:** "In with the new, out with the old" is a philosophy many of us subscribe to. Those new phones, tablets, and personal computers, with their speedy connections and improved capabilities entice us to quickly ditch our old devices and pass them along generously to others. But simply deleting our data from the hard drives isn't enough to divert persistent and tech-savvy crooks, though. With enough technical know-how, someone can access personal files, downloaded bank statements and more.

- **Employee files:** I said this earlier, and it bears repeating: A great many identity thieves are employers or employees who steal personnel file data or records captured in the course of doing business. The FTC says that 90 percent of business record theft pertains to employee records, not records collected from consumers. Frequently, temporary workers secure short-term positions intentionally to access employee data files; the worker has not undergone a background check or other measures that would have been exercised for permanent employees. The work ends within a day or two, and the employee is long gone before anyone realizes what's happened. The International Risk Management Institute reported a case from 2002 in which two temp employees at Children's Hospital of Arkansas were part of a large identity theft ring and were charged with theft of employee records.

In other situations, disgruntled workers leave the company planning to "get back" at employers by taking unsupervised records, cleaning crews root around in trash cans, or third-party contractors with access to files take advantage of that.

- **Address changes:** In Chicago, one man worked the postal service's change of address form to his advantage. He managed to have mail intended for UPS corporate headquarters in Atlanta rerouted to his own personal home address. Though he was eventually charged with mail theft and fraud, it was only after he'd deposited about $58,000 in forwarded checks. So much mail came to him for UPS that the postal service had to put a tub outside the man's door.

That change of address form is shockingly easy to manipulate. All a would-be crook would need to do is purchase a post office box with cash, fill out the form from the Movers Guide Packet changing your home address to the new post office box, stamp the letter, and pop it in the mailbox. Before long, your mail is being rerouted to John Q. Thief. The U.S. Postal Service is supposed to send a Moving Validation Letter to the old address, to confirm that the change of address is valid. But if you miss it (assuming, for instance, that it's a solicitation and not official business), bam, your mail stops coming.

According to National Public Radio, postal inspectors received more than 17,000 complaints in 2017 regarding fraudulent address changes.

How You Know You're a Victim

So with all these possible means for stealing your identity without being discovered or caught, how do you discover that you've been victimized so you can begin the long and arduous process of recovering your identity? Here are some warning signs:

- You get your credit report, and it ain't good. This is the number one way identity theft victims have discovered that they have been victimized, as nearly a quarter of them report finding unauthorized accounts on their credit reports, according to the Identity Theft Resource Center. Experts tell us to check our credit reports at least once a year and to scour them for errors, and the good news is that many more of us do this—but it's often not enough. CNBC reports that one in five credit reports contains material errors, and they may not be the result of fraud but simply bad or incomplete reporting. It behooves you to correct these errors to maintain good credit ratings, which are essential for securing loans, getting insured, or even being employed. If something doesn't look right to you, that may be a sign that you've been targeted for identity theft. Be particularly cautious about addresses you've never had or credit accounts you've never used or signed up for.

- Your bank accounts don't jive. If you're frequently checking your bank balances online and reconciling all your transactions (and you should be), you should be able to spot any transactions that don't look familiar, or that charge amounts different from those you remember. This is the second most common way victims learn about the problem, with 18.2 percent of cases being uncovered this way.

- Your mail stops coming. If bills you usually receive with regularity stop coming, or your mailbox is unusually empty, you may have been victimized by a change-of-address scam.

- You're getting bills for things you didn't buy. Don't write it off as a fluke; even if the criminal can't be caught, if you report it early, you go on record as the victim of identity theft, which can help keep you from liability in future incidences.

- You're receiving unsolicited credit cards or credit card statements that you know aren't yours.

- You're getting calls from debt collectors. When people start saying you owe money that you know you don't owe, that's a major red flag.

- Your bank contacts you about suspicious charges. Sometimes, the charges were legitimately yours—say, you went out of town on a spontaneous vacation and decided to splurge on some art—and sometimes they're not.

- You're denied credit. Your cards are denied, your checks won't clear, and your attempts to obtain credit accounts fail, despite the fact that you know you have good credit. That's a sign you need to get a credit report and find out who might be abusing your credit information.

- Your health care provider charges you for services you didn't receive. We tend to trust doctors, labs, and hospitals for providing accurate information, and we also frequently don't know the medical or scientific terminology referenced on our bills, so we may pay them without thinking (*"I mean, I know I saw the doctor a few months back. I guess this charge is from that?"*). But health care fraud is on the rise, and a thief may have used your information to obtain services he or she couldn't access normally.

- Related to this, your insurer sends you a notice about a denied claim or type of coverage. If it's a condition or treatment you've never had, that may be a sign of identity theft.

- A company where you have an account or have done business is the victim of a data breach.

- You receive word from the IRS about additional income that doesn't sound familiar, your IRS refund doesn't come, or you learn that more than one tax return was filed in your name. Or you receive word that your electronically filed tax return was rejected, which might mean that someone tried submitting false information under your name.

- You get an alert about a two-factor authentication requirement. Sometimes this is a legitimate request because you've opened a new account, or it's your bank wanting to verify your identity. But sometimes it's someone trying to lure you into a scam.

The worst part about all this is that once it's started, stopping it becomes nearly impossible. The Identity Theft Resource Center conducts an annual study that examines the aftermath of identity theft. It reports that victims' actions to resolve identity theft included borrowing money from friends and relatives and selling possessions to pay bills, as well as closing financial and online accounts. A majority (almost 62 percent) said they had yet to clear up their cases and resolve their issues even *after five years.*

More than 53 percent felt powerlessness or helplessness as a result of being victimized, and 7 percent actually reported feeling suicidal. Resulting financial problems included being denied credit, loans, mortgages, and rentals, with some of the most minor problems including increased interest rates on their credit cards. Sharing your life takes a toll.

In some ways, it's good that almost half—42.5 percent—learned about the problem within three months of it starting. This shows that consumers are becoming increasingly vigilant when it comes to this problem.

But still, the chances of prosecuting these criminals is very low. The government needs to step it up before these criminals present even more of a challenge.

"The impact of identity theft can be devastating and long-lasting, impacting the victim's financial wellbeing in many ways, ranging from bad credit to outright bankruptcy. Years of data breaches, culminating in the Equifax breach, have left millions of people exposed to identity theft. Quite simply, it has become one of the most important challenges of our time." — Matt Cullina, Board of Directors, Identity Theft Resource Center and Industry Expert

Chapter Six

Dialing for Dollars

Scammers Play the Game of Phones

CASE #4: *The Sweepstakes That Wasn't*

Eighty-five-year-old Vivian Murphy of Worcester, Massachusetts, had fond memories of Publishers Clearing House, the 65-year-old purveyor of magazine subscriptions, household items, online games, and, of course, the annual sweepstakes that enlisted television pitch man Ed McMahon and an enthusiastic team called The Prize Patrol to deliver ginormous checks to sweepstakes winners before a live audience. Every year for decades, Murphy told the *Boston Globe*, she had eagerly entered and watched the sweepstakes, which to date has provided more than $380 million to lucky winners.

One day, she received a call that she thought meant all her dreams were finally coming true. The caller, who identified herself as Deborah Holland—a name Murphy had frequently seen printed on those PCH letters that showed up at her home—asked first if Murphy was alone.

When Murphy confirmed that yes, she was alone at home, Ms. Holland offered her warm congratulations. Murphy was the winner of $1.5 million in the PCH sweepstakes!

Murphy was ecstatic. After decades of entering the contest, all that time and all those high hopes had finally paid off. Now she could help her children and grandchildren by paying off their mortgages, even provide some seed money to start bank accounts for her great-grandkids.

"You can't tell anyone about this yet," Ms. Holland warned. "It has to stay confidential for now, or you will risk losing the prize."

Holland's voice grew serious. First, they needed to get down to business. PCH could not present the prize to Murphy until some taxes and fees were paid. They would need a check for $890.60.

Murphy promptly cut the check to get the ball rolling, but she soon learned that was just the tip of the iceberg. The woman, who now had begun calling her "sweetie" and "dearie," called the next day to say they needed $3,000 more, just to "keep the process moving," and the next day after that, they needed another $3,890. The following week, Ms. Holland called one morning asking for $5,000, and later that afternoon they needed another $5,000.

But there was nothing left in her checking account, Murphy argued. She couldn't afford to pay anything else. So Holland suggested that maybe her retirement accounts had some money in them she could access.

Spurred on by the incentive of that $1.5 million prize, Murphy got in touch with her financial advisor and asked if she could have some money transferred.

"What do you need it for?" the advisor asked her, but Murphy remained firm to her commitment to the PCH and refused to comment, saying only that she couldn't reveal the details yet, but that soon it would all be made clear.

The details Ms. Holland had given her were clear, and Murphy made sure to follow them to the letter, writing the checks from her credit union account to the names of people she was told worked for PCH. But Holland was adamant that she write nothing about PCH on the check's note line.

When she finally received an official note of congratulations and a copy of a check for $1.5 million from PCH, Murphy breathed a sigh of relief. Finally, *finally*, all the money she had spent was coming back to her in the form of her sweepstakes winnings. Ms. Holland said she couldn't wait to present the check in person so the two women, who by now had become good friends, could finally sit down to have coffee together.

Two weeks from the day when Murphy had learned of her winnings, after she'd already spent roughly $18,000 to grease the skids on this sweepstakes delivery, Holland called again to request $10,000. Murphy, growing concerned and anxious, did as she was asked. Calls came every day, including one day when there were eight calls—Holland urgently needed $20,000 to comply with the IRS's tax demands. The date for her sweepstakes delivery kept getting pushed back, and she couldn't get paid back until she did what she was told. Murphy held her nose and wrote the check.

The *Globe* reports that by this time, Murphy had written seven checks totaling $47,780.60. Finally, PCH was ready to deliver the prize money on April 27, 2018. Murphy had to cancel a long-planned doctor's appointment so she could be home to receive her Prize Patrol visit. When Murphy's daughter, who had planned to take her to the doctor that day, asked why her mother had cancelled, she was told, "I can't tell you."

Her daughter, Maureen Sanderson, became worried and went to check on Murphy, and finally the woman could stand it no longer. Beaming with pride, she pulled out the letter of congratulations and revealed the secret she had been bursting to share with her daughter. But Sanderson was nonplussed. Her first question was whether they had asked her mother for any money. Yes, Murphy replied, she'd had to pay some fees.

After that, Murphy's daughter took matters into hand. She called the credit union and put a stop payment on the $20,000 check. The rest, they learned, was unlikely to ever be returned.

"It took a while to convince my mother this wasn't real, and she's not usually gullible," Sanderson told *Globe* reporter Sean P. Murphy. "Obviously, they took advantage of her."

The checks were traced to St. Paul and McKinney, Texas, and Murphy and Sanderson reported the situation to the police, the FTC, PCH, and the Massachusetts attorney general. The number Ms. Holland had provided to Murphy turned out to have been generated from Kingston, Jamaica—a common origin point for scam calls because of the proliferation of U.S. companies' call centers in that country, which is nowhere near Publishers Clearing House. Murphy was left bewildered, depressed, and out nearly $28,000.

Here's another case:

The phone rang on an afternoon in 2012. Seeing a phone number with a Southern California area code and thinking that she knows several people who live in that area, the woman answered the phone without a thought.

"Yes, ma'am, I am calling from the Internal Revenue Service regarding the case that is being brought against you and the money you owe the IRS. This call is being recorded. May I please get your attorney's name and contact information so that we may contact him or her regarding this case?"

"Uh... I'm confused. What case is this referring to?" the woman asked, suspicious. But if this was a scam caller, why would he be asking for her attorney's phone number?

"Ma'am, I'm not able to discuss that information with you. Let me give you the name of the deputy in charge of this case, and you can contact him to discuss this. We suggest you contact your attorney immediately, as a warrant for your arrest has been issued in this matter."

The woman took down the name and phone number for the "deputy" that the caller provided, and then she promptly called me, an attorney who happens to be a good friend. "Do you know anything about this? Could this be legit?" she asked me. "They said they want to speak to my attorney."

"Yeah, that's a hoax," I told her. "You're fine. The IRS doesn't call people."

It was a sophisticated plan, I thought. The "IRS" calls I'd heard of before had merely been recordings, computerized voices threatening hitherto unknown horrors if the call recipient didn't call the number provided and pay up immediately. Since my friend called and told me about this bizarre phone scam, I've received a few such messages myself, and so have my family members, friends, and colleagues.

The scam is so pervasive that in a survey of one thousand people that was conducted by First Orion, a telecommunications company dedicated to caller identification and call management solutions, IRS impersonations were the number-one scam call reported, with forty percent of survey respondents saying they had been contacted by someone impersonating the IRS.

About 75 percent said they had received calls they believed to be scams. First Orion projected that consumers would receive *nine billion calls* from known scammers that year.

Truecaller, another caller ID and spam-blocking telecommunications company, reported that 95 percent of people had been targeted by phone scams in the last six months. The average user, it determined, received 20.7 scam calls per month. In most scams (70 percent), the scammers asked for money by phone. The average loss was $430.

Folks, we are almost to the point where the number of scam calls received by the average person rivals the number of legitimate calls we get. First Orion projects that almost half of cell phone calls will be from spammers in the future. The National Consumers League's National Fraud Information Center reports that more than half of all consumer fraud involves the phone.

How did something as seemingly harmless and old fashioned — technology that's been around for almost one hundred and fifty years — become the preferred method of perpetrating scams? Well, probably by being old technology that's easy to use and abuse. First, whereas in the "olden days," when our phones were attached to our walls at home, where we left them behind whenever we left the house, now we have our cell phones in our pockets and purses all day, even beside us when we sleep at night. We're more likely to answer calls on our cell phones.

Plus, it's attached to a ten-digit number that is given out so frequently you don't even think about it. You give it to the cashier at the grocery store to access your club card account, you use it at retailers to access frequent-shopper discounts or receive coupons by text, and you provide it to log in to online services. And every time that number gets disbursed across the internet or punched into a register or computer, it provides an opportunity for a potential scammer to get hold of it and use it to reach you and your personal information. Your number may just have been added to a list (what *Frauds, Scams, and Cons* author Duane Swierczynski calls "the sucker list") that fraudsters sell to the highest bidder.

Remember what I said earlier? If you've fallen for a scam before, you're more likely to fall for it again, so if your name is on such a list, you're being targeted as an easy mark.

Incoming call numbers are easier than ever to mask. Dialing *67 allows anyone to mark their own number as blocked or private. Scammers are increasingly becoming more sophisticated, too, and they now frequently engage in something called "spoofing." They may be calling from somewhere on the other side of the world, but they have cloaked themselves with phone numbers that appear to be from cities nearby, or even in your own area code. Seeing a phone number that could be from a neighbor—maybe your child's school, a possible customer, your doctor's office—tricks you into answering, and before you know it, you're unwittingly engaged in a phone call with someone who wants to take your money or your identity.

And phone scammers will say—and they have—absolutely *anything* to get what they want out of you. AARP researchers worked with law enforcement agents in early 2018 to get actual recordings of scam callers on the lines with victims, or on their answering machines. The things they said will astound you. Here are some examples:

- Actual oil and gas investment pitch: "Most of the big boys can put $150,000 in the fireplace, burn it and not lose an ounce of sleep. And this is a big-boy game, so if you're going to play this game, you've got to be able to just lose money and not think twice about it."

- From a scammer who was speaking (unknowingly) to an undercover agent who was asking too many questions: "Are you stupid? I'm not trying to insult you, but are you mentally ill? ... I'm going to pass you to my manager 'cause you are making me sweat, and if you were in front of me, I would have slapped you by now, OK?"

- From a scammer who had already collected hundreds of thousands of dollars in a prize fraud who was finally being told no: "You're going to your grave a loser. A big loser. I think you are terrible."

You think that's bad? They get worse, way worse, because the people making these calls have nothing to lose. These phone scammers are nearly impossible to catch and will pull out every trick in the book if it means they can get hold of your money. The crazy part is that when someone talks to a normal, reasonable person this way, the psychological effects can include intimidation, anger, fear, or shame, and that's exactly how these people extract what they want from their victims.

There are new phone frauds being created and executed every day, so there's truly no way to provide an exhaustive list of all the possible methods by which phone scammers can rip you off. All you can do is stay informed about some of the methods these crooks use, recognize the patterns and try to stay one step ahead.

Who's Calling, Please?

There's no doubt that there are telemarketers out there working every day in legitimate enterprises. I would never choose that as an occupation, but it is legal to conduct some business this way. This fact, however, makes it harder to distinguish the real ones from the fakes. Here are some of the tactics used by phone scammers—I'm sure many of these are familiar to you.

- **The good ol' IRS or court warrant scam:** This is what we call the scam of choice among phony callers. It happens in a number of ways, but the bottom line is that the caller manipulates the average person's fear of the law and government by trying to convince you that the IRS or a federal marshal is coming for you because you owe money. Sometimes it's just a robotic voice warning you to call the number provided or else. Sometimes it's a live person. Sometimes the caller says you've missed a court appearance and someone is on his way right now to arrest you, unless you settle up right now on the phone with a credit card, a prepaid debit card, an iTunes gift card (yes, this is a real thing), or wired money via the Western Union office down the street from your house.

The following was captured in the AARP recordings and is typical of these types of calls—just like the one my friend received: "This is officially a final notice from IRS, Internal Revenue Service. The reason of this call is to inform you that the IRS is filing a lawsuit against you. To get more information about this case file, please call immediately on our department number ..."

Please know this: The IRS and other government entities will rarely, if ever, initiate contact with you by phone. Ninety-nine percent of the time, they will reach out to you through the U.S. mail. In some rare circumstances, such as long-overdue tax bills or impending audit appointments, the IRS representative will call a citizen, but this is only after contact has been initiated by mail, and in the case of outstanding balances, several pieces of mail will already have been sent. It will never be a surprise that comes out of the clear blue sky to have the IRS call and tell you that you owe money. The IRS is never going to demand a particular type of payment, and they won't insist that it be made right then and there while they have you on the phone. And they certainly have no need for your iTunes gift cards.

They also won't threaten to call in immigration authorities or sheriff's deputies to come arrest you. In fact, the IRS has no jurisdiction in matters of immigration and cannot revoke immigrant status. Neither will federal marshals look to extract money from you in order to help you get out of trouble for missing jury duty (Um, hello... can you say bribery?). My friends in Paraguay say this does happen there. But in the US, if a collection agent calls you on behalf of the IRS, you will have been notified by mail about the name of the firm and, again, not be surprised by the fact that you owe money the IRS is trying to collect. And any payment owed to the IRS should only be made to the U.S. Treasury—not the name of some debt collector or middleman.

- **You've won a trip!** Second in frequency only to IRS scams, among all telephone frauds, is the cruise or vacation scam, accounting for a full 25 percent of scam calls reported in the First Orion survey. While the IRS scam plays on that fear motivation that works so well on us law-abiding citizens, the travel scam plays on our greed, the deep desire to get something for nothing. The caller announces, "Congratulations, you've won an all-expenses-paid Caribbean cruise!" All you have to do is pay for the taxes, fees, or other perks by handing over your credit card information. The caller may ask for a credit card simply in order to verify your identity (hey, isn't that ironic?) before you can collect your winnings. The details are likely to be pretty murky—it's just a "five-star" resort or "luxury accommodations," but they're hard-pressed to provide any names. They'll push you into signing up for a travel club in order to receive the prize, but it's a "great deal" because it gets you discounts on future travel. And many times, they're recorded messages or "robocalls."

  Some of these recordings are pretty darn good, too. One time I answered the phone with my customary "hello," and a woman with a young-sounding, pleasant voice said, "I'm sorry, what was that? I couldn't hear you." So I repeated my hello, and she said, "Oops! Sorry, my headset must be malfunctioning!" She giggled childishly and began launching into her spiel about the trip I'd won. I only realized it was a recording when I tried interrupting her and she barreled on through the call without even stumbling. I promptly hung up as the recorded voice prattled on.

- **Bank and credit card calls:** The third most frequent telescammer tactic, accounting for 16 percent of calls in the First Orion survey, is the credit card or bank call. If you're like me, you are on a first-name basis with "Rachel from Card Services." She always likes to call at dinner time, doesn't she? She's calling to tell you that you might be eligible to lower your interest rate on your credit card. Unfortunately, she is lying to you. She has no such power, and she'll probably try to charge you a few thousand bucks for trying.

Sometimes the caller says you've been selected to receive an interest-free credit card, a credit-monitoring protection plan, or even a low-interest loan by your bank or credit-card company. "Guess what?" the caller will say, explaining that the credit laws have changed—instead of the $50 standard liability, now you might be responsible for all unauthorized charges on your account! What are you going to do? Fortunately, XYZ Company is offering credit insurance, which covers you in the likely event that a scammer gets hold of your credit card numbers and tries to rip you off! The problem is that none of this is true and credit insurance is a completely unnecessary provision. If fraudulent charges are suspected on your account, under the Fair Credit Billing Act, a simple call to your bank should be able to take care of it, and you still are only responsible for up to $50 of any fraudulent charges. Beyond that, those charges should automatically be refunded back to your account.

Same goes for the bogus "card security" call, in which a representative from Visa or MasterCard calls to verify your card's protection features by asking you to provide some personal information; or the advance-fee loan scam, where the fraudster promises you a hefty loan with no credit check or references needed, and all you have to do is pay the $250 administrative fee to process the loan. I'm here to tell you, you ain't never gettin' that money. There isn't a legitimate bank, credit card, or loan provider in the world that insists on charging a fee to provide you with "free" money.

- **The prize bait and switch:** I hate to tell you, but no, you didn't win a free trip without any strings attached, and you didn't win a lottery or cash prize, either. Unless you're holding the winning ticket in your state's lottery—which you know because you just heard the numbers called on TV—allow me to be the one to break the news to you. You're not a winner. Like the trip or advance-fee loan scam, the common tactic employed is to ask you to pay a fee or taxes in order to take delivery of your prize. Think about this one: Have you ever legitimately won a prize for which you were asked to pay something first? How would that be a prize? It's either free or it's not, and if it's not, it's not for real. No one needs your credit card number in order to give you something. Even casinos won't promise you'll win before taking your money.

- **Challenging charity calls:** It's hard to give to charities these days, when so many disreputable people are standing by, ready to rip you off. Sure, nonprofit organizations are starting up every day, for every cause imaginable, and some of them take up issues that tug at the heart strings. The problem is that it's becoming harder and harder to distinguish the real ones from the fakes. One prevalent example is the call asking for donations for the Police Foundation in Washington, D.C., or for any police or firefighters' benevolent society. The caller is usually pretty skilled at convincing you of the dangers of this important public service work, and how these generous heroes put their lives on the line every day. What would their families do in the event of their death? They're likely to thank you for supporting in the past (you didn't). These so-called charities pretend to give these donations to the families, when in actual fact they may give only a small percentage—if any at all. Have you heard of the "Police Survivors' Fund,"? It purported to collect funds for the survivors of slain police officers. Between 1999 and 2002, the organization collected $441,000 from donors, and only paid out $14,500 to six families. As you can imagine, in a post-9/11 world, the callers were likely to reach sympathetic ears with stories of widows and children left behind.

As hurricanes, wildfires, floods and pandemics seem to have proliferated in recent years, so have the vultures claiming to represent worthy charities for helping those victims. After Hurricane Harvey slammed into the Texas coast in the summer of 2017, a swirl of rumors went around terrifying or confusing victims who were already feeling lost and displaced. One such rumor was that the National Guard had established an 800 number for people to call and get direct, immediate help. Gosh, wouldn't that be nice? It was a hoax. Though thousands of National Guardsmen had been mobilized to help with the flood response, the number being publicized was for an insurance company trying to take advantage of people in their time of need.

The same goes for post-disaster calls claiming to be from contractor, adjusters, attorneys, FEMA inspectors, government workers, or anyone from a charitable organization who wants to "verify" personal information like your Social Security number, driver's license number, or insurance information. Like looters, these are the bottom-feeders of the con artist world, preying on people desperate for help and seeking answers, but it happens a lot. And anyone claiming he or she can do repairs on your home should be registered with the Better Business Bureau and should be able to provide license information. They should be prepared to deliver a contract that you can read and sign in person. And they should never be asking for all the money up front.

Simply uttering the words "police" or "firefighter" or "disaster" or "pandemic first responder" doesn't make what they're doing legal or worthwhile. Any legitimate fundraiser calling on behalf of police or firefighters—or victims of wildfires or hurricanes or domestic abuse—will a) be able to mail you information or literature about what it does, b) provide you with a name for themselves and the organization, as well as a phone number, and c) never use threats, guilt, or intimidation tactics. Don't be afraid to take names and numbers and call to verify the fundraising efforts before giving a single red cent. The FTC also suggests reading up online about any charitable organization to find reviews or reports of scams.

- **Political Action Committee Fraud:** An Austin, Texas man raised money for Democratic candidates. He also raised money for Republican candidates. Political philosophies did not get in his way. Why would they? He raised $500,000 and spend $495,000 on himself. Travel, liquor and lap dances were all his supposedly legitimate political expenditures. The court did not buy his arguments. He was sentenced to three years in jail.

There are over 7,000 Political Action Committees (PACs) registered with the Federal Election Commission. They are not charities and their contributions are not tax deductible. But like some charities, PACs are a fertile ground for scamsters. Instead of raising money for political causes these sham PACs raise money for personal causes – the enrichment of the promoter.

There are three key tips for donating to a PAC:

1. If a PAC doesn't list the names of the management and the contact information on its website, call BS and walk away.

2. You can check out a PAC and how is spends its money at the Federal Election Commission's website: www.fec.gov. If the group sounds like a charity but is regulated by the FEC, know the difference. Again, you won't get a tax deduction if the organization is really a PAC. Legitimate charities can be checked at www.guidestar.org.

3. Do not place money with a PAC that doesn't ask you to confirm you are at least 21 years old and a U.S. Citizen. Foreign nationals are not allowed to contribute into our political system. (There is a whole other book to be written on that scam topic).

- **Foreign lottery fake-outs:** "Congratulations! You may receive a certified check in the amount of $5,000,000 USD in one lump sum!" These solicitors promise the call recipient a one-in-six chance of winning in a foreign lottery, thanks to a secret for beating the lottery system. Plus, the money is tax free! You just have to buy the tickets by phone, so you'd better get out that credit card. It's a sure thing, right? Wrong. Suppress that urge to believe you've found a way to harmlessly beat the system. You're being scammed, and trust me, this is illegal. Not to mention the fact that, even if you somehow managed to get hold of an actual foreign lottery ticket, you've just wound up on the sucker list and are bound to receive plenty more offers where this one came from. Congratulations.

- **Tech support:** Remember the story I shared a couple chapters ago about my friend who received a fake tech support call from someone pretending to be with Dell? This type of scam is used frequently, as it plays on people's natural intimidation around technology. In this type of scam, the person calling will say he or she is with a reputable company such as Microsoft, Apple, or Dell, and will warn you that your computer is vulnerable to some sort of attack or malfunction. The person is likely to try to gain remote access to your computer, at which point he or she may implant a virus, malware, or spyware into your computer, gain access to personal files or information, or try to get you to download some "fix" or "software" that will correct the nonexistent problem. For this kind service, they are also likely to charge you a hefty fee, enroll you in some kind of monthly plan, or direct you to a website that asks you to provide credit card or bank account information. Some even tell you they want to offer you a refund, and that they will deposit the money in your bank account, but instead of giving you money, they will take it. The caller may sound legitimate, even providing identification numbers for your computer or information about your date of purchase, but don't fall for it. If you suspect something is wrong with your computer, call the tech support number provided on the company's website. Never call a number that comes up in a pop-up ad. This is malware, and it's a scam. This is not how true computer or software companies operate.

- **Sham business or investment "opportunities":** Sure, it's a nice idea that you could potentially make $10,000 a month stuffing envelopes at home. Is it likely to happen? No. That doesn't stop scammers from trying it on you, though. Callers may promise such staggering returns for a low initial investment to set yourself up with supplies. Other callers may guarantee returns on can't-lose investment opportunities. Guess what? There's no such thing. I'll talk more about these kinds of scams ahead, but suffice it to say that no business or investment is a sure thing, and anyone considering jumping into such an opportunity should do a lot of homework, over a much longer period of time than it takes to complete a phone call.

- **Checking your benefits:** One scam that currently is gaining some traction is a Medicare scam, which takes advantage of the fact that new Medicare cards were set to go out to members in 2018. Here's how it works: The caller identifies him or herself as a representative from the Centers for Medicare and Medicaid and explains that a new membership card will be arriving soon. The person receiving the call typically is elderly. The caller says that until this new card comes, the old card is invalid, and the call recipient will need to purchase a temporary card or his or her health benefits may go away entirely. This card may cost anywhere from $5 to $50, but regardless of the amount, this is a hoax. The CMS will never call and threaten to cut off your health benefits. Similar tricks are being used on veterans, in light of new laws allowing vets to go to approved health care providers outside the VA—all they need to do is call a number to verify eligibility. Scammers have set up fake phone lines that mirror these real ones, and when the caller asks to verify eligibility, the scammer on the other end promises a rebate in medical expenses if the caller can verify some credit card information. Folks, this is not how our government works.

Some of the "information verification" requests can be downright intimidating, too. Here's one that was captured in the AARP recordings: "Ma'am, it's illegal to hang up on a verification. Do you understand this? This is the law President Bush passed himself, ma'am. You cannot hang up. We have to go through with this. We have your information. We just have to verify it, OK?"

Call BS on that. Hang up the phone.

- **Utility calls:** When cold weather sets in and heating and electric bills go up, this scam increases in pervasiveness. The caller pretends to be from the power company and wants to suggest a way they can lower the recipient's power bills by enrolling them in a federal program. All they need is a little identifying information to verify this is the right account. Once the caller has this information, he or she has enough to commit identity theft. In other situations, the caller says that the recipient has an overdue power bill and needs to immediately call an 800-number in order to keep from having their power shut off. It bears repeating that this, like the IRS or legitimate corporations, is not how power companies do business. If you are overdue on a power bill, you'll know it—you will have received several notifications by mail, including perhaps a couple in a nice bright pink. It will never come as a big surprise that all of a sudden you're facing the loss of power unless you pay up.

- **Phonejacking scams:** Con artists have grown quite savvy at turning your sorcerer's stone against you. Occasionally, they will call to try to convince you that your phone bill was too high last month and that you are owed a refund ("We'll just credit that back to your credit card/bank account—can I please have that number?") or that they just need to verify your personal information before they can credit your account ("And what's your birth date? And your Social Security number?").

The caller may also pull the long-distance-carrier trick on you, or what's called "slamming." Believe it or not, in this day and age of cell phones, this is still a thing. Here's how the scam works: Your traditional wire-line phone service is switched to a local, local toll, or long-distance carrier without your permission. The slammer may do this by getting you to sign a coupon or sweepstakes form. It's illegal, but it happens, and it's hard to catch because it involves reading a lot of fine print and combing your bill each month—something that, let's face it, a lot of us don't do as carefully as we should. Fortunately, the FCC has made laws about this, and you don't have to pay a bill that a slammer charges you for the first 30 days of service. Report the issue to your local telephone carrier and ask to be switched back with no "change charges." Do the same for your long-distance carrier. Call the slamming carrier and ask that the charges be moved to the carrier you agreed to pay in the first place, and then report them to the FCC or National Consumers League. The FCC's website (www.fcc.gov) provides detailed information about dealing with slammers.

Scammers also use your phone to trick you. They may "smish" you, or phish with SMS, or text, messages. In a smishing scenario, the scammer will send you a text with a link that indicates some "problem" with your financial accounts that you need to fix. You go to the site and provide personal data to "confirm your identity" and the fraudster gets hold of it.

It used to be that our area codes were associated with where we were calling from. A 212 area code meant you were in New York. San Francisco, Oakland and Walnut Creek were all 415. That's a remnant from a bygone era that no longer means anything. Scammers now can use software to make it look like they're calling you from local numbers—sometimes even your own or a neighbor's number! They know you're more likely to answer if the call looks local. Or they'll call you, ring only once, then hang up, and do this repeatedly to make it look urgent, banking on your curiosity to get you to call back. But when you do, it's a long-distance number with massive charges associated with it. When they answer, they may even put you on hold for long periods of time so you rack up expensive charges.

Don't Call Me a Sucker

Though anyone can be a victim of phone fraudsters, it may surprise you to learn that Millennials—the most tech-savvy generation—tend to be the most gullible to "vishing" (a new term for telephone fraud, so named because it mashes up "voice" with "phishing," the email equivalent that we'll discuss in the next chapter).

First Orion's survey found that although the Millennial generation, also called Gen Y, is more averse in general to answering their phones at all, they are six times more likely to give away credit card information on the phone when asked for it. They received fewer scam calls in general, but were most likely to be suckered into giving away information they shouldn't. They're almost twice as likely to give away Social Security info over the phone. When callers provided the last four digits—the part that's most accessible to anyone who does a little digging—17 percent of Millennials surveyed gave up the rest of the numbers, whereas only 3.2 percent of Gen Xers and 2 percent of Baby Boomers did so. And female Millennials seem to be hit harder than males. More than half of these young women had received bogus IRS calls while only one-third of men had.

Yet, ironically, it's this group that seems less convinced that they'll be suckered. Only 35 percent of Millennials in the survey said they thought they were susceptible to scams, while half of Gen Xers and more than half of Baby Boomers thought so.

Knowing how prevalent vishing scams are, it's tempting to swear off the phone altogether. But before you do that, here are some tips that might help mitigate the problem:

- The National Do Not Call Registry is operated by the FTC and is intended to keep you from being deluged by telemarketing calls. It won't stop all calls, unfortunately, but it will stop many. If you're still getting calls, they're scams. Sign up at DoNotCall.gov, or you can verify that your number is registered. If you're still getting calls, report the callers to the FTC on this website. Tell any telemarketer that you want to be taken off their call lists; they have to do this, by law. Again, if they still call you, it's either scammers or they're breaking the law. Hang up without any guilt.

- Know that legitimate telemarketers have to restrain their calling times to the hours between 8 a.m. and 9 p.m. If anyone calls outside those hours, it's likely a scam.

- By law, telemarketers are required to tell you when they're making sales calls. They also have to provide you with the names of the sellers and what, exactly, they're selling before they make their pitches. If you don't get this information right off the bat, hang up. Anyone who proceeds to pitch you without doing this is probably about to try a scam.

- I've said it before and it bears repeating: Scammers use high-pressure tactics and the false urgency of time to get you to make bad decisions. They want you to decide NOW, not to wait, not to gather more information. A legitimate enterprise will take the time to prove its legitimacy and will allow you to think it over.

- Authentic businesses will not hesitate to send you more information by mail to help you make up your mind. But scammers will.

- Scammers like to ask you to "verify your information" or collect fees and personal details up front. Typically, a real business won't do this—and they probably won't contact you by phone this way, anyway. Don't agree to this, and don't provide any information or money up front. If they can't take the time to mail you something or to allow you to think something over or make payment arrangements at another time, they aren't for real.

- There are plenty of services you can use to help combat phone scams. First, block any number that is making unwanted calls to your phone. Your smartphone should have this capability in its settings. Second, report any such number to the FTC. Third, try downloading an app that not only blocks unwanted calls but can even possibly provide you with phone number blacklists or tell you where a call is coming from. These apps include Call Blocker, Sync. ME, Call Control, Mr. Number, YouMail, and Hiya, but dozens more can be found in app stores.

"Listen, why don't you pick up the phone? I know you are there. Pick up the phone and stop playing games. Want me to come over there and set your home on fire?" — *A scammer talking to a victim who had lost $75,000 to fraud and had stopped sending money. From the AARP report on audio recordings of actual scam artists.*

Chapter Seven

Gone Phishin'

*Internet and email scams hack away
at our privacy and well-being*

CASE #5: The Man of God and the Nigerian Email Scam

Fifty-seven-year-old John W. Worley had a Ph.D. in psychology. He was a Vietnam veteran, ordained minister, and busy Christian psychotherapist with a thriving practice in Groton, Massachusetts. In fact, as part of his practice, he had developed Worley's Identity Discovery Profile (WIDP), a tool for psychological profiling based on a person's temperament in social and vocational situations, leadership, and relationships. It was intended to reveal a person's needs, desires, and likely behavioral responses, which he told *New Yorker* reporter Mitchell Zuckoff would have impressive results: "The individual's understanding of self will be greatly enhanced, increasing the potential for a fulfilled and balanced life." Worley had even been the keynote speaker at his granddaughter's graduation, warning students of the dangers of temptation, a trick Satan used to destroy us.

In June 2001, he sat at his desk reading through his emails, and one addressed to "CEO/Owner" caught his eye. The message was from a Captain Joshua Mbote, and the message was a strange entreaty. Mbote was chief of security for the Congolese president, Laurent Kabila, and Kabila had sent Mbote to South Africa to buy weapons for his elite team of bodyguards. But before Mbote could complete his mission, he said, Kabila had been assassinated. Now Mbote claimed he was stuck in South Africa with $55 million USD in cash.

"I quickly decided to stop all negotiations and divert the funds to my personal use, as it was a golden opportunity, and I could not return to my country due to my loyalty to the government of Laurent Kabila."

But in order to complete his plan, he needed help from someone who could keep a secret and had access to an overseas bank account. This partner would be richly rewarded for his assistance. Perhaps Worley was just this person?

"With regards to your trustworthiness and reliability, I decided to seek your assistance in transferring some money out of South Africa into your country, for onward dispatch and investment."

Unlikely as he seemed to be lured into such a plot—a therapist and staunch warrior against temptation—Worley was determined by his own tool, WIDP, to be a private person, needy and stubborn, as well as somewhat egotistical. He was the perfect mark. Within minutes he had typed a reply.

"I can help and I am interested."

He asked only one question of Mbote. How had he found Worley? Mbote offered a quick explanation that the South African Department of Home Affairs had provided Worley's name among a list of ten. Someone named "Pastor Mark" had pulled the name out of a hat. That Mbote had found him was God's divine intervention, Worley believed, and was sold on the idea immediately.

As Worley told Zuckoff of *The New Yorker*, the plan Mbote proposed was complicated. Worley would pay up-front costs, including fees for the storage facility where the cash was being held, and he might need to travel to South Africa to pick up the money. If he would agree to these terms, he would receive 30 percent—$16 million USD.

Worley was torn. This didn't sound like a legitimate transaction. He told Mbote that as a man of God, he was always concerned about behaving with integrity. And despite the fact that he resided in a mansion and had claimed a six-figure income to the IRS, Worley was still recovering from a bankruptcy in the early 1990s. He also had no retirement money saved, and what little he had put away was intended for his grandchildren's college education. Mbote offered assurances that investors could provide up to $150,000 for expenses such as airfare. Worley needed only to be the curator of the funds. Mbote would see to it that Worley was sent money to get the ball rolling.

Within two months of the original email, a check from one of these "investors" arrived in Worley's mailbox for $47,500. The account from which the check originated was Syms Corporation, a discount clothing chain, and the account was with Fleet Bank in Portland, Maine. Worley grew suspicious and placed a call to Fleet Bank, where a representative explained to Worley that the check was an altered duplicate of a check that Syms had actually paid to a vendor.

Worley was disheartened. He asked Mbote for a replacement check and received no reply, so he announced that the partnership was over. Mbote disappeared. But a few days later, Worley received another email from a man named Mohammed Abacha, who claimed to be "the eldest surviving son of the Nigeria's late dictator General Sani Abacha," a man who was reported to have stolen billions from the Nigerian treasury. Mbote had screwed up, Abacha told Worley. He had been working on the Abacha family's behalf but had managed to mess things up so badly that Abacha himself now had to step up and intercede. The whole story about buying weapons had been a ruse to protect the Abachas and their wealth, which was being hidden in Ghana. General Abacha's widow, Maryam Abacha, contacted Worley via phone and email, repeatedly begging him for help. Worley was needed by a woman in distress, and he had a chance to be a hero.

In November 2001, Worley hired the services of an international tax-planning attorney to assist with this task, and the attorney warned Worley of the scheme. The warnings were dismissed casually. By this point, Worley had invested not only time but money, so there was no turning back. He explained to the Abachas that he had found a way to ship the cash secretly to Bermuda, to a bank that would allow a huge deposit of cash without question and tax free. He invested $4,300 of his own money in January 2002 to open the account at Bank of Butterfield.

A series of requests followed: For $8,000 to hire a Nigerian lawyer and pay bank and late fees, for him to travel to Amsterdam to collect the cash. When Worley adamantly refused to travel, they tried another tack, asking him to help claim the $45 million hidden in the Federal Ministry of Aviation at the Central Bank of Nigeria.

Worley sank deeper and deeper into the plot; the "man of integrity" agreed to allow these partners of his to file false documentation that he was a private aviation contractor who was owed $45 million by the Nigerian government. He was incessantly being asked for money from many people—at one point there were nine correspondents—and each time, he consented. He even sank so low as to ask a client if he could borrow $15,000 for a business venture in Nigeria. The woman agreed and paid him the same day, and he immediately wired it via Western Union to Nigeria. (He eventually repaid her with interest by borrowing on his credit card.)

Worley was draining his bank accounts and desperate that he'd lost so much and had received nothing he'd been promised. He begged Ms. Abacha—who spelled her first name in a number of different ways (Maryam, Miriam, Maram)—for help, even making a bid for her sympathy by claiming to have cancer. It didn't work. Finally, Worley broke down.

"To date, I have lost nearly fifty thousand dollars chasing a rainbow with a pot of gold at the end of it. I cannot go any further. It will take me two years to recover from this, and I will probably be dead by then."

Still, Ms. Abacha managed to wrangle another $13,000 from him over the course of three more months, and he finally wrote her this:

"I must stop this financial torment and anguish and pray that God forgives me for my pursuit of money, simply put, greed."

He didn't speak to the Nigerians for five months after that, but as we've said before, once a mark, always a mark. In September 2002, Worley received a fax from someone ironically calling herself "Mercy Nduka," who claimed to be the confidential secretary at the Central Bank of Nigeria who was working with the Abacha family. The $45 million was still waiting for him at the Aviation Ministry, but in order for him to claim the money, they would need $500,000 to bribe five Nigerian bank officials, and another $85,000 to cover fees. When Worley replied that he couldn't pay it, Nduka said she and her boss, Usman Bello, would borrow it from investors. Once everything was paid, the three would split the reward for delivering the $45 million to the Abachas.

Soon the "investors" were calling asking for credit references and collateral—a measure he found comforting, a sign of legitimacy. In November 2002, he received a check for $95,000 from an insurance company in New York. It seemed so legitimate that he deposited the check and promptly wired $85,000 to Nduka. Thus, it continued, with checks coming and Worley depositing them, only to then turn around and wire money for bribes and fees and so forth.

It continued like this for another year, with more requests for funds, more wiring of money to Nigerians, more strange checks coming from random U.S. companies. Every time Worley pleaded for help, begged for them to let him be, cried that he had no more money, that he was now being investigated by banks, they only asked for more, offered more of a sob story. Nduka replied in February 2003:

"I am quite sympathetic about all your predicaments, but the truth is that we are at the final step and I am not willing to let go, especially with all of these amounts of money that you say that you have to pay back."

All she needed was one more thing: $3,000. Mercy was merciless.

Worley's actions caught up with him in May 2005, when he went on trial in U.S. District Court in Boston. He was charged with money laundering, bank fraud, and possession of counterfeit checks. His Nigerian partners were never caught, and in the end, Worley lost $40,000, though with bank fees, credit-card interest, and wiring charges, Zuckoff reported, the losses may have actually been double. Worley was found guilty and sentenced to two years in prison and restitution of $600,000. He was given five weeks to close out his affairs and turn himself in.

When Zuckoff interviewed Worley at his home prior to his departure for prison, Worley still seemed confused about having been scammed, and was legitimately confused about how his work with the Abachas had gotten mixed up with these fraudsters.

He said he still hoped to hear from the Abachas, who were supposed to send $600,000 to cover his restitution.

Here's an email case:

From: Randell Digel
Sent: Friday, July 27, 2018 6:45 AM
Subject: RE: <Password formerly used by Recipient>

I'm aware that <Password formerly used by Recipient> is one of your personal password and Lets get straight to the point. You do not know me however I know you and you're probably thinking why you're receiving this mail, right?

I actually placed malware on porn vids (sex sites) & guess what, you accessed same adult website to have fun (if you know what I mean). While you were watching video clips, your web browser started functioning as a RDP (Remote Computer) with a keylogger which allowed me access to your screen as well as your web camera access. Right after that, the malware obtained all of your contacts from your messenger, social networks, as well as e-mail.

What have I done?

It is simply your bad luck that I got to know about your blunder. Later I invested in more days than I probably should have looking into your personal life and generated a two screen video. First half shows the video you had been watching and next part displays the recording of your webcam (its someone doing dirty things). Genuinely, I'm ready to delete all about you and let you continue with your life. And I will present you a way out that will accomplish your freedom. These two option is either to turn a deaf ear to this email (bad for you and your family), or pay me $ 1950 to finish this chapter forever.

What can you do?

Let us understand those two options in more detail. Alternative one is to turn a deaf ear to my e-mail. You should know what is going to happen if you choose this path. I will send your video recording to your entire contacts including members of your family, colleagues, etc. It will not save you from the humiliation your household will feel when friends learn your sordid sextape from me. Wise option is to send me $ 1950. We'll name it my "confidentiality fee". Lets discuss what will happen if you select this choice. Your secret remains private. I'll keep my mouth silent. Once you pay, You move on with your daily life and family as if none of this ever occurred. You will make the transfer via Bitcoins (if you don't know this search "how to buy bitcoin" on google search)

Amount to be sent: $ 1950

BTC ADDRESS IS: (33 jumbled characters)

(It is CASE sensitive, copy and paste it)

Important: You have one day to make the payment. (I've a special pixel within this email, and now I know that you have read this email). DO NOT TELL anybody what you will be utilizing the bitcoin for or they might not give it to you. The procedure to obtain bitcoin will take a short time so do not wait. If I do not get the BitCoins, I will, no doubt send your sextape to all of your contacts including members of your family, co-workers, etc. having said that, if I receive the payment, I will destroy the video immediately. If you want proof, reply with "yes!" and I will send out your sextape to your 5 friends. It is a non negotiable one time offer, so kindly don't waste my time & yours by responding to this e mail. You should know that my software will be recording what action you take when you're done reading this email. Honestly, if you search something inappropriate then I am going to send your sextape to your close relatives, colleagues even before time ends.

Recently, I was speaking with a woman who works as a personal assistant to a colleague of mine. She and I were exchanging pleasantries and I explained that I was working on this book about scams and rip-offs.

"Ha!" she laughed. "I ought to show you the email I got the other day. It was one of those email scams, kind of a creepy one. They said they'd been spying on me with my webcam and had recorded a sex tape of me! It was actually pretty funny, but it was the first time I ever got one of those."

Intrigued, I told her I'd like to see it, and she pulled it out of her email trash and printed it out, and I've included it here for a number of reasons. First, part of me thinks it's hilarious. The terrible grammar and the utter improbability of the technology involved actually made me laugh out loud—well, that and, to be frank, the idea of this sweet woman accessing porn from her front desk computer. I've heard of email scams, and I've received plenty of outlandish solicitations via email myself, but this one was a brand-new storyline for me.

When I went looking online for information about such scams, to see what I could find about them, I had a good, hearty laugh reading an article in the U.K.'s *Mirror Online* about the increasing frequency of this scam abroad. "I do not presume to judge you... I do not think that caress oneself is very bad, but when all your acquaintances see it – it is obviously very bad," read the email received by a man who calls himself "Reader Sam" in the article. The email goes on to make a threat similar to the one my friend received. "The most interesting point that I created video," the email went on, "on one side it shows your screen record, on second side your cams record. Its very funny. But it wasn't so easy ,so I proud of it."

That last part had me roaring with laughter, I admit. He's proud of his hard work.

Jeez, how would someone fall for that? Also, by the way, those grammatical and punctuation errors were taken directly from the email—don't blame my editor!

It's instinctive for us to laugh at some of these things, but to be honest, it's no laughing matter. My research uncovered the fact that KrebsonSecurity.com, the cyber security website run by author and security expert Brian Krebs, had already been tipped off to this formulaic email. Three of his readers had received some version of this email within the same 72 hours, and in every case, the readers indicated that the passwords the senders had provided had, in fact, been their passwords at some time at least a decade ago. Krebs suspects that the information had gotten out in a data breach around that time; the victims' passwords had been compromised and put on a list that the modern-day hackers had in their possession.

"I suspect that as this scam gets refined even more, perpetrators will begin using more recent and relevant passwords—and perhaps other personal data that can be found online—to convince people that the hacking threat is real," Krebs warns. "That's because there are a number of shady password lookup services online that index billions of usernames (i.e. email addresses) and passwords stolen in some of the biggest data breaches to date."

This isn't quite so funny anymore, is it? My friend recognized her old password and opened the email, curious about why she was seeing that in the subject line. But she's not gullible and knew immediately that it was a hoax. Others haven't gotten so lucky, and as the scam grows more sophisticated and full of ever more relevant and recent data, the likelihood of them believing it grows, too.

The FBI's Internet Crime Complaint Center (IC3) released its "2017 Internet Crime Report" to highlight trends in internet scams. The data in the report were drawn from 301,580 complaints that were received by IC3 in 2017, with losses totaling $1.42 billion. On October 12, 2017, the agency received its four millionth internet crime complaint. IC3 received 14,938 extortion-type complaints that year, with adjusted losses of more than $15 million. But that's just one of dozens of types cybercrime committed each year. The IC3 reports that these were just the top ten internet crimes reported in 2017:

1. **Nonpayment/nondelivery of merchandise:** With more than 84,000 victims reported every year and annual losses of over $141 million, this crime is a type of auction fraud. You've already met some of its perpetrators in this book so far. In a nutshell, the premise is about as simple as it gets: It's a nondelivery scam. The victim pays for something that the scammer never delivers, like Brett Johnson's satellite transmission cards. Sometimes this is done with a sham auction established solely for the purpose of getting credit card

information from buyers, but just as often it's done merely to steal buyers' money by not completing the transaction. In a nonpayment scam, the reverse is true: The victim is selling something, for instance on eBay. The scammer orders the item, receives it, and never pays. They might, for example, use a fraudulent credit card or bank account, or someone else's PayPal account. By the time the victim has shipped the item, the "buyer" is long gone.

Associated with this type of scam is the online auction site, in which the scammer misrepresents a product it advertises for sale. In many of these, such as DealDash.com (which promises "fair and honest auctions"), the site charges visitors for every bid. So while it may be advertising low, low prices for high-value items, you're also paying just to bid—you're not even guaranteed to win. Some of these are flat-out fake sites designed to get your money or credit card information, but the scammer behind the site has no intention of sending you any of the merchandise. Be especially cautious when the seller is outside the country, has no customer reviews, provides no information about a return or warranty policy, insists upon wire transfer or some other type of payment besides credit card or third-party payment site (like PayPal), or asks for such information as a driver's license or Social Security number. Credit cards and PayPal are best to use for these types of transactions, because you can make secure payments and won't be held responsible if the information is used fraudulently.

2. **Personal data breach:** Responsible for over 30,000 complaint reports to IC3 and losses totaling more than $70 million, the data breach is the 21st Century plague—the victim's personal information, stored on a computer or in the victim's online accounts, is hijacked by a cyber thief who gains access to the computer or accounts remotely.

3. **Phishing/vishing/smishing/pharming:** The use of email and websites to fraudulently extract money or personal data was responsible for over 20,000 reports to IC3 in recent years. You've

probably heard by now of "phishing," in which a scammer sends an email pretending to be someone trustworthy in order to obtain anything from usernames and passwords to credit card information or other personal data.

Ironically, this morning, I received one of these in my personal email inbox. In the "From" line of an email I found in my inbox was the name of my email server. The subject line "Unpaid Bill." The message, which was cleverly designed to look like something official, read that they had received notification my bill was unpaid. To clear it up, I was to click the link provided. I know that my monthly email bill is paid automatically from my debit card at this time every month, and I also know that my bank recently sent me a new debit card (which I mentioned earlier), so it took me a minute to realize that the card the bank replaced was not the card on file for my monthly payment to my email server. When I checked into it further, I found that yes, indeed, my monthly automatic payment for the month had been processed. And the email address where this strange message originated from was NOT for my email provider at all. I quickly marked the message as spam and deleted it. I'm glad I didn't click on that link provided, as it was almost certainly malware or, at the very least, a method by which the scammer would have collected credit card information. But it was a great reminder for me about how easy it is to convince unsuspecting victims to give in to scam tactics. Thousands of these types of exchanges happen every single day. They should stop.

Phishing scams, like the sextortion email I shared earlier, are estimated to cost American businesses about half a billion dollars a year, according to a recent *Forbes* report. Interestingly, attorneys' offices (like my friend's) and title companies seem to be the primary businesses that are victims of such attacks. I've covered vishing and smishing, which involve extracting this information by phone or text. And pharming, like the email I received today, involves scammers directing you to click on a link or go to a website in order for the criminal to obtain user information, including financial or personal data. This can be done in a number of ways, from changing the hosts file on a victim's computer or rerouting traffic to a legitimate site toward a sham site—for instance, the 2005 attack on the large New York ISP Panix in which the site was hijacked to point traffic toward a website in Australia.

4. **Overpayment:** Remember my Dell story involving the "tech support representative" who promised to refund my friend's money, and then claimed to have mistakenly given her way too much? He had asked if she'd mind wiring back the extra money so he wouldn't lose his job for the mistake. The problem was that he never gave her any money to begin with. In this kind of scam, the scammer somehow pretends to have sent an overly generous payment (perhaps a fake receipt from PayPal, forged check, credit card, or fraudulent bank transfer of your own money between accounts), then kindly asks if you'd refund the excess. The problem is that the only money that ever changed hands was your own to the scammer.

5. **Identity theft:** This one earns tens of thousands of complaints to IC3 and is complex enough to have earned its own chapter in this book. Email and the internet make this one easier now than at any time in history.

6. **Advance fee:** Responsible for losses of nearly $58 million and more than 16,000 IC3 complaints, the advance-fee scam is just what it sounds like: You are promised you will receive money, products, or services as part of some special deal, event, promotion, or activity. You pay a little bit up front (a membership, administrative, handling, or delivery fee, or maybe taxes) and your rewards will be plenty on the back end—at least, that's what you're promised. The truth, as we've already learned, is much different. These come in MANY forms. Of course, you've seen in our vishing scams how that looks in IRS, lottery, trip/prize/sweepstakes, or investment propositions. Other scenarios include the debt-elimination fraud,

where a scammer claims to represent a debt-elimination service that can help you get debt free with just a small out-of-pocket fee to get started.

Another one that is highly popular is the Nigerian email scam—named for the country where this scam really originated and still seems to be most popular. Chances are, just like John Worley, this is one scam every reader of this book has encountered: The scammer poses as a government official, a member of royalty, or a service member in the military, and emails the victim asking him or her to help transfer millions of dollars out of Nigeria in exchange for a cut of the proceeds. Sometimes this involves princes or other royals in exile, or even millions of dollars' worth of gold bullion. The victim, once hooked by the promise of a payoff and sympathy for the poor Nigerian, sends money to cover the necessary bribes or legal or bank fees.

The scheme dates back to the 16th century as something called the "Spanish Prisoner Letter." A scammer would write to wealthy Englishmen asking for help in freeing someone who had been imprisoned in Spain. The scam resurfaced in the 1980s as a postal mail scam when oil prices collapsed in Nigeria, leaving its people unemployed and facing poverty. The scam was similar in that it typically involved royalty or government officials needing to get funds out of Nigeria. When emails began to proliferate in the new millennium, making it easier and cheaper to send such messages, email harvesting software enabled these scammers to find their marks. Some believe that the outlandish stories and requests made by the scammers are intentionally strange. They serve the purpose of weeding out the suspicious, more reasonable people, leaving them only with the perfect, most gullible targets. The interaction typically involves the presentation of official-looking documents, government titles that look authentic (but really aren't), and a promise for a big payout if only the victim will front the money. They may even request that the victim travel to Nigeria or other countries, where they fall prey to kidnapping or worse. But the scam's most sinister quality is that it will never let the fish off the hook. The scammers relentlessly demand more money, and then more money, and still more. As long as they can squeeze a drop of blood from the turnip, they will continue to try. They have nothing to lose and everything to gain, and they are so treacherous because they almost never get caught. Its victims fall prey to that craving for a "good deal," the fast win that plays such a huge role in scam victimization. As long as there's a promise of a payoff at the end, victims have been known to take the most outrageous actions in its pursuit. I'll share one such story with you at the end of this chapter.

7. **Harassment/threats of violence:** The costs of this cybercrime may certainly have resulting financial losses, but it's more likely the greatest ramifications for these crimes are emotional in nature. The internet, emails, and social media have many wonderful uses, but they also are used with dark purposes as well, to cyberbully victims, to share revealing or purely falsified videos or photos of victims, to steal information, to harass or stalk, to threaten, or to spread rumors.

8. **Employment:** The ad features a photo of a lovely young woman at a computer, smiling and content because she now has a great job that pays well and which she can do from home. The ad promises that you, too, can have this job, and it guarantees you'll make between $5,000 and $10,000 a week, no special skills or education required. *Whoa,* you think. *I could stay in my pajamas all day. Set my own hours. Spend more time with my family. No more boss, no more morning commute. Sign me up!* They're all the same—the promise of unbelievably high income, no skills needed, start right away, work from home. In short, it's the American Dream. You click on the ad or the link provided in the email to learn more about this great opportunity. You're then asked to pay something—maybe you need to purchase supplies to get started with your envelope-stuffing or your customer call list, or maybe you need to pay for a

certification—but you won't ever get that job. Instead, you'll get a list of job search advice you didn't need or a sham certificate that's worthless... and that's if you're lucky. Mostly, you'll get nothing except broke. That money-back guarantee was a big fat lie. You might even be instructed to call a 1-800 number to learn more, and calling it will get you to a prerecorded message designed to rack up your toll charges. Or the instructions for this "work" will be an incomprehensible series of directions intended to get *you* involved in selling the scam to other people.

The work-at-home pitch is just one type of employment scam perpetrated online. There's also the vending machine scam promising that you can own and distribute your own vending machines that become a passive income stream for you, but the machines (if you get them) are terrible and are placed in such bad locations that you'll never make money on them. There's the "employer list scam" in which you're asked to send a "small fee" and the scammer will send a list of companies that are looking for great employees like you. What you'll get is a directory of businesses—just their names and addresses, as valuable as a phone book. That's if you get anything. You might even encounter the government job scam: Pay us a small fee and we'll send you a form guaranteeing you a great government job. I think you can guess how this one turns out.

As Robert B. Reich, former U.S. labor secretary and researcher into consumer market behavior, pointed out to *The New Yorker*, "American culture is uniquely prone to the 'too good to miss' fallacy. 'Opportunity' is our favorite word. What may seem reckless and feckless and hapless to people in many parts of the world seems a justifiable risk to Americans."

9. **BEC/EAC:** Business email compromise (BEC) and email account compromise (EAC) may only be ninth on this list in terms of number of complaints, but together they were recently responsible for a whopping $676 *million* in losses. This is one type of cybercrime the FBI is acutely concerned about, and for good reason. In BEC,

business email accounts are hijacked using social engineering or computer intrusion tactics. The unsuspecting users, who typically work with foreign suppliers or companies that frequently use wire transfer payments, receive emails from these hijacked accounts requesting that they send fund transfers. Somehow the victims are identified as those who are capable of, and frequently deal with, wire transfers. Typically, a phishing email will go out, asking for additional details about the business or individual being targeted (for instance, travel dates or names). The victim is asked to click on a link that downloads malware into the victim's computer that gives the scammer access to all kinds of sensitive data. The information enables the scammer to transmit fraudulent transaction instructions and execute those unauthorized transactions, which as you might imagine in the case of certain large companies can be rather a lot.

In EAC, the technique is the same, but rather than the email accounts and financial accounts belonging to the business and going to its employees, the account belongs to an individual who may frequently conduct large wire transfer transactions, perhaps with financial institutions, lenders, real estate firms, or law firms. The email sends fraudulent wire transfer instructions to financial institutions, thereby draining the victim's account. The emails are cloaked to look legitimate, as if they are coming from a business that the recipient is used to conducting transactions with, but they definitely aren't.

According to a recent report from Verafin, a fraud-detection and anti-money-laundering software developer, the majority of BEC and EAC fraud directs funds to China and Hong Kong, followed by the U.K., Mexico, and Turkey. Signs that BEC or EAC is being attempted include seemingly legitimate email transaction instructions that have different language, timing, or amounts than previously used; the instructions come from an email account that looks *similar* to those sent previously, but somewhat altered, perhaps with one or two characters being different; the account information for the beneficiary is different from the norm; the wire transfers are directed to a foreign bank account; the instructions direct payment to an unknown beneficiary; the language includes words like "urgent" or "confidential"; or the instructions are delivered in a way that gives the financial institution little time to verify authenticity.

10. **Confidence fraud/Romance:** I'll deal a bit more with this type of phishing in the chapter on vanity fraud later on in this book. But know this: It affects a lot more people than you might think, with more than 15,000 annually reported cases of it going to the IC3 in recent years. In this type of internet or email crime, the fraudster takes advantage of the victim's trust or confidence, forming a relationship with the victim under false pretenses in order to get that victim to give him or her money or to perform some sort of illegal activity. It abuses trust, capitalizes on the lonely or depressed, and can, as you'll see, make anyone, even the most intelligent and sophisticated of people, victims.

Of course this isn't the extent of email and internet scams. There are the promises of financial awards for passing along chain emails or sharing social media posts. There are the spam messages we get from "friends," names we recognize, who send us bizarre emails or social media messages telling us they have something we "have to see" or that they thought we'd enjoy, instructing us to click on a link or download a video. All you'll get from clicking are viruses and malware.

There are the social media phishing scams involving "free coupon" or "free gift card" offers to customers who just "follow these simple steps," which include completing a pretty specific survey to collect your personal information such as address, date of birth, email address, and phone number. You may even be asked to enroll in a subscription program in order to receive the free gift card. But logos, company colors, and established brand appearances are pretty easy to mimic online, and legitimate companies don't ask for credit card numbers or banking information, and if they ask for other personal information, they should also provide a privacy policy.

Don't buy into the promise that a dollar is donated to some child's kidney transplant every time her photo is shared on social media—no one would do that. And celebrities don't give away money, cars, or other items based on how many likes or shares a Facebook post gets.

Insecure networks also leave us vulnerable. Anytime you connect your device to an insecure network—the free Wi-Fi at the airport lounge or that coffee shop down the street, for instance—you open yourself up to the possibility that a hacker will seize the opportunity to gain access to your system and everything contained in it. Be especially careful conducting private conversations, banking or financial transactions, or email exchanges on these connections, as these networks are usually left unprotected. Meanwhile, malicious hackers can easily find free programs on the internet that enable them to access critical files or information on the network. Don't open Wi-Fi you can't trust, and seek out secure, password-protected connections when working at local businesses. If you absolutely must connect to a public Wi-Fi network, don't perform any bank transactions or access any critical information while connected.

To Err is Human

Before I move on, I want to take this opportunity to suggest that there should be no shame in coming forward with the fact that you have been victimized. As you've already seen by the astonishing statistics I've provided, it has certainly happened to people of all ages, income levels, education levels, races, genders, and backgrounds. Email and internet attacks are particularly insidious because they often mirror the legitimate transactions and exchanges we conduct on a daily basis, especially now as our reliance on our electronics grows and grows. Distinguishing the truth from the scam can be challenging, even for people who make a study of scams.

But the more people who come forward to share their stories, the more we can minimize the impacts of such crimes. Please use our Fight Back information found in Appendix A. Being a victim doesn't reflect badly on you, it reflects badly on the criminals, so don't forget that. And some even say that your susceptibility means you have some wonderful traits. There is always a silver lining. Just be sure to include skeptical as one of your traits.

In October 2014, Colin Barras wrote an article entitled "How Con Artists Trick Your Mind" for BBC.com. In it, he shares some of the commonalities that victims share—including our deference to authority, our tendency to follow the herd, our inability to make good decisions under time constraints—and how scammers have turned these tendencies into weapons to use against us. Barras spoke to Frank Stajano, a security and privacy researcher at the University of Cambridge, who points to other "weaknesses" often blamed for scammers' ability to victimize, such as our empathy for others and natural desire to provide assistance (for instance, when scam emails beg for help).

"[M]any of the vulnerabilities that scammers exploit are actually human strengths rather than weaknesses," Barras writes. "[Stajano] points to the work of psychologist Robert Cialdini at Arizona State University, who is famous for his work on the psychology of persuasion. 'He's explained that the authority principle, for example, is actually very helpful for surviving peacefully in human society,' says Stajano. 'We shouldn't see scam victims as stupid—they're acting in a way that's beneficial for our survival most of the time.'"

So there. Consider yourself human. But, again, add skepticism to your humanity. And don't ignore your BS Detector, which has helped us survive over the eons.

David Modic, a researcher in the field of internet fraud psychology at the University of Cambridge, says that having intelligence and experience don't seem to offer any protection against this type of crime: "If it did," he told Colin Barras in his BBC article, "then better educated people and older people would be less likely to fall for scams. And that is not supported by my research."

Yet it seems that as the pervasiveness of scams grows, so too does the amount of blame foisted upon victims. When people click bad links, unknowingly give money to scammers, unthinkingly reveal personal data to would-be thieves, open emails that look authentic, these victims are actually blamed for the crimes committed or computer damage done. How many times have you sheepishly had to explain to your company's grumpy IT specialist how you accidentally clicked something you shouldn't have, only to be met with an eye roll?

Security expert Stajano says that others in his line of work are more likely to blame security breaches on the people using their systems as they are on the criminals. "Too many security professionals think: Users are such a pain—my system would be super-secure if only users behaved in the proper way," he told Barras of the BBC.

It's an unfortunate reality that because cybercrimes can be committed by people on the other side of the world, who are not likely to ever be caught, it's easier to blame the poor sap sitting in front of you who fell for the tricks. The sooner security systems and those in charge of implementing them can take our humanity into account, the safer we'll all be. And, the sooner governments go after the real criminals, the better off the honest will be.

"I hate being taken advantage of by you evil bastards... This is all lies?... Your day will come that you will be judged by God, and so will I. And I am ashamed, and shamed, and an embarrassment to my family, who are so precious and Godly people. What a terrible model of a Christian that I am. Thoughts of suicide are filling my mind, and I am full of rage at you despicable people. I hate living right now, and I want to die. My whole life is falling apart, my family, my ministry, my reputation and all that I have worked for all my life. Dear God, help me. I am so frightened." — *John W. Worley, victim of a Nigerian scam, in a message to his persecutor, "Mercy Nduka."*

Chapter Eight

The Young, the Rich, and the Vain

Vanity Scams prey on ego

CASE #6: Grape Expectations

Rudy Kurniawan was a slight, soft-spoken twenty-something with glasses who looked more like an upstart app developer than a wine snob—pretty much the last guy you'd expect to have the most sophisticated wine palate in any room. But for a few years in the early 2000s, he was the guy every wine aficionado turned to for hints at what wines were worth buying, who possessed what one auctioneer called "the greatest cellar in America," and who nearly single-handedly drove up the value of old wines.

Those who knew him—or at least thought they did—had learned that his love affair with wine began in 2001, while celebrating his father's birthday at a restaurant on San Francisco's Fisherman's Wharf. As Benjamin Wallace of *New York Magazine* reports in his 2012 article "Château Sucker," the moment the celebratory 1996 Opus One touched his lips, Kurniawan was hooked and began avidly collecting it, before long amassing nearly 200 bottles of Opus One and diving headlong into a personal education on California wines, then Bordeaux, then the granddaddy of them all, Burgundy. He began attending weekly wine tastings, acquiring rare bottles, and honing his palate. By early 2002, he was seen at a charity auction steadily holding his paddle high until securing a case of California Syrah Sine Qua Non—that same year, The Wine Advocate, Robert Parker, often considered the world's most influential wine critic, gave that vintage a score of 100, and today a single bottle of it can go for anywhere from $600 to $1,000. Kurniawan could name any wine in a double-blind tasting—meaning he could identify the wine without even knowing it was in the room—and reportedly spent $1 million a month at wine auctions. His collection was the envy and inspiration of wine lovers everywhere.

Meanwhile, few knew much about him. They deduced, from hints he gave, that he was a trust fund kid who received a hefty monthly allowance from his family back in Indonesia, though no one knew Kurniawan's own provenance. Some had heard he made $1 million a month; some had heard $2 million. His Chinese family owned a beer distributorship, but which beer was not clear. Few knew more than what he showed them at tastings or auctions. They just loved that he kept pouring.

Soon he was rubbing elbows with some of the world's wealthiest wine collectors and noteworthy critics, including Robert Parker himself, as well as auctioneer John Kapon, Burgundy importer Paul Wasserman, and a group of New York wine collectors who called themselves "The 12 Angry Men," occasionally paying long visits to them to astound them with his generosity by pouring million-dollar cases of rare 1945 Romanée-Conti like he was pouring water. He provided cases for a $17,500-a-head wine weekend, hosted charity dinners showcasing his wines, and started consigning cases from his magical cellar at auction. He even managed to provide enough wines for not one but *two* single-cellar auctions, bringing in a total of more than $35 million.

But all was not well. By fall 2003, there already were rumblings that Kurniawan's wines didn't add up. At a $4,800-per-person tasting of Kurniawan's rare treasures in Santa Monica, wine importer Paul Wasserman, who previously had never tasted a Pétrus older than 1975, found himself drinking a 1947 and a 1961 and doubting the veracity of both. A buyer on the auction site Winebid was threatening to sue over some bottles he believed were fake, purchased from a consignor named

Rudy Kurniawan. A 2007 wine dinner in New Jersey hosted by a wine collector, with a sommelier and winemaker present, resulted in the group finding six of the eleven Kurniawan wines being poured to be clearly fakes. As some demanded repayment, the market for buyers began drying up, and Kurniawan started running out of money and asking his friends for loans. Then in 2008, Laurent Ponsot, from the Ponsot family of winemakers, made an interesting discovery. Bottles of 1945 and 1971 Clos St. Denis from Domaine Ponsot began hitting the market, which Ponsot found interesting since his family didn't even make that particular wine until 1982. He heard that the bottles would be coming up for auction in April 2008 and attended the auction to ensure they were not sold. Auctioneer Kapon was forced to withdraw the wines, "at the request of the domain and with the consent of the consignor."

Kurniawan backpedaled, evading questions about where the wine had been purchased and claiming ignorance, managing to convince some that he'd been duped as well. When pressed by Ponsot, he relinquished phone numbers for his source, someone named "Pak Hendra in Asia," but when the numbers were called, they went to an Indonesian airline and a shopping mall in Jakarta.

"Winemakers don't like to talk about counterfeiting, for fear of the taint," writes Wallace. "Also, one thing not high on the FBI's list of investigative priorities: Billionaires getting snowed by wine forgers. It's clear to everyone on this rarified circuit that wine fraud is rampant. It's also clear not many insiders feel an urgency to do anything about it."

In fact, despite the growing body of evidence against Kurniawan, many of those who stood to lose the most and who were most well-equipped to sniff a forgery were those who turned the other cheek, hailed Kurniawan a hero, and proclaimed that his detractors were dead wrong. In fact, auction houses were still taking consignments from him.

Right about this time, billionaire Bill Koch of the famous Koch brothers uncovered fakes in his wine collection. He hired a private investigator and filed suit against Kurniawan. When authentication experts found highly suspect auction consignment records, the FBI intervened. In 2012, they raided the home Kurniawan shared with his mother in Arcadia, California, and found its notorious resident in his bathrobe. Thousands of wine labels bearing such names as Pétrus and Lafleur filled shopping bags. The kitchen was a laboratory, the sink filled with old, empty bottles soaking in water, on their way to gaining new lives as pricey new bottles of Burgundy. Strewn about were bags and bags of corks, glue, stencils, pattern scissors, foil capsules, and sealing wax, not to mention instructions for faking wine labels.

Investigation revealed that Kurniawan had for years been collecting old, empty bottles that had once held rare wines, shipped to him on his request from the Greenwich Village restaurant Cru—acquired after he explained he was creating a bottle museum in his garage—and asking brokers to find him "third-tier, worst vintage of just really old Burgundy." He had been performing chemistry in his kitchen, blending cheap wines, getting hold of various vintages and calibrating them to approximate the taste, bottling them, sealing them factory style, and selling them by the case. Meanwhile, details of Kurniawan's background are still hazy, but it was clear that his name was taken from an Indonesian badminton star. His real name was Chinese: Zhen Wang Huang.

Many have hailed Kurniawan as a sort of Robin Hood figure, someone who stole from the rich, a victimless crime. Nonetheless, he was sentenced to ten years in prison for selling counterfeit wines. And in spite of the glaring evidence against him, many of those who lost the most to Kurniawan's scheme refused to concede their errors, so concerned were they with saving face.

In a 2016 article for *The Guardian*, Ed Cumming wrote of the then-recent release of *Sour Grapes*, a documentary film about Kurniawan's rise and fall, made by Jerry Rothwell and Reuben Atlas. Cumming describes scenes from the film and what they reveal about the great wine scam:

> Those duped were almost exclusively male. These were men showing off, including Jay McInerney, the Manhattan literary enfant terrible who has mellowed into a wine critic. There is "Hollywood" Jef Levy, a red-nosed sunglass-clad producer of films you won't have

heard of. There's a drawling suit-clad investor, swirling a glass in a taxi across town.

"Buy '06 Champagne," he tells us. "If you can't afford that, buy '02. If you can't afford that, drink f*****g beer."

It's striking how easily those in the boys' club were prepared to believe in the character of Kurniawan—an ingénue immigrant with plenty of cash, who wanted to be part of their gang. "Everyone in the story could play themselves in the Hollywood movie," says Atlas. "They were all so perfectly cast: You pick up on who they are very quickly."

The Price of Vanity

The most well-remembered scam story in history is one we're all taught as children. In Hans Christian Andersen's "The Emperor's New Clothes," a haughty ruler cares only for fine, expensive clothes and loves to parade them before his subjects to receive their praise. When a pair of weavers come to town and start boasting about their incredible, handcrafted clothing, made of magical fabrics that are invisible only to those who are "unusually stupid" or unfit for their positions, the emperor, desperate to prove his superiority to his subjects, is intrigued.

Certainly, he would be able to discover which of his loyal subjects are unfit for their posts, and he could demonstrate his own fitness to rule by seeing and wearing this coveted magical clothing. But when the clothes are pronounced finished and he can't see them, it becomes plain to him that he must, after all, be unfit and hopelessly stupid—a fact he simply must not reveal. Instead, he allows the weavers to proceed with their great show of dressing him and flattering him with praise about how fine the clothes look on his person. The emperor proceeds with the show, strutting his stuff into town. Certainly no one would dare accuse him of wearing nothing if he behaves as if he can see the clothing, right? And none of the townsfolk can see the clothes either, but no one will admit as much and risk a dressing down by the emperor himself.

That is, until a child, innocent and lacking in pretense or a desire to impress, cries out, "But he hasn't got anything on!"

The story points out one of the greatest truisms in the world of cons: No one is easier to fool than a vain, wealthy man.

Some of the biggest, most astoundingly successful cons in history have been committed against those with deep pockets and shallow minds. Recall from Chapter 4 that among the shared traits most frequently seen in scam victims are that they're white men, possess an insatiable craving for a good deal, lack self-control, have a tendency to be dreamers, are too trusting, are likely to be lonely, and may even be coping with personal difficulties. Sorry guys. It's a truth.

In other words, they are deeply flawed humans who may rely too heavily on the approval of others and are more willing to strut naked into town than to reveal ignorance or vulnerability. And they may have more money than sense.

Throughout the course of this book, I've shared stories about con artists who have capitalized on these foibles, preying on fear and greed and using flattery to deceive their victims and compel them to hand over their confidence, their information, and their money. There's one needy culprit that gives con artists the ultimate power: Ego.

A whole breed of scams have been created simply to play to the needs of the ego—some that promise everlasting youth and beauty, some that promise riches and power, and some that promise love and adoration. We saw it in the story about John Worley, who was victimized in a Nigerian scam and whose own psychological diagnostic tool determined him to be stubborn and egotistical. We saw it in Charles Ponzi's victims, who boasted of being in the know and part of his elite clientele, never questioning his nonexistent business model. It's obvious that without the need to feed the ego, scammers would be a lot less successful. And part of the reason for this is that feeding the ego means denying that you're susceptible. According to an article entitled "Who Gets Scammed: Why

Some People Are More Vulnerable," in *Consumer Reports*, "The most dangerous attitude any consumer can have is what social scientists call the 'illusion of invulnerability'—as in, 'I'm too smart to ever fall for a con.'"

But even the emperor can walk outside naked.

I Love You, Goodbye

In the internet age, one scam gaining traction every year is the romance scam. Online dating sites are now prime hunting grounds for con artists looking to take advantage of vulnerable, hopeful people eager to make connections. Typically, the scammer finds the victim on an online dating site, sparks up a correspondence, and uses deception tactics to convince the victim to engage in illegal activities or send money. It works so well because online dating sites are full of lonely, optimistic people who are eager to make connections, coping with rejection, and often struggling with low self-esteem.

According to the FBI, American consumers have lost more than $230 million annually to romance scams. The number is likely considerably higher than that, but victims are often too embarrassed to come forward and report it. And a *Consumer Reports* survey found that 12 percent of people who had used online dating sites had been scammed and 35 percent believed they had been grossly misled by someone's online dating profile. Part of the problem is that these sites rarely vet their users, so a person whose motives are genuine has no assurance that the prospects presented are sharing true details about themselves. With a few carefully curated photos and creatively written details, a scammer can be anyone.

This was exactly the scenario when Paul Frampton, a lonely, recently divorced theoretical particle physicist and professor at the University of North Carolina, Chapel Hill, logged onto Mate1.com in November 2011 and met a beautiful young woman who claimed to be the famous Czech bikini model Denise Milani, who was ready to settle down and start a family. As Maxine Swann explains in her March 2013 story about Frampton in *The New York Times Magazine*, the two quickly started online chatting, sometimes spending hours on Yahoo messenger. Milani was attentive, calling Frampton "honey," telling him numerous times that she loved him, and expressing a fervent desire to escape her life of glamour and become his wife. For his part, the 68-year-old calculating scientist had dreams of marrying a beautiful woman—someone between the highly fertile ages of 18 and 35—who would bear him children.

But every time Frampton suggested that they talk by phone or meet in person, Milani had some reason for not doing so—it wasn't a good time, she couldn't rearrange her schedule. Finally, she conceded. She put him in touch with her agent, who spoke with Frampton by phone and arranged to send airline tickets for him to meet Milani in Bolivia, by way of Toronto, Canada, and Santiago, Chile, in early January 2012. Thinking it would only be a short trip, Frampton packed a small bag, left his car at the airport, and left for Toronto. When he arrived, he learned that the e-ticket he'd been sent for the next leg of the trip, to Santiago, was invalid. Worried, he called Milani, who assured him another would be sent immediately. After four days of travel difficulties, he arrived in La Paz, Bolivia, but Milani was already gone—called away to a photo shoot in Belgium. A ticket for him to join her there was being expedited, but she needed just one thing from him: Pick up the suitcase she'd accidentally left behind in La Paz. He was to fly to Buenos Aires with the bag and then await the ticket to Brussels.

In an email correspondence with a friend, Frampton explained the situation he'd found himself in—still fully believing Milani was on the up and up though he'd been in Bolivia for over a week—and the friend put it in plain terms: "Inside that suitcase sewn into the lining will be cocaine. You're in big trouble."

Frampton disregarded the warning as melodramatic and picked up the bag as instructed, from a Hispanic man on a dark street. Finding it surprisingly nondescript and empty (it had "sentimental value," Milani explained to him), he packed it with his dirty laundry and boarded the plane to Buenos Aires without incident. He sat waiting for a ticket to Brussels, but before long he realized he could no longer continue the journey; his life had waited too long for him back home. A friend purchased him a ticket to Raleigh, and after 15 days futilely hoping to meet Milani and having his hopes dashed, he checked his bags for North Carolina and headed home, hoping that his beloved would eventually join him there. When his name was called over the loudspeaker, he approached the ticket agent's desk and found policemen there ready to arrest him for the 1,980 grams of cocaine found in the suitcase, the value of which came to almost $400,000.

He was arrested and sent to Devoto prison in Buenos Aires, where he spent the next ten months awaiting trial for drug smuggling. Though his defense team made a compelling case for the fact that Frampton had no idea about the cocaine and meant only to meet up with a woman, his lack of precaution and apparent willingness to participate damned him in the end. He was found guilty on November 19, 2012—almost exactly one year after he initially met and began corresponding with Milani—and sentenced to four years and eight months in prison.

A few weeks into his stay in Devoto, his fellow inmates had managed to convince him that the person he'd believed to be world-renowned bikini model Milani wasn't her, and likely wasn't even a woman at all. After all, friends argued, why would a beautiful young woman like that (who is married, has a son, and claims never to have heard of Frampton until the media reported his case) fall for a 68-year-old physics professor?

"Well," Frampton told Swann in an interview, "I have been accused of having a huge ego."

Frampton was a perfect mark for this dating scam that lured him into drug smuggling. Lonely? Check. Inflated ego? Check. A dreamer with illusions of grandeur? Check, and check. Additionally, there are a number of other hallmarks of classic dating scams that appear in Frampton's story and should serve as red flags for the lovelorn:

- **Poor-me profiles.** Part of the reason romance scams are so hard to catch right away is that many of the reasons people use online dating sites is that they are lonely and find themselves in circumstances that prohibit them from meeting people organically. So it's not uncommon to find divorcees, widowers, single parents, and caregivers on these sites. Unfortunately, these are also some of the trademark qualities scammers possess. Their profiles are designed to elicit sympathy, to make you, the potential victim, feel needed, as if you're all that person has. That's step one in the plan. This is a frequently used tactic among men to bait nurturing women. I'm not saying a divorce or dead spouse should be an automatic deal breaker, but never take an online dating profile at face value, either.

- **Provocative pictures.** To bait men, one tactic often used is posting sexy, provocative photos of beautiful women. They may be single and unattached, but often there's a person relying on her—perhaps an aging or sick parent. Again, it may all be true, but it should be a red flag, enough for you to reserve judgment until you've done some more research on this person. And you should definitely examine any photos you see closely; they may have been doctored or just snagged from the internet. Do a little web search to see if the photos you find of her online jive with what's on the profile.

- **Strange language.** Maybe there are frequent misspellings or odd, foreign-sounding turns of phrase. Maybe he or she claims to be an American citizen—an odd thing for an actual American to put on a profile. If the person is claiming to have a college education but can't write a good sentence, that's a problem. Many of these scams are conducted outside the United States, and their writing can be easy to spot.

- **Taking the chat off site.** A site such as eHarmony or Match has the capability of spotting problematic language or behavior and booting the scammer off the site before trouble starts, and would-be victims can report suspicions. When a romantic prospect suggests continuing the conversation elsewhere—perhaps because his or her "membership to the site is about to expire"—consider that a warning that he or she may be planning some behavior that isn't totally above board.

- **An unexpected pairing.** Beware the hot young twenty-something breathlessly chasing the middle-aged teacher or humdrum retiree.

Tread lightly when there's constant flattery and someone wanting to sweep you off your feet. Use caution when the words "I love you" make early, insistent appearances. Sure, it's possible that a sexy young thing like Milani could find a man forty years her senior attractive, but let's be realistic: It's not likely, and the chances are even smaller when the pair meet online. The academic journal *Cyberpsychology, Behavior and Social Networking* reported the findings of a psychological study of romance scam victims and found that they tended to be well-educated, middle-aged and older, and more often women. This population tends to be more nurturing and struggle more with self-esteem issues. Scammers will target those who seem to be vulnerable, dejected, lonely, or feeling past their prime. And, frankly, they're less likely to be knowledgeable about technology and cybersecurity. They may be struggling with issues associated with weight gain, wrinkles, and other physical traits that come with aging. Scammers know these people are likely to respond favorably to overtures from the young and beautiful. This is all part of the grooming process, laying the groundwork to strike at a victim.

- **Too good to be true.** Frampton's "Denise Milani" imposter was beautiful, but so was her glamorous life of jet-setting around the globe, doing photo shoots in exotic locations, with an agent arranging all her travel plans. But like most things on social media, the life being presented isn't often the truth. I had a British real estate broker high jack my photo recently, which means they'll misuse anyone's likeness. Scammers will troll the internet and steal anyone's photos, including yours, which they place on the web to convince their marks that they are wealthy, successful and have a pulse. This is an important part of a scam that involves the victim sending money. It's all a highly orchestrated effort to convince the victim that they do indeed have the money, they just can't immediately access those funds for some inexplicable reason. Showing you visual evidence of wealth is a sort of proof of eventual repayment—a key in getting the victim to let his or her guard down.

- **Continual drama.** In real life, few of us have to suddenly drop what we're doing and fly off to another country, but in dating scams, that's to be expected. Scammers talk a good game about how you're meant to be and they can't wait to be with you. They'll indulge fantasies about settling down together, tell you they love you, and say all the things you've wanted to hear someone say to you. But then when you insist upon meeting in person or speaking by phone, poof! They're gone. Despite a profile that says they live nearby, they're oddly in the Philippines or Brazil. A family member abroad is in crisis and they had to fly away to be with them. A last-minute work situation meant hopping the next plane. A military action forced their disappearance. Geographic problems. Natural disasters. Work crises. And then they need your money for emergency surgery, or they're stuck in a foreign country and need money for a hotel room and food or to cover legal fees. They may not ask for it directly, but they're banking on your investment in the relationship, hoping that by saying they need money, you'll offer it willingly. They may even show you photos of where they are or the dire straits in which they find themselves. Don't buy it. They have access to the same Google searches you do, and it takes only minutes to find photos of Brazil.

- **Asking for personal details.** There's no reason why anyone you meet on an online dating site—which should have options for chatting on the site—needs your email address, and certainly they don't need details like an address or other personal information. A legitimate prospect may ask for a phone number, but never demand it, and you should never give it if you haven't done some due diligence. Anyone who asks for any of these things should be viewed with a critical eye, blocked from seeing your profile details, and reported to the site administrators.

One lesson to be learned, regardless of the type of scam, is this: If it seems too good to be true, it probably is.

The Search for the Magic Pill

The same maxim holds true for most scams... and for life, really. Sure, we'd all like to lose a little weight, mask our physical flaws, enhance our natural beauty or vibrancy, and become more attractive to the opposite sex. Advertisers know this, which is why so many of them promise "unbelievable weight loss" or "lose thirty pounds in thirty days" or "watch the miracle fat-burning power." Occasionally, I'll catch one of these infomercials on TV when I'm up late, and they always make me chuckle. I like to think most people have become savvy enough about commercials by now that no one actually falls for them.

But, unfortunately, they do. At heart, we are humans and we are weak, and we often choose to believe the things we want to hear. Plus, there's a reason that nearly 40 percent of Americans are considered obese, according to the Centers for Disease Control and Prevention: Losing weight is hard work, and we've grown more and more accustomed to not working that hard. We have cars that stop for us, and we can push a button and have dinner delivered in minutes... isn't there just a pill we can take to lose weight?

No. No there's not. Think about it: If there were, wouldn't every doctor on the planet be prescribing it? Would we really be seeing 60 percent of American women and nearly 75 percent of American men still overweight?

Combine this innate desire to take the easy way out with many of the other traits of successful scams—persuasive language, a target who's susceptible, confusing and easy-to-manipulate technology, methods for quickly snagging your personal information—and our general lack of understanding about health, medicine, and the inner workings of the human body, and you can quickly see why weight-loss and other vanity scams work.

Today's weight-loss or health product scams may feature the following characteristics:

- **Celebrity endorsements:** Researchers at the University of British Columbia developed a screening tool to determine whether a weight-loss or health claim on the internet is likely to be a scam. They call it the Risk of Deception Tool. (Remember, we call it the BS Detector.) Their detector assigns points to a variety of characteristics that are likely to correlate to a scam. A celebrity endorsement gets a point, and it's one of the most frequent tactics used because we trust them. Scientists have found that when we see celebrities who are familiar to us, our brains make a connection to the products they're endorsing, which also seem familiar. Similarly, if we see a celebrity we believe has good taste or whom we associate with high quality endorsing a product, our minds make the leap to associate that product with high quality as well.

- **Fake news:** Don't get all hissy here. The political talk about "fake news" is based in truth: The internet makes it entirely possible to present information in a way that looks like news, acts like news, reads like news, and IS NOT actually news. While innocently reading an article online, you're likely to encounter a link to a story about a celebrity who just discovered a miracle diet or a beauty product she can't live without. The link takes you to a fake news site, created intentionally to tell you about the celebrity's "dramatic weight loss" or to describe a reporter's "investigation" into the hype on a particular product, as well as his or her amazing discovery that the product does indeed do all that its manufacturer claims. It may provide you with an opportunity to purchase the product right there on the page. There may even be a way to order a free trial of the product. Remember that legitimate news organizations don't promote products in their stories. Also know that there are plenty of illegitimate "news organizations".

- **A friend's recommendation:** We have previously pointed to one of the latest tricks used by scammers—taking advantage of our trust in friends. Hackers can cloak phone numbers to appear to be from neighbors, or send emails and social media messages in a way that they appear to have been sent by friends. Be wary of the email from your long-lost friend insisting "you've gotta try this" diet pill or that beauty cream. That's not usually how friends operate.

- **Pseudoscientific language:** Many scammers take advantage of our innate trust of medical authorities by sprinkling in language that sounds sufficiently scientific and complex—no matter that it makes no sense. Have you heard of the new product that speeds up your metabolism and knocks out fatty tissue? The active ingredient in this incarnation is a seaweed mold called "focus," (which interestingly rhymes with "hocus" and "pocus"). Anyone who's ever heard one of those two-minute commercials for a new medication knows it's common to hear scientific terminology that's unfamiliar and even funny-sounding. That's why the presence of pseudoscientific language—language that sounds based on real science, like that of astrology or alternative medicine, but in fact is not entirely based on science—earns a point on the Risk of Detection Tool. Seaweed mold sounds like it could be a real thing, right? Well, doctors deny the existence of this miracle mold and the claims made by its makers are as murky as the waters where this supposed seaweed mold might be found.

- **Outrageous, magical claims:** You know how to lose weight? Eat right and exercise. Any claim that this can be done in any other way is magical thinking. The FDA says beware of language such as "secret ingredient," "all-natural miracle cure," "one product does it all," "new discovery," "scientific breakthrough," "quick fix," "lose weight without diet and exercise," or "rare and in short supply." This sort of language scores a point on the Risk of Detection Tool, because it's highly likely to correlate to a scam.

The following claims made in weight-loss and beauty scams should serve as red flags to you when you encounter them:

Lose 30 pounds in 30 days! The product Skinny Coffee Club promises to help you lose weight dramatically—a dress size in four weeks—not to mention clear up your skin and reduce wrinkles, thanks to green tea extracts ("extracts" are a big part of weight-loss scams) and other magical ingredients. It's managed to gain huge traction, selling in 145 countries to a cult following, thanks to its photos on Instagram and website. Studies of its veracity have turned up nothing to support its claims. Dramatic weight loss of this magnitude, especially without any real dieting or exercise, just isn't possible, and certainly isn't healthy.

Lose up to 50 pounds! "Up to" is code for "you won't get anywhere near this number." The FTC says that sometimes advertisers only give their one best customer's incredible and highly unusual results. Watch for fine print that says, "Results not typical." One bizarre example of this is the Fat-Be-Gone Ring, whose maker claimed that you need only slide the coiled ring on the finger that, through acupuncture and acupressure principles, corresponded to the place where you wanted to lose weight. A paunch around your belly? The index finger does the trick. Wide hips? Put it on your thumb. Its ads claimed the wearer could gain the same benefits as running *up to* six miles a day. Well, a walk across the room to go to the bathroom counts as "up to six miles," right?

Eat whatever you want! Lose weight while watching TV! The weight stays off, even after you stop using it! Promising substantial weight loss no matter what or how much you eat and whether you exercise or not just isn't possible, and certainly wouldn't be recommended by a doctor. Weight loss is a lifestyle, not a two-week or thirty-day plan.

Contains fat blockers! Have you heard of products that contain a plant fiber that blocks fat from being absorbed into the body? Currently, there's only one FDA-approved fat blocker on the market. It's called Orlistat, and it's the only one that science has actually shown works, and it should only be used on the advice of a doctor. Avoid any other product claiming to block the absorption of fat or calories. It won't work, and you won't know what else the product might contain that could actually do you harm.

Rub the fat away! Yes, it supposedly is that easy with Miracle Thigh Cream which promised its users would obtain "the smooth beautiful thighs you want, and the Defat Seaweed Soap that would enable users to "watch the fat go down the drain!" (Poor seaweed, so maligned by the weight-loss industry.) To be clear, you cannot lose weight by rubbing anything on your skin. It's not scientifically possible. At least in this universe.

The weight-loss industry isn't the only victim of today's magical-thinking scam artists. The health care industry in general suffers from outrageously false claims at the hands of people who take advantage of our ignorance, fear, and desire to be healthy and beautiful. A whole industry exists for these people to hawk their wares to those who are desperate for quick, easy, affordable solutions to health problems. They include such useless (and often expensive) products as:

- Arthritis remedies including copper bracelets or magnets
- Anti-aging creams or pills (nothing yet has been proven to reverse time)
- Diagnostic tests that aren't approved by the FDA
- Over-the-counter treatments for sexually transmitted diseases—the real ones are only available by prescription, and without it, you may be unintentionally transmitting a disease to others
- Herbal remedies to prevent or treat flu

The jury is still out on many of these illnesses and conditions, so unless it's recommended by a doctor, purchased at a pharmacy, or approved by the FDA, it's likely not to work and to be a waste of your money and hopes.

Get Over Yourself

A University of Exeter psychology professor, Dr. Stephen Lea, has spent years researching the psychology of scams and how they work, and his findings are interesting. We often disregard scams as being the domain of the ignorant—only a fool who had no knowledge of weight-loss strategies, for instance, would fall for such obviously false claims that a ring worn on your finger or a soap made of seaweed can help you magically shed weight. Yet there's a reason why the weight-loss and diet products industry takes in over $60 billion a year: Americans are more overweight than at any time in history. The reason is this: A little bit of knowledge is a dangerous thing. People who are focused on weight loss, who have spent considerable time looking into what mechanisms in the body can help us to lose weight, are the ones who have an overinflated sense of their own knowledge and are, ironically, more susceptible to a claim that seaweed mold can help you melt fat away.

Lea's research proved that most people overestimate their competence in areas in which they have interest and *some* knowledge. This "overconfidence effect," as psychological researchers have dubbed it, points to a great disparity between what people actually know and what they think they know. This bears out as truth when you see that most drivers rate their own driving abilities as superior to their peers. A *Psychology Today* article by Rolf Dobelli explains the phenomenon. "What's surprising is this: Experts suffer even more from the *overconfidence effect* than laypeople do. If asked to forecast oil prices in five years' time, an economics professor will be as wide of the mark as a zookeeper will. However, the professor will offer his forecast with certitude."

This is the entire basis on which con artists conceive vanity scams. Ego isn't just a fatal flaw in literature—it's a fatal flaw in life too. Beware the self-proclaimed expert. And be especially aware of the expert's vain acolytes. As you saw in the case of Rudy Kurniawan, his staunchest supporters were those who had frequently been hailed as having the keenest palates and the greatest bank of knowledge about fine wines. Vanity obscures objectivity.

The overconfidence effect is responsible for a breed of scams all aimed at stroking the ego. People will pay enormous amounts of money in order to gain bragging rights and save face. Consider the oldie but goodie found on city streets: The counterfeit merchandise scam. A Fendi handbag sure would impress your friends, but you're not-so-impressive wallet won't allow it. But this knockoff being sold on the corner sure looks like a Fendi—it's a deal, right? The entire scam is premised on the customer's desire to impress.

Beware this latest rash of scams created to puff up your ego and take advantage of the overconfidence effect:

- **Vanity business awards:** "You've been selected by your peers for the prestigious Businessperson of the Year Award! Only a small percentage of people in your field have achieved this distinction!" It's possible you've received one of these letters and your heart swelled with pride to think, "Me? They picked *me*? What an incredible honor! I must really be good at this!" The letter goes on to explain that, as a winner, you'll receive a plaque (that you must pay for) and have your name published in the organization's annual publication (to which you must subscribe), not to mention the honor of being able to claim this impressive award on your resume and bio (a meaningless designation that no one will recognize). You might even be hit up to join this mysterious organization that you've never heard of (*But wait! My peers have joined! Maybe I'm missing out!*) Don't be fooled. If you want your business to stand up and be noticed, invest those thousands in a sound marketing campaign spearheaded by experts. Don't drop that same bundle on a bogus award. Typically, there will be fine print that explains that while you certainly don't have to *pay* to be a winner, you're getting what members pay annual fees for, so the least you can do is pay for the plaque to hang in your office and impress your colleagues. Don't get me wrong, there are legitimate awards given by real, well-intentioned organizations that prize talent and hard work, but those awards are given freely to well-deserving recipients. They aren't used in a bait and switch designed to make money off you.

- **Who's Who directories:** Every adult I know can probably remember receiving a letter just prior to their high school graduations congratulating them for being selected for the "Who's Who Among America's High School Students." We, and our parents, felt enormously proud at having made the cut. Eager to strike out in the world and show off our talents, grasping at anything substantial that served as proof of academic achievements (so small in number at that age), students and families were eager to shell out the hundreds of dollars for the hard-bound book in which our names would be printed, just so we could point to something that legitimized us in the eyes of future colleges and employers.

  Even as adults, we may receive similar letters congratulating us for being selected for the "Who's Who in Business" or "Executives of the Year." They boast that these are excellent networking tools, and that selection is based on outstanding achievement or philanthropic work, yet where are the Fortune 500 companies, the major nonprofit organizations, or your community's largest donors? It's not that the work you're doing isn't valuable, but that's not why you were selected.

  In fact, there's usually no selection "process," because no one is turned down. If you're willing to pay, you get a listing. Trust me, no one is buying or reading these listings to select business partners or make hiring decisions. Not only that but the "next to nothing" cost of receiving these listings—if indeed you ever receive one— can be upwards of $700 or more. There's a reason why the Better Business Bureau does not endorse a great many of these Who's Who businesses.

- **The starving artist scam:** There's a long-cultivated belief that in order to work as an artist, one must be broke. The myth of the starving artist says that you should consider yourself lucky to be seen, read, or appreciated at all, and if you make a single red cent, you should pat yourself on the back. You should have to claw your way to the top, suffer for many years, earn your stripes, receive rejection after rejection. After all, you got to follow your passion.

Isn't the joy in the *making* of the art? Earning any money at all is just a perk, right? Even artists themselves have bought into this notion. So when an opportunity comes around to be acknowledged, to be selected for a gallery exhibit or see our written work in celluloid, the pull of something to put in the ol' portfolio and bragging rights becomes too strong to ignore.

Consider the letter that photographer Mathieu Stern received from someone with The Brick Wall Gallery in London congratulating him for selection to exhibit in its "rentable gallery space." With further research, he concluded that for the exorbitant rate of about $800, he might receive about nine or ten feet worth of wall space in a basement. Of course, the gallery promised that paying the fee up front meant that he would retain all rights and royalties on any paintings sold. But there was no promotion, there were no opening receptions… no way at all to sell the work.

And as it turned out, many artists hungry for attention had fallen for the gimmick and been sorely disappointed. Similar scams capitalize on writers eager to build a portfolio of published works: Pay for Amazon reviews on your latest self-published book; pay $2,000 for a 10-minute radio interview about your work; pay $1,000 for someone to make a trailer for your book ("You'll make that money back in a month with sales of your book!"); pay a Hollywood screen writer to create a screen play based on your book; pay the low low rate of just $50 to have a professional editor edit your book!

Then there are the content mills that ask writers to crank out content for the slave-labor rate of $10 per 100 words that you must wait for six months to receive. That's a whole other problem, but at least they're getting paid, not paying for the work. Worse is the International Association of Professional Writers and Editors (IAPWE).

Writer Tamara Gane received some notoriety when she shared the story on Medium.com about how, as a newly minted freelance writer, she came across a Craigslist ad exclaiming that the IAPWE—an organization with a closed, paid membership—was hiring freelance writers. She needed only to submit a writing sample—not a resume or proof of publishing, which was music to a newbie freelancer's ears—and await acceptance before the assignments could come rolling in.

When she received her "Congratulations! You've been selected as a freelancer!" email, she anxiously awaited her invitation to IAPWE's page on Basecamp, a project-management and team communication site, so she could start fielding assignments. The woman whose name had appeared on the congratulatory email, Amy Wilkerson, explained at the end of the letter that although the exclusive IAPWE rarely accepted new members, they wanted to invite Gane to join, and were even willing to waive the standard $119 annual fee and offer her the limited-time rate of just $17.85 a month.

When she explored the link provided in the email, she discovered that IAPWE was willing to grant her a free 30-day trial membership. No harm, no foul, right? Gane thought, "I'll just cancel before the 30 days is up." She figured becoming a member might improve her chances of getting more assignments, though the email had indicated that the job and the membership were two separate things. She signed up on PayPal, inputting her financial information, and waited for a Basecamp invitation that never came.

Suspicious, Gane conducted a bit of online research into IAPWE and quickly discovered that numerous writers had similarly been duped. Elsewhere, a number of so-called successful freelance writers had sung the praises of IAPWE and the enormous amount of work they'd received from the organization, but when Gane grew curious about whom these people actually were, she could find no actual trace of their work, nothing that substantiated their claims that they were "successful, published freelance writers."

Emails to Amy Wilkerson over several days finally yielded an invitation to Basecamp, where it was clear to Gane immediately that no assignments had ever been posted there for her. And, as you might have guessed, they never were. She went right to the IAPWE website to cancel her membership and had quite a few hoops to jump through in order to do it, including the puzzling request that she confirm her subscription.

After taking every step indicated that was supposed to lead to cancelling her membership, she landed at a notice that a 50 percent discount would be applied to her membership; if she did nothing, the 50 percent discount would be applied. She still wasn't cancelled. Doing so involved an exhausting eight-step process that included cancelling her eventual automatic payments through PayPal.

Further research revealed to Gane that the photos populating the IAPWE website had been stolen from the internet or severely doctored. As a test, she attempted on two other separate occasions to obtain writing jobs under false identities—one time uploading a writing sample that was garbage and another time not even bothering to upload one at all. Both times, she received the same congratulatory letter welcoming her to IAPWE's team of freelancers. Dozens of comments on Gane's Medium.com article thanked her for calling out this sham organization that had also fooled others into giving up money to get assignments that never had come.

No legitimate organization will insist that you *pay* to get work. They should be paying you, no matter what. The amount of pay you will accept in exchange for your talents is all up to you, but know this: Even as an artist, you have the right to be paid for providing a product or service. Not the other way around.

"In the rare-wine world, doubts are endemic; murkiness is built into a product that is concealed by tinted glass and banded wooden cases and opaque provenance and the fog of history. At the same time, the whole apparatus of the rare-wine market is about converting doubt into mystique. Most wealthy collectors want to spend big and drink famous labels, not necessarily ask questions or hear the answers. Guests at tastings don't want to bite the hand that quenches them."
— *Benjamin Wallace, "Château Sucker,"*
New York Magazine, *May 13, 2012*

Chapter Nine

There's No Place Like Home

The rise of bank and real estate scams

CASE #7: The Dream Home Nightmare

The median home price in Santa Clara County, California, is generally over $1 million.

The San Francisco Bay Area is notorious for its sky-high real estate prices. In San Jose, the heart of the Silicon Valley and county seat of Santa Clara County, an 1,100-square-foot ranch home recently sold for $1.2 million, over $1,000 per square foot.

Those who already own homes in San Jose may be eagerly counting dollar signs, but this was certainly not the case for Cindy Bernal, a grandmother who was renting a home for herself, her husband, Richard, and her youngest son for $1,500 a month, in San Jose, where the median rent for a two-bedroom apartment was $2,640 in late summer of 2018.

Richard, who was on disability, relied entirely on his wife to support him, but the school district where she'd been employed for fifteen years let her go. Nervous about the prospect of rent increases—expected to soon double—and far away from her daughter and grandchildren, who live in northeastern Ohio, Bernal decided it was high time to get out of the Bay Area's rat race and buy herself something affordable and close to family.

She and her husband had been barely making ends meet in San Jose, but thanks to her 401K, which she'd cashed in, she was ready to put it all down on a fixer-upper home in the rural Midwest, near family, where housing prices were rock bottom and probably would remain that way.

In spring 2018, Bernal and her husband found a 980-square-foot home, just south of Cleveland and ten minutes away from her daughter's home, whose owners were asking just $28,000. Money like that would barely qualify as a down payment in San Jose, but in Ohio, Bernal could afford to pay cash out of the gate and skip the mortgage process altogether. Working with her real estate agent, Brent Karlen of RE/MAX Edge Realty, she made an offer of $24,500 that day, and it was accepted.

The papers were signed and the transaction was under way. The next step was wiring the money to the seller's agent, Jeff First of First Realty. On May 10, Bernal's agent received an email containing detailed instructions for wiring the entire $24,500 to the seller's bank.

But an hour later, Karlen received a strange email. The seller's agent was making a change to the earlier instructions, which he claimed had been "a mistake." *These* instructions were the correct ones. Karlen was instructed that Bernal should instead wire her money to a Texas bank whose account and routing numbers were provided in order to complete the transaction. Karlen told Bernal about the mix-up. So excited for this promising future, she followed the new instructions to the letter and began preparing for her new life in Ohio.

But the seller never received the money, and on May 14, Bernal received a call from Karlen, instructing her to go immediately to her bank. "It was a fraudulent account. The other realtor's account was hacked," he told her. "You need to run to the bank now and stop the transaction." The hackers had taken over the seller's agent's email and given instructions for wiring to his own bank account rather than the seller's.

Again, Bernal did as instructed, without delay, and believed the transaction had been stopped and disaster averted. Unfortunately, that wasn't the case. Days of correspondence between the two banks led to one unified conclusion: The scammer's account was drained, the money long gone and untraceable.

"It's ruined my life," Bernal told the Bay Area NBC affiliate who interviewed her about the ordeal.

When she was interviewed by the reporter, Bernal sadly said that she was left with only $244 to her name, out of her entire life savings. And when she turned to the professionals for help, everyone pointed the finger at the other guy and claimed they weren't at fault—the seller's agent claiming he couldn't be held responsible for the hack, and the buyer's agent claiming he had no idea the instructions given weren't real. All denied culpability, blaming each other and Bernal for falling victim. And Bernal was left holding the very expensive bag.

Her family started a GoFundMe account to help Bernal and her husband rebound from the incident, cover their living costs, and find a new place to live. The Santa Clara County district attorney caught the story on the NBC station's report and is now investigating the matter. And Bernal has filed suit against the real estate agents who she claims did not perform adequately in protecting her money.

But at the time of this writing, Bernal is no closer to getting her money back.

Maybe the most insidious of all scams is the one that happens right in the zenith of your happiness, the one that capitalizes on your life's work and your hopes and your investment in what most think of as the American Dream.

You've just gone through the exhaustive process of walking through homes, let a bunch of strangers pore over and judge your credit and spending habits, endured weeks of inspections and incessant phone calls, and experienced highs and lows in which your payment went up, down, up, and down again. You've packed all your belongings, given notice to your landlord or put your own home on the market, experiencing the exhaustion from both sides of the table. You've signed paper after paper in a seemingly never-ending series of steps to buy the home you've pinned all your hopes on. You've carefully determined how much of your life savings you can spend on a down payment, dotted every i and crossed every t, and the day has come to finally, *finally* pay them that money, get your keys, and take possession of your new home.

Then the crushing truth hits you like a brick wall: That life savings has been taken from right under your nose, with your own blessing even, and there's no way to get it back.

According to the Federal Trade Commission, bank and lender fraud was the sixth most frequently reported fraud of 2019, with almost 150,000 reports that year alone. Many of these include predatory lending practices perpetrated by fraudulent institutions marketing themselves as legitimately working on your behalf—for instance, payday loan companies or advance-free frauds in which a lender offers a loan for which you must pay fees up front for "good faith" or "processing." However, an increasing number of them target financial institutions. The FBI calls these FIFs—Financial Institution Frauds.

These schemes involve the misappropriation of customer accounts and personal information for use in identity thefts, and consumers always end up the unwitting victims. Fraudsters performing these acts may be acting on the outside, but they also may be working on the inside. As we've discussed, about 70 percent of identity theft starts with an employee stealing information from his or her own company, and six out of ten American companies and government agencies have been hacked.

FIFs may include the following scams, which are seen with alarming regularity by the FBI:

- Stolen or counterfeit checks
- Account fraud or identity theft
- Credit/debit card fraud
- Email hacking leading to financial loss

And although FDIC backing ensures that banks will perform due diligence and prevents some amount of fraud, the unfortunate truth is that scammers are just really good these days, and technology makes them even better at getting away with it. The amount of home buyer fraud alone has skyrocketed lately; according to the FBI's IC3 office, 9,645 prospective home buyers lost nearly $1 billion in 2017 alone due to wire fraud situations like what Cindy Bernal experienced, and that number is way up from the mere $19 million lost just a year prior. In other words, about $2.65 million in real estate funds were stolen from home buyers *every day*. And the FBI reports that email compromise scams like this are a $12 billion (and growing) industry.

Any time you plan to make a major purchase with high dollar figures involved, you run the risk of encountering a scammer who wants to hijack your dreams. In comparison, Cindy Bernal's loss was small.

A Denver, Colorado, couple sold their home and planned to use the $272,536 they made on the sale toward a down payment on their new $504,000 home. But somewhere along the way, the couple received email instructions for wiring the cash, like Bernal, and the entire down payment was lost.

Another woman in San Jose—who chose to remain anonymous in the fallout of her loss—approached retirement and was looking to downsize. She found a home that met her needs and agreed to put $400,000 down on the new house. But when it came time to send the down payment, she received emails from a scammer that appeared to have come from both the real estate agent and the title company. The messages said that the seller had changed the purchase agreement and instructed her to wire all the money rather than getting a cashier's check. She did as she was told and realized, just two hours later, that the money she'd spent ten years accumulating had vanished.

Even that loss is small compared to the $1.57 million lost by a Washington, D.C., couple whose transfer of settlement funds was diverted to a hacker's own account when the thief broke into the title and escrow company's email system.

Hackers are finding openings in title companies' or realtors' email accounts in order to track upcoming purchases that are scheduled to close—the higher the price, the better—and then appear to be those trusted sources in order to provide fraudulent wiring instructions that the recipient will believe. Then the funds go directly to the scammer's own bank account, which is promptly emptied and closed, then gone without a trace. Shouldn't the government actively pursue such criminals?

The problem is so widespread that the California Association of Realtors now requires its agents to provide the following printed warning on every real estate contract:

DO NOT EVER WIRE OR ELECTRONICALLY TRANSFER FUNDS PRIOR TO CALLING TO CONFIRM THE TRANSFER INSTRUCTIONS. ONLY USE A PHONE NUMBER YOU WERE PROVIDED PREVIOUSLY.

The Denver couple has hired an attorney to sue their title agency, real estate agency, and mortgage lender for negligence and other transgressions, under a little-known caveat known as the Financial Fraud Kill Chain. Under this rule, the FBI may be able to stop a transfer and recover lost funds exceeding $50,000 if the transfer is sent internationally, the bank issues a recall notice, and the FBI is alerted within seventy-two hours.

The bottom line is to exercise abundant, even excessive caution when engaging in a large financial transaction of any kind. A home purchase involves putting every one of your personal financial details on the table, so you're always at risk at every step of the way.

When I buy real estate, I get a cashier's check from my bank and drive it directly to the title office. The $5 check fee and a little gas are safer for me than any wire transaction would be.

According to a *Forbes* article, Dale Dabbs, CEO and president of EZShield, an identity protection firm, says that email is easily hacked and not secure, so the first warning for any potential victim is that instructions of any sort come through email. None of these transactions should be conducted this way.

Prior to even beginning the process, consumers should ask how all their personal information will be protected, ensure that the check is covered by fraud protection services, and send payments by certified mail. Dabbs also suggests that realtors and mortgage professionals offer professional data protection.

A lot of these scams happen on Fridays, especially before a long weekend, for a couple of reasons. First, people are eager to close at the end of the week so they can begin the moving process over the weekend, so they may be inclined to rush through the transaction without performing due diligence. Plus, banks and financial institutions aren't conducting business over the weekend, so by the time the home buyer can report it, several days have passed. In this situation, every minute counts. Often, these scams involve a series of transfers and accounts, making the trail nearly impossible to follow, and once it's gone out of the country, you can say goodbye to that money.

Home buyers should pay attention to how wiring instructions are sent—only accept instructions that are secure and encrypted, says the National Association of Realtors. Buyers should confirm every single number personally, by phone, throughout the process, and then call to confirm receipt of the funds immediately afterward. One single call or email should never be the thing that tells you where to send your money; there should be a series of conversations about this transfer, with every detail double and triple checked. Wiring instructions rarely change, so any indication that these instructions will vary is a red flag that buyers should take seriously and take extreme caution with. Multiple checkpoints at every phase can help prevent this fraud from taking place.

The IC3 website indicates that some of these victimized home buyers were targeted by phone, so the FBI's recommendation is that consumers establish code words with everyone involved in the transaction to ensure that anyone who calls looking for information or transmitting instructions is legitimately involved.

But once the scam has occurred, the best thing a person can do is contact the bank immediately to report it—there is a chance the money can be retrieved if too much time hasn't passed.

Unfortunately, this is only one type of real estate and property scam gaining traction. Here are some of the biggest scams people encounter when it comes to conducting large financial transactions to purchase or rent property.

- **Foreclosure rescue fraud:** In this type of scam, the perpetrator identifies a homeowner who's in danger of defaulting on a mortgage or who is already in foreclosure, and then indicates that he or she can help the homeowner save the home by putting the title for the home into the name of an "investor." The homeowner may even be told that he or she can rent the property and then repurchase it once his or her credit has been re-established. Of course, none of this happens. The scammer instead sells the property to an investor or "straw borrower" (an identity created by a scammer that's not attached to anyone, or is stolen from someone), using equity drawn from a false appraisal, then steals the fees paid by the homeowner and disappears. Of course, the "investor" never makes a payment, the home goes into foreclosure anyway, and the original homeowner is left homeless and out even more money due to the money lost to scammers.

In some of these cases, the scammers promise to help negotiate lower monthly payments in order to stop the foreclosure—a service for which they charge high fees and deliver nothing.

According to the *South Bend Tribune* in Indiana, the state's General Assembly created its Consumer Protection Assistance Fund in 2011 to help victims of this increasingly devastating scam recover their losses through legal action, and by 2018 it had helped them recover nearly $1.4 million. Thirteen of these victims suffered from foreclosure relief frauds.

"Real estate and foreclosure relief scams can be particularly devastating because they often involve large amounts of money, and the victims tend to already be in a tough financial spot," said Indiana Attorney General Greg Zoeller in the *Tribune* story.

Kicking people when they're down is a common theme among scam artists, because the down-and-out are usually the ones looking for Hail Marys and will do almost anything to get out of trouble. But remember when I talked about what makes a good mark? They're desperate, and they're making last-minute decisions that aren't reasonable. Scamsters, ever despicable, gleefully defraud the downtrodden.

- **Loan modification schemes:** Along these lines, homeowners facing foreclosure or who have trouble making their mortgage payments are contacted by scammers pretending to be representatives of financial institutions or lenders. They may offer to refinance your mortgage at a much lower interest rate than what you're paying—often in 24 hours or less and without closing costs. Or they may offer alternatives to foreclosure that may include negotiating with your bank to reduce your mortgage payments. First, though (you can see it coming already, can't you?), you have to pay a fee, often something like one percent of the mortgage to "guarantee" the loan. These advance-fee type scams may also be associated with consolidation loans or business loans, since these may be consumers looking for quick infusions of cash.

  Once you pay it, they tell you, your application will be processed immediately. It won't—but you knew that already, right? Be on the lookout for any sketchy-sounding refinancing option or anything that involves an upfront fee. Any actual mortgage broker worth his or her salt would never charge an advance fee—the only fees you might have to pay are for a credit report or a property appraisal, and you'll get legitimate paperwork on that. The best thing you can do to avoid becoming a mark is to once again use your BS Detector. Know when something smells fishy and hang up the phone, delete the email, or throw away that direct mailer. If you're facing the loss of your home, you don't need a savior, you need a lawyer or a realtor.

- **Illegal property flipping:** Similar to the foreclosure rescue scheme, an illegal property flip involves the purchase of a property by someone looking to make a quick buck. The property owner somehow gets hold of a false, overly inflated appraisal, then turns around and sells the property at way more than its value, presenting fraudulent information to home buyers in what's supposed to be a good-faith transaction. The scam may also include falsified loan documents, inflated buyer income, or kickbacks to others involved, such as buyers, investors, brokers, appraisers, or title company employees, says the FBI.

Freddie Mac reports a similar fraud called cash-out purchase fraud. Markets where homes are rapidly appreciating, or, conversely, where homes are remaining stagnant and sitting on the market for long periods of time, may see this type of scam, in which a buyer offers way more than asking price, with the stipulation that the additional amount over the asking price be given in cash to the buyer at closing—something documented in an addendum in the contract—which is purportedly to cover the home improvements that the scammer claims will be made (and likely got a falsified estimate for). The buyer gets that extra money, but the sale often is predicated on falsified information. So the buyer usually disappears and the home goes into foreclosure.

- **Builder bailout/condo conversion:** In situations where a builder has a lot of inventory sitting unsold and is facing declining demand, the builder may employ a bailout scheme in order to show bankers—who loaned him the money to build—that the inventory is moving. In this kind of scenario, the builder offers to sell the property for no money down—but at an inflated price, based on a phony appraisal. The buyer—usually a straw buyer to apply for the loan but who can't be traced, or an employee of the builder or developer—gets a loan at that price. Then the builder takes out a second mortgage for what remains of the cost, but represents it as a down payment, so the financial institution gets what it's owed, the buyer gets all the financing on a home worth less than the price, and the builder not only pays off his costs but makes a profit to boot. The problem is that the buyer defaults on the loan that he or she either didn't know about or never planned to pay, and the bank eats the loss. The buyer may have received some sort of payoff, whether it's being allowed to stay employed, getting a nice cash bump, or even being allowed to live for free in the property for a period of time.

A condo conversion scheme works similarly. A hot housing market provokes the builder, seller, or developer to turn apartment complexes into condo properties. But when the market cools, the developer is left with an excess of units and promotes them as "no-risk" investment properties, with little to no money down, to people with excellent credit. It may also include incentives such as cash back at the closing table, guaranteed mortgage payments for a fixed period of time, or even turnkey management on the property. Like the buyer bailout scenario, the sale price on the property is inflated based on a fraudulent appraisal, so the bank funds the loan, the developer uses the extra cash to fund the incentives. And the buyer is often straw, so his or her income has been inflated to get loan approval.

According to Freddie Mac, the hallmarks of these scams include buyer incentives built into the sale price, which are often a red flag that the price has been inflated and built on a faulty appraisal; the builder's willingness to "do anything" to sell the property; no-money-down promotions; buyers being recruited from out of state; HUD-1 forms indicating that a portion of proceeds go to unrelated third parties; comparable listings in the appraisal all being from the same complex or development; the source of funds being questionable; renovations being either superficial or nonexistent; or the occupancy form for a condo stating that the property is owner-occupied when it's a rental.

It isn't just the banks who pay the price for these cons. Neighbors pay too when the property's non-existent owners don't take care of the homes and they fall into disrepair, driving down property values.

- **Equity skimming:** The "straw buyer" is a classic real estate con. In this scheme, the ideal buyer is constructed using false credit reports and other income information in order to qualify for a home loan. Once it closes, the straw buyer immediately signs the property over to an investor with a quit claim deed, relinquishing all claim on the property. Then the investor just rents out the property, collecting a nice monthly check from unsuspecting renters, until the bank comes knocking and eventually forecloses.

In other scenarios, the buyer offers to take over the mortgage payments while the homeowner pays rent. But the buyer does no such thing, and the foreclosure happens anyway.

Swierczynski writes about one equity purchaser fraud that took advantage of a 79-year-old Bronx woman who had fallen behind on her payments and was facing foreclosure. A con artist appeared under the guise of a savior, promising that if she could pay him low monthly payments, he'd hold off the foreclosure for her and then refinance the house at a lower interest rate for her. She paid him about $24,000 over the course of a year, and he sent receipts that made it all look legit—until she got a letter from the bank telling her to vacate the property within thirty days. It turned out that the bank had never received any of that money.

HUD warns consumers of some signs of equity skimming:

- The prospective buyer doesn't look very closely at the property, just gives a quick, even dismissive glance and immediately makes an offer.

- The prospective buyer doesn't put up any money—just a piece of paper that basically serves as a glorified IOU.

- The buyer offers a very small sum of money as a down payment but promises there will be more "when the house is resold."

- **Commercial real estate loan scams:** This is an instance of a real, credible transaction that's been manipulated by con artists looking to work the system and make a quick buck. As the FBI explains, loan scams involving business properties may work in a few ways:

  - Owners of commercial properties that are distressed—or others working on their behalf—secure loans based on fraudulent values. This may be done by exaggerating the company's profits, thereby inflating the property value, which tricks lenders into offering overinflated loans to borrowers who ultimately default.

- Scammers posing as commercial loan brokers hawk products that call for advance fees. Actual, legitimate loan brokers only get paid when a deal closes, so like any advance-fee scheme, the request for money upfront should be a huge red flag here.

- Cash-advance lenders prey on struggling business owners by offering quick cash, with little to no paperwork and no credit check, but in exchange they feature unmanageable terms and exorbitant interest rates and fees. Make no mistake, a lender offering "cash in advance" will come out on top, every time, and you'll be left even broker than before.

- Credit-repair offers promising to help get your credit back on track in order to get you qualified for a business loan usually charge hefty upfront fees and pretty much give you nothing in return. And remember that no lender can "guarantee" approval for a business loan. Ever. If they aren't doing their due diligence on your financials, they aren't for real.

- **Air loans:** This is exactly what it sounds like—a loan secured based on nothing. There's no collateral, no business, no home, nothing. It's all fabricated, a made-up property with a made-up value and a wholly imaginary borrower. The borrower falsifies documents— they may even create new phone numbers and voicemails in order to receive calls from lenders or creditors. The loan comes, the borrower takes off with the money, and there's nothing to foreclose on. Like the property itself, the borrower is gone into thin air.

You would think that the level of checks and balances that exist in the mortgage industry would make this type of thing impossible, and for certain it's more difficult to pull off than ever before. But crafty con artists have been known to go to great lengths to pull this off, faking title records and ownership documents, falsifying account information, and employing phony references.

- **Discount scam**: This scam typically involves a home with a serious problem that an inspector likely would catch—mold? termites? flood damage? —and an unscrupulous owner willing to do anything to avoid paying for the repair. The seller, who typically opts not to work with a licensed realtor (red flag #1), offers to sell the home at a screamin' deal (red flag #2), usually at a 20 percent discount or more, if the buyer agrees to make the deal on site, without getting any of those pesky inspectors or money-hungry realtors involved. The seller may offer the excuse that he or she needs to move quickly or that it's a fixer-upper—in which case the seller may reveal that it needs certain minor repairs, which is an attempt to mask the major ones. Well, there's a reason not to involve any professionals in such a deal: A licensed realtor or broker would lose their license if they engaged in such practices. Never make an on-site, deeply discounted mortgage deal—at least, never without representation by a licensed real estate expert.

- **Title fraud**: How do you steal a house? You steal or manufacture an identity, put that person's name on the deed, and then use that title to claim ownership. This often happens in situations where homes aren't occupied, or where the owner has died. Consider the 2014 case of Jennifer Merin of New York, who inherited a home that was unlived in. But when she started receiving water bills, she probed the matter and discovered that a man named Darrell Beatty had forged a deed to the home and was living there as a squatter. It took Merin more than a year and $100,000 in legal fees to get Beatty out of the house she legally owned, plus her property suffered extensive damage and she lost numerous family heirlooms—meanwhile, the convicted thief was sentenced only to a year in prison.

  In some cases, a scammer steals the homeowner's identity, then uses the title to get a mortgage in the homeowner's name, then makes off with the loan money and leaves the actual owner on the hook. And in others, the person uses a forged deed to sell the property out from under the owners and run off with the cash.

Title insurance helps prevent this type of scam, and so does safeguarding your identity, as we've discussed. And if you own a property that doesn't currently have residents, watch for unpaid bills, make frequent visits to the property to check for signs of life, and consider a surprise foreclosure notice a tipoff, rather than a mistake. Many counties also provide a consumer notification service whereby you can register for free and be notified by email or text any time a document is recorded on your property.

- **False-listing scam:** Helene Nessenthaler of Saranac Lake, New York, was surprised one day to find a man climbing over her fence. When she stopped him, he said he wanted to buy her house—but it wasn't for sale. It turns out Nessenthaler had been the unwitting victim of a false-listing scam. The perpetrators of such a crime troll sites like Craigslist, Trulia, or Zillow looking for homes. They create false real estate listings that look just like the real thing and put the home up "for sale" or "for rent." If it's a sale, the scammer asks that interested buyers wire money for the purchase; if a rental, the scammer asks for first and last months' rent plus a security deposit. Then, money in hand, they disappear, leaving the "buyer" without a place to live and the actual owner struggling to cope with the fallout, which may include belligerent, angry victims insisting that they be let in. It often happens in cases of empty homes or homes that actually are for sale. In Nessenthaler's case, the assumption is that the scammer screwed up and got the house number mixed up with her neighbor's house, which really was for sale at the time.

Obviously, the vital link in the chain here is reliable communication with a verifiable seller or landlord. Wiring money to anyone, sight unseen, is just plain foolish.

Don't Get Taken on Vacation

Nationally renowned consumer expert Clark Howard made a name for himself by cleverly hunting down deals and sharing his knowledge with shoppers. His syndicated *Clark Howard Show* is full of great tips to help consumers be more savvy shoppers and make better decisions about their money.

So you'd think his name would have set off alarm bells when a scammer posing as the owner of a vacation rental home tried to pull the wool over his eyes. Howard and his wife were planning a trip to Hawaii, and true to form, they were hunting down great deals on homes where they could stay in Maui. While on VRBO.com (Vacation Rentals by Owner), he came across a great property that looked like it was being offered at a reasonable price. VRBO asks prospective renters to fill out an inquiry form, which is sent to the owners, who use that to determine the rate or discounts they'll offer. He submitted the form and heard back from the owner through an authentic-looking email from HomeAway (the parent site for VRBO). In it, the owner was offering a 25 percent discount. It was a good deal, but not suspiciously so, so he was ready to act on it... until he read the fine print about where to send his money. The instructions read that he was supposed to do a bank transfer to an account in Poland.

Being the consumer expert he is, Howard immediately recognized this as a scam and alerted the folks at VRBO as well as the actual owner of the property. The owner informed Howard that he was the fifth person to have contacted the owner about the scam, but Howard had been lucky— the other four had lost money in the deal.

It turns out that taking money from vacationers is quite a business. Travel, vacation, and timeshare scams are frequently ranked on the FTC's list of the ten biggest frauds.

How the hoaxes are perpetrated varies. They may peruse real rental listings, pull the owner's contact information off the listing, replace it with their own, then place the ad on a different site and wait until the offers come rolling in. In other cases, like the one Howard stumbled into, the scammer hijacks a property owner's email through a reputable website such as VRBO, HomeAway, or others, then takes over communication with prospective vacationers.

And in some cases, there's not even a rental at all—the scammer just makes up a place that either doesn't exist or isn't even for rent at all. Then they offer too-good-to-beat rental prices or promise fantastic amenities (*"Oh, you want a pool and a gym? Yeah, we definitely have those here."*) It only needs to be believable enough to get you to pay the deposit before you find out the truth. And the average person loses about $1,700 on a deal like this, according to the FTC.

In other cases, it's the owner, not the traveler, who's being scammed. VRBO warns owners against inquiries in which the prospective renter can't, for some reason, pay by credit card and insists upon paying by cashier's check or wire transfer, which can be falsified. In some cases, they may engage in an overpayment scam, in which they send more than the requested amount to the owner, then request a refund. As I've discussed previously in other chapters of this book, overpayment is a classic scam intended to get the victim to refund money that they never had in the first place.

In other cases involving travel destinations, the loss is more significant. While on vacation, we've all been presented with the "opportunity" to attend a free "orientation" breakfast, during which timeshare developers pitch us on what a great investment opportunity a timeshare at this fantastic destination would be. They may even offer you the chance to spend a free weekend in one as an incentive. But an owner may wind up thousands in the hole for a property he or she only gets to use one week out of the year. AARP reports that today there are more than 1,500 timeshare developers in the U.S., and more than 9.2 million timeshare owners.

Sure, many find it a great alternative to buying a second home, but many have questioned the industry's somewhat unscrupulous sales tactics as well as the benefits of a very-temporary home that owners must pay maintenance fees for and can't easily unload when they want to. The difficulty of selling a timeshare gave birth to a new kind of scam a little over a decade ago—the fraudulent timeshare sales broker.

It works like this: The scammer poses as a representative of a company that helps owners sell their timeshare properties. He or she will say, "I've got a buyer already lined up, you just need to pay these upfront fees to cover the processing costs." The forms seem legit, you sign on the dotted line, you pay the "broker's fee" for the sale, and poof! He's gone with your money and you're still stuck with that timeshare.

But even this loss doesn't measure up to the $310,000 that Frank and Rebecca Balluff lost in a second-home real estate scam. And they aren't alone—others lost their entire life savings after falling for the ads on Bloomberg News, Fox News, and infomercials offering the opportunity to get in on the ground floor of Sanctuary Belize, Sanctuary Bay, and the Reserve, a proposed 14,000-total-acre project on the Caribbean coast of Belize. Buyers who chose to invest in this real estate opportunity would enjoy such fabulous amenities as fine restaurants, a luxury hotel, a marina, retail stores, an American hospital, a championship golf course, a casino, and an airstrip.

Plus, if buyers chose to sell their parcels of land, they were guaranteed speedy and impressive profits. The developers pushed a "no-debt" approach—rather than relying on lender funds, they would take sales revenues and put them immediately into finishing the project, which was projected to happen within two to five years. Capitalizing on wealthy consumers' desire to live in luxury and the prospect of retirement on an exotic beach, the developers raked in over $100 million selling the one-thousand-plus parcels of land in what buyers thought was a shrewd real estate deal.

But the funny thing was, nothing ever was developed there. The Balluffs, eager to escape Michigan winters, kept checking on progress, and six years in have still seen none, according to *The Washington Post,* in a November 2018 article. When questioned, the developers refused to offer refunds and simply resold the lots to other buyers. An FTC investigation revealed that the man behind the scheme, Andris Pukke, is a known felon who had been sued by the FTC for fraud in a debt-counseling scheme—he had even conducted some of this scam from prison. The lesson? Buying into a resort development, whether it's overseas or on a Florida beach, is a risky investment to begin with. It's worth your time, money, and effort to carefully research anyone pushing such an investment.

Before you get taken for a ride on any vacation or second-home scam, remember the following:

- As many times as it's come up in this book, it bears repeating: Wiring money as payment isn't a good idea. Neither are prepaid or gift cards. None of these options allow you to retrieve your money when it's gone. If they won't take a credit card, skip it.

- If the owner or developer wants you to act now, skip it. Don't invest your well-earned vacation or retirement dollars in something that has to happen fast. Remember that fast decisions rarely make for good ones.

- If it's too good to be true, it almost certainly is. Beware the amazing deal, the below-market rent for a premium property. Research prices in the area and confirm the deal is legit.

- Don't pay anything without a contract. I shouldn't have to say this, but I will: Confirm that the property address listed on the contract actually exists. Call the owner to confirm. If there's a resort office, call it and confirm the contract details.

For Rent... Not

According to data reported by *Forbes*, U.S. renters recently lost an annual $5.2 million to rental scams. And an Apartment List study reveals that 43.1 percent of American renters—nearly half—have encountered or fallen victim to rental scams. Though its victims range in age and characteristics, the Apartment List study found that victims are 42 percent more likely to be between the ages of 18 and 29—a population that tends to be inexperienced, in need of affordable short-term rentals, and with less household income to start with. This is a demographic that might need to rely on renting a place sight unseen, especially in the case of students from out of state or starting internships in strange cities. The below-market rental listing is likely to appeal to this group. Plus, as we've discussed, though Millennials are tech savvy, they tend to be surprisingly trusting when it comes to scams, and they're not likely to perform much due diligence in securing a rental.

Apartment List says the following are the standard rental scams that it found in its study:

- **Bait and Switch:** Sure, there's a property for rent, but it's not the impressive one advertised. The scammer collects a deposit and a signature on a lease, but once the renter signs, he or she is stuck with whatever overpriced hovel the landlord actually provides the keys to. But even that is preferable to the alternative—at least there's a place to live, unlike...

- **Phantom Rentals:** Like the vacation rental scam, this one banks on a poor schmuck who needs a place to live. The scammer creates a fake listing for a place that doesn't exist, isn't actually a rental, or that he/she doesn't own. The relatively low rent lures renters, who wind up with nothing to show for their money.

- **Hijacked Ads:** Like in the case of Nessenthaler, a scammer gets hold of a listing for an actual property for sale or rent, tinkers with the ad, then reposts it on another site with his or her own contact information.

- **Missing Amenities:** The Apartment List study found that laundry, heat, and air conditioning are the amenities most lied about in rental listings. Others include outdoor spaces (such as balconies), dishwashers, gyms, and pools. In a missing-amenity scam, the landlord dolls up the listing online by claiming it has amenities like these and others, which it doesn't have, in order to justify a higher rent. Similar to a bait and switch, the renter doesn't discover what's lacking until he or she has already signed the lease and paid the deposit. (*"A gym? No, no, I said Jim. My name is Jim. Sorry about that. Here's your key."*)

- **Already Leased:** It's already leased, but a scammer or a crooked landlord doesn't care—he'll keep right on advertising the property, collecting application and security and deposit fees all day.

In a variation on this theme, some scammers "rent out" properties that are temporarily sitting empty—a crime that involves two victims, the homeowner and the innocent person who just needs a place to rent. The scammer scours neighborhoods looking for homes with no occupants, such as those that operate as second homes or those sitting empty between renters. They may even go so far as to change the locks or steal spare keys the owners may have "hidden" nearby. Once they're in, they might just stay there.

Sixty-nine-year-old Beverly McKinney of Central Indiana was on a fixed income. She went on Facebook to find a rental for herself and her two great-granddaughters. Using a page intended to connect homes with renters, she found a great three-bedroom home in Anderson, Indiana. She reached out to the landlord, who asked her to fill out a contract and send the $500 deposit via MoneyGram. Once that was sent, the woman told McKinney, she'd send the keys. But no keys ever came, because the property's actual owner, Steve Wagner, had already rented the property and had no idea who McKinney was or what had happened to her $500.

According to The Indy Channel, her local ABC affiliate, McKinney reported the incident to the police, whose investigation uncovered that the Facebook page—containing numerous grammatical errors, frequent pushes for more money, and a suspicious friend total of one—had been taken down, and the MoneyGram had been picked up by a man at an area Walmart. Chances are slim that she'll see that money again.

"I just don't want anybody else to get burned," McKinney said to the TV reporter who interviewed her for the story. "It's terrible... I lost $500 and my dignity."

The problem with rentals is that they can be tough to find, especially in a hot market, and often involve your need to move quickly. So before you jump head first into a sweetheart rental deal, take a few precautions:

- Say it with me now: *If it's too good to be true...* Trust your gut. You probably aren't just getting really lucky with that low rent, world-class amenities, perfect location, and no-screening process. If your gut says something is off, listen.

- Check for that listing on other sites to see if it's corroborated elsewhere. Sometimes scammers hack a listing on one site and repost their own versions on other sites. Confirm that the contact information is the same in every instance. Sometimes they're even found in multiple cities and at widely varying prices.

- Don't make decisions on the fly. Your landlord should be methodical about doing a lot of checking on you, and you should exercise the same discretion. Anyone who eagerly promises to get you in quickly and skip the background check isn't operating honestly.

- Never rent anything sight unseen. Never send money or share personal information unless you've met the person and visited the property. It's also a good idea to take someone with you. Avoid anyone from out of state or overseas, as that's usually a way to justify asking you to wire money to a foreign account.

- Watch for listings without photos or addresses, and double check addresses on Google Earth, or just drive by, to be sure it matches the listing in quality and appearance.

- Avoid deposits that seem out of proportion or higher than normal, and never use cash, MoneyGrams, or wire transfers. That's just asking for trouble. Use credit cards or checks only.

- Some websites are more reputable than others when it comes to finding quality listings. Craigslist is often problematic and filled with false ads and bait-and-switch tactics. Stick with higher quality sites such as Apartments.com or StreetEasy.com.

- Use a professional. This means finding an agent to help you locate a quality rental, or working with a reputable property management company.

In a Fix

Buying, selling, and renting property isn't the only way to turn a home into a scam opportunity. Home repair, improvement, and product scams are very prevalent. All it takes is a person with a truck or van who looks handy to pull one over on unsuspecting homeowners. Seniors, who often rely on younger professionals to do home repairs and improvement, are the most common victims of this scam.

It's perpetrated in a few different ways. The scammer may knock on your door and say, "I just happened to be driving past on my way to a job at your neighbor's house, and I noticed your roof needs a bit of repair. I'd be happy to do that for you. In fact, I'm doing the same work at your neighbor's house, so all the equipment is already in my truck. I'd be happy to offer you a deal if I can do it today."

Or maybe he stops by to say he's offering a deal on that repair today, at a price so low you'll want to jump at it. If you hesitate, he'll go even lower.

Maybe he's offering to do free mold testing. Mold is a scary business, so it sure would be nice to know you were clear of it. But of course he'll find some, then take your money, do some sort of unofficial busywork on the "job site," or maybe even take your money, leave to go get "equipment," and never return. And by the way, you probably don't have mold.

In some areas where natural disasters have created multiple victims who are having trouble getting help from insurance companies or are tired of waiting in line for the "real contractors" to get back to them, distraught victims receive unannounced visits from people posing as contractors, offering to do the work for cheap out of the goodness of their hearts. They'll take your insurance money, do a crappy job, then disappear.

Some shady contractors will insist on large deposits before beginning work, but then never actually show up to do the work, or never finish what they started. They may offer low-ball bids, a red flag that they either don't fully understand the project in front of them, or they'll make up for it by charging high, unexpected costs at the back end.

Then there's the "electrical breaker swap," in which property flippers try to skirt modern building code requirements for arc fault breakers—

which cost about $800 each—by sneaking in and removing them, then replacing them with cheaper traditional breakers in order to add to their profits.

It's hard to believe, in this day and age of electronic communication and internet scams, but home repair scams still heavily rely on door-to-door contact. So beware anyone knocking at your door trying to sell you something—especially home repair products or services.

If you're genuinely interested, do yourself a favor. Fire up the BS Detector and don't make decisions in a hurry. Perform your due diligence before plunking down any money:

- Research any contractor, including license, Better Business Bureau reviews, references, and portfolio of work. Be sure the contractor is licensed, bonded, and insured.

- Get bids in writing and compare costs and services.

- Know your state's laws regarding allowable deposit amounts. For example, California law states that contractors can't ask for more than 10 percent down or $1,000, whichever is lowest. A high upfront fee could be a tipoff that something isn't quite right.

- Be sure you get a contract detailing exactly what work will take place and with what supplies, a schedule for performing it, start and completion dates, a payment schedule, a contractor signature, and full contact information.

- Get written copies of warranties and guarantees, and keep all records related to the project.

- Be wary of any contractor who finds unexpected problems—like a load-bearing wall. A good contractor does due diligence, just like you should. But surprising discoveries are usually a way to tack on unexpected fees that couldn't be included in the estimate.

- Never make a final payment until you're satisfied that the work was performed as promised and that all vendors and subcontractors have been paid.

When all else fails, check the peephole: If you don't know who's at the door, don't answer it.

What a Disaster!

Talk about kicking people when they're down... some scammers prey on folks who have already endured devastating circumstances—wildfires, floods, tornadoes, earthquakes, hurricanes. These are the folks least able to afford quality, reputable professionals, and who are least able to make reasonable, critical decisions. And while these circumstances often galvanize communities and demonstrate the very best of humanity, they also, unfortunately, can bring out the worst as well.

Here are the most common ways that scammers take advantage of disaster victims:

- **The door-to-door solicitation:** They're ready right away to offer their know-how and services. But as I said above, you should never make a split-second decision to pay someone to work in your home. Contractors don't typically just drive around looking to offer homeowners deals. Are their good Samaritans who sometimes are willing to do this? Sure? But if they're legitimately able to help, they'll still be willing to do it after you've done your homework.

- **The public adjuster:** The person at your door will work with your insurer to get you the full amount possible—for a fee, of course, or a percentage of your claim. Double check that anyone claiming to be an adjuster is licensed and can be verified by the Department of Insurance.

- **Contractor collusion:** An adjuster refers the homeowner to a specific contractor—usually someone he or she is working with in a joint scam. Like I said above, do your homework on any contractor, regardless whether the adjuster recommends him or not.

- **The disaster official:** You may face someone at your door claiming to be a disaster official who demands money in order for you to obtain relief funding. Does that make sense to you? Yeah, me neither.

- **Water and clean-up:** Some scammers pose as debris-cleaning professionals or water-quality experts. They may try to sell you useless water-purifying products or promise to remove debris that they just push around onto neighbors' yards or nearby parking lots—for which you may even be fined. Your water utility company should be able to provide information about water quality and offer solutions, if any are needed, and you should be sure that you know where all debris is disposed of, and pay only when the job is done.

- **Price gouging:** It's illegal to jack up rates more than 10 percent on essential services in the event of a natural disaster, unless they can show that supply costs went up by that amount. Don't let anyone tell you that the demand means you should pay any more than that.

- **FEMA endorsement:** Gosh, it sounds great that FEMA has endorsed that contractor—except it isn't true. FEMA doesn't certify contractors.

- **The lockdown excuse:** Fraudulent vendors will request an ACH (Automated Clearing House) payment, also known as direct payment, instead of a check. During the Covid-19 pandemic, they used the excuse that they couldn't get to their bank to request such payments. Of course, the vendor disappears (pandemic or not).

- **Donation scam:** Even if you aren't a disaster victim, scammers will find a way to prey upon your generous nature by convincing you to donate to the survivors. Only donate to charities you know, through reliable channels. Beware of copycat organizations that *sound* familiar but aren't. They chose those names to lend an air of authenticity to their pitch. You can check whether a charity is reputable with the Better Business Bureau or the National Association of State Charity Officials.

Where's My Stuff?

If you've finally managed to complete a genuine real estate transaction and are ready to move, you aren't out of the woods. Moving scams are popular because they work, and about 40 million people move each year, according to the U.S. Department of Transportation. A crooked mover with all your belongings on his truck is in a convenient situation to hold those belongings hostage. Even if you've paid what was quoted, it's hard to know what's happened on the truck or what difficulty the movers had to endure that were unexpected and costly, and many such scammers know that people will pay an exorbitant amount of money to get their stuff back, because what choice do they have?

Beware the over-the-phone estimate—estimates should be based not only on mileage but on weight, so the mover should see your belongings. And when the mover arrives, he or she should ask lots of questions, look inside cabinets and inside closets, being careful to be accurate. If all you get is a cursory glance, that's a sign of trouble. Be cautious of any mover who wants money up front. You shouldn't pay anything until the items have been safely delivered to your new residence. And like you would with any contractor, check references and reviews. Many movers change names to avoid getting busted for misdeeds, so look at reputation and longevity.

Car Cons

Before I conclude this chapter on real estate scams, it's important to touch on scams affecting another pricy purchase: Your car. Though cars cost less than homes (at least in California), obviously, they're still a high-dollar item whose purchase can invite greedy tricksters to behave in less-than-honorable ways. The FBI's IC3 has received nearly 27,000 complaints with losses exceeding $54 million since it recently started tracking this issue.

Typically, the way this works is that the scammer lists a car for sale, but he or she needs to unload it quickly, for some reason—maybe he's being deployed overseas by the military, maybe she's moving, or maybe a dead relative left the car to him. This explains the deeply discounted price. Then the seller will ask for payment in the form of a wire transfer or maybe even a prepaid gift card. When you learn the car was stolen, they are long gone.

Other car-related scams have gained traction as well. In July 2018, the Better Business Bureau released an alert warning consumers of the VIN report scam. In this hoax, the scammer trolls car listings and contacts sellers, then asks to see the VIN report. Typically, this is evidence that a buyer is performing due diligence, which is why it works. But the "buyer" in this instance convinces the seller to buy the report by going to a website created by the scammer. It may be just a way to steal $20 from the seller, but even more frightening is that the site may have been designed to capture credit card or other personal information used to steal your identity. Remember that the National Motor Vehicle Title Information System, a division of the Department of Justice, exists to help consumers by tracking information from insurance carriers, junkyards, and salvage yards. You can access odometer readings, sales and damage history, and title information using this free website.

Other vehicle scams include:

- **Title washing:** The scammer offers to clear the title of "salvage" status or clear any worrisome events from its history, such as floods or serious accidents. It's not legal, so don't fall for it.

- **Odometer fraud:** It's not easy to do, but it happens. Scammers find ways to tinker with a car's odometer in order to make the mileage appear lower in order to sell it at a higher price.

- **Escrow scams:** The seller asks the buyer to put the purchase money into a holding, or escrow, account. Once the money's there, the scammer, the car, and the money vanish.

- **Security deposits:** If a private seller asks for upfront money to take the car off the market, run away. That seller will only take your money and disappear.

- **VIN cloning:** The thief steals another vehicle's identification number and slaps it on the car offered for sale. This allows him to hide the fact that the car was likely stolen.

As with most large transactions, all business should be conducted face to face. Prospective buyers of vehicles should carefully examine reports and ensure that VINs match registration information, that sellers' addresses are fixed (not a P.O. box, for example), and that the seller's driver's license matches the car title. Ask for vehicle maintenance records to ensure they're consistent with mileage and reports. And, as always, know that if it seems too good to be true, it probably is.

"Scammers and hackers want to target you when you're either scared out of your mind or extremely happy," says Ryan O'Leary, vice president of the Threat Research Center at WhiteHat Security, to CNBC. "Real estate is the perfect one-two combo, and there's a lot of money at stake."

Chapter Ten

Top o' the Pyramid

Protect yourself from investment schemes
and business manipulation

CASE #8: *The Guy Who Madoff with All Their Money*

The American Dream is that you work hard, you pay your dues, and in the end, for all you've endured, you will have earned that pot of gold at the end of the rainbow. It is ironic that many scamsters have used the same motivation in justifying to themselves that it's okay to take innocent people's money. It's almost as if they feel they are owed. Entitlement can be a sickness.

Perhaps that's what led Bernard Madoff to become the most notorious fraudster of the century, and certainly the most successful promoter of a Ponzi scheme in history. Madoff was the son of Ralph, who had been born to Polish immigrants, and Sylvia, a housewife and the daughter of immigrants from Romania and Austria. The two had married at the height of the Great Depression, which, upon reflection, may have been what drove them to get involved later on in finance, and even perhaps to influence their son to do the same. A parsimonious life is perhaps at the root of Madoff's mad drive to sit at the top of the heap and experience a level of wealth few could ever even comprehend.

In fact, Sylvia Madoff had become a registered broker-dealer in the 1960s for a company registered by the name of Gibraltar Securities, which the U.S. Securities and Exchange Commission (SEC) eventually shut down for its failure to disclose its true financial condition. The family's home was revealed to have had a tax lien for more than $13,000, which went unpaid between 1956 and 1965.

Bernard, or Bernie as most called him, married his high school sweetheart, Ruth Alpern. He attended the University of Alabama and, eventually, Hofstra University in Long Island, to complete his bachelor's degree in political science. A brief stint at Brooklyn Law School ended when Bernie decided he'd rather save up to start his own business. By lifeguarding and installing sprinkler systems on the side, he saved up $5,000—enough to start an investment firm called Bernard L. Madoff Investment Securities in 1960, where he got his start as a trader in penny stocks, or stocks for $5 per share or less that are traded outside the major stock exchanges.

At first, his clients were friends of his father-in-law, Saul Alpern, who referred his wealthy circle of friends and their families from within the Jewish community to Madoff. Unlike firms that were members of the New York Stock Exchange, Madoff Securities captured the growing zest for technology that Madoff himself could sense would overtake Wall Street. His firm developed and began using an innovative computer technology that enabled them to disseminate computerized quotes to investors by phone—the precursor of what eventually became the National Association of Securities Dealers Automated Quotations, or the NASDAQ, which was founded in early 1971 and has since gone on to become the second-largest stock exchange in the world. Madoff Securities, not surprisingly, was at one point the largest buyer and seller on the NASDAQ, of which Madoff himself was a three-term chairman.

The firm grew in unprecedented fashion, and the Madoff family's involvement grew as well, with Bernie's brother Peter coming on board as senior managing director and chief compliance officer; Peter's daughter, Shana, joining as compliance attorney; and Bernie's sons, Mark and Andrew, working in the trading department of the company.

The firm operated two separate entities—a trading division and an investment advisory operation. This had some scratching their heads in concern about the possibility of "front running," in which a brokerage firm engages in investment activities based on advance, non-public knowledge about the investment. Concerns were frequently squashed because of the logistics: They were not only physically separated, on different floors of New York's Lipstick Building on the corner of 53rd and Third, but each employed its own staff and utilized a completely separate and distinct computer system, to ensure compliance with laws forbidding front running.

From the beginning, Madoff had established a reputation for his good instincts as a trader, dealing not exclusively in big, well-known stocks but in small, unlisted stocks. He operated like a wholesaler, dealing only with big, established stock trading firms that wanted to trade their customers' money quietly, rather than with the average, off-the-street, individual retail investor. His clients' portfolios showed a diversified set of investments, ranging from Walmart and General Electric down to the smaller upstarts, about which he was knowledgeable.

And his clients were an exclusive bunch—friends of friends, primarily from Jewish enclaves such as Long Island or Palm Beach, Florida, and celebrities including director Steven Spielberg and actors such as John Malkovich, Kevin Bacon, Kyra Sedgwick, and Zsa Zsa Gabor. You couldn't even approach Madoff, it was said, unless you were prepared to invest $10 million. Madoff had an aura, a mystique, and clients (led, not surprisingly, by their egos) were convinced they had been specially chosen, allowed to become members of an exclusive club. His business became so profitable that a London office, Madoff Securities International, opened and employed a staff of twenty-eight.

Clients trusted him. Known for his quiet politeness, his tendency to listen rather than talk, his abundant warmth, and his desire to take care of those he loved, his company was craved by people, who were excited just to brush shoulders with this man with a Midas touch. He has been described as shy, it was well known that he never drank, and people spoke often of how he always wore a smile. He made benevolent gestures to those in his inner circle and was known for his philanthropic efforts. A 2009 *Vanity Fair* article describes how he once arranged for a helicopter to transfer an ill friend to a hospital. He had created a multimillion-dollar private foundation that would give money to hospitals and theaters, and he sat on the board of Yeshiva University.

Clearly he was a successful investor, but, in a method reminiscent of Charles Ponzi, Madoff couldn't seem to explain accurately how it was that he could guarantee his exclusive clientele steady returns of 10 to 12 percent. He never had a down month—*ever*, no matter the economy's ups and downs. Fate is never so kind.

His strategy? A split-strike conversion, sometimes called a collar. Boiled down to its simplest form, this involves buying and selling different sorts of options, or the right to buy or sell assets at certain agreed-upon prices, during specified periods of time or on predetermined dates, for a "strike price." This method helps clients to minimize volatility and risk, as Madoff explained. In 1992, he told *The Wall Street Journal* that in the 1970s he had put funds that had been invested with him into "convertible arbitrage positions in large-cap stocks, with promised investment returns of 18 to 20 percent."

It was terminology no one understood. As Warren Buffet has always counseled, if it doesn't make sense, ask for an explanation. But with Bernie Madoff, no one did. Instead, they blindly trusted the chair of NASDAQ, a successful, philanthropic investor with a highly successful career of more than three decades.

In the same *WSJ* interview, Madoff explained that he didn't think what he was generating for clients was that big a deal. Standard & Poors 500-stock index, he said, generated average yearly returns of about 16 percent at that time. "I would be surprised if anybody thought that matching the S&P over 10 years was anything outstanding," he said.

Many concluded that his use of options helped cushion clients against the occasional blows of the market.

And he was true to his word. With a client list of roughly 4,800 investors, he was unusually consistent and successful in his returns—so much so that some clients were worried about pulling their money out, for fear he'd never let them back in.

It was in the early '90s that Madoff's business strategy started raising eyebrows. One of its feeder funds, Avellino & Bienes, was investigated by the SEC in 1992 under suspicion that they were selling unregistered securities, and the firm indicated to the SEC that its fund with Madoff had seen "curiously steady" yearly returns of 13.5 to 20 percent. Avellino & Bienes had deposited $454 million from its investors with Madoff.

Financial analyst and portfolio manager Harry Markopolis approached the SEC about his suspicions that Madoff was operating a Ponzi scheme, even eventually releasing his own seventeen-page report claiming, "Bernie Madoff is running the world's largest unregistered hedge fund. He's organized this business as a 'hedge fund of funds' privately labeling their own hedge funds which Bernie Madoff secretly runs for them using a split-strike conversion strategy getting paid only trading commissions which are not disclosed. If this is not a regulatory dodge, I do not know what is." Markopolis said this was "unsophisticated portfolio management" at best, front running, or, most likely, a Ponzi scheme.

Under pressure, Avellino & Bienes agreed to return the money to investors, shut down their firm, and undergo an audit, but the comments regarding Madoff were never pursued by the SEC. Michael Bienes himself even continued to invest several million with Madoff until 2007.

In fact, numerous people stepped forward over the years to raise questions about Madoff's strategy—the numbers no one could make add up, the offshore accounts, the inability of anybody to comprehend his investment strategy. Markopolos' allegation that this was a Ponzi scheme even led the SEC to investigate Madoff in 2006-2007, but the investigation turned up nothing untoward. But in 2007, the Financial Industry Regulatory Authority (FINRA), the trading industry's watchdog, released a statement, without any explanation, that parts of Madoff's business actually had no customers. Yet the SEC staff responded, "At this point in time we are uncertain of the basis for FINRA's conclusion in this regard."

And even as the market began its collapse in 2007, Madoff never suffered a bad month. In November 2008, he was, strangely, up while the S&P fell 7.5 percent.

But warning signs continued piling up, and the mystery surrounding Madoff's inner workings mounted, provoking curiosity from certain officials and the media. Its stock holdings were liquidated each quarter, which was believed to help him avoid reporting certain numbers. Clients and even fund managers were denied online account access.

And the investment end of his business was what *The Economist* in 2009 called "a black box, run by a tiny team at a very long arm's length from the group's much bigger broker-dealer." The article goes on to describe the air of mystique surrounding Madoff:

> Clients too were kept in the dark. They seemed not to mind as long as the returns remained strong, accepting that to ask Bernie to reveal his strategy would be as crass as demanding to see Coca-Cola's magic formula. Mr. Madoff reinforced the message by occasionally ejecting a client who asked awkward questions.

Madoff's fall from grace began in early December 2008. He had already been hitting up pals for money, claiming to be starting up a new investment vehicle. The firm that in its heyday had well over $5 billion in its accounts was down to $234 million. Banks weren't lending in this failing economy. The well had dried up. And on December 9, Madoff told his son Mark that he wanted to pay employee bonuses totaling $173 million early that year—in December instead of February. Mark, known for his conservative, nervous demeanor, expressed his concerns about his father's request to his brother, Andrew, and the two confronted Madoff about it on December 10.

He was finished, he told his sons. He had absolutely nothing. "It's all just one big lie," he told them. "Basically a giant Ponzi scheme" at the astronomical scale of $50 billion. He had some money to distribute to employees and friends, then planned to turn himself in to authorities.

That evening, Madoff hosted his annual employee holiday party, where he announced to his New York office that they were "going to have a great year!" remembered employee Julia Fenwick.

But the legal machinery was in motion, with the FBI's financial crime team already mobilized. Early on the morning of Dec. 11, 2018, Madoff confessed his crime to the investigators who arrived at his door, and he was arrested.

Everyone, even his family and closest friends, were stunned and claimed to have had no idea of the epic proportions of this fraud. "When everybody thinks your dad's a god, why shouldn't his own sons think that?" Mark Madoff had once said to a friend.

One unnamed investor told *The New York Times*, "The returns were just amazing and we trusted this guy for decades—if you wanted to take money out, you always got your check in a few days. That's why we were all so stunned."

"Doubt Bernie Madoff?" Bienes told a reporter in a 2009 interview. "Doubt Bernie? No. You doubt God. You can doubt God, but you don't doubt Bernie. He had that aura about him."

Yet as the extent of the scheme continued to reveal itself, it became clear that, despite Madoff's insistence that he had worked alone, you can't pull off a scheme of this size without help. He had gotten this from a number of sources, including his bank of choice, J.P. Morgan Chase, where he had routinely deposited clients' money rather than investing it. In fact, the investigation has revealed that all investment had effectively stopped back in the early '90s, if not earlier. In a classic rob-Peter-to-pay-Paul scheme that lasted nearly two decades, Madoff had simply plopped his clients' money into the account, then withdrawn it to pay off investors when they came calling. Investigations led to the 2014 charge of two felony counts against the bank for failing to maintain adequate controls, though the feds agreed to drop charges if the bank adopted a proper compliance system and paid $2.6 billion in fines and penalties.

Others were eventually implicated, including Frank DiPascali, Madoff's right-hand man, the chief financial officer for Madoff Securities. DiPascali caved under pressure from federal prosecutors and pled guilty in 2009 to ten felony counts.

In 2013, DiPascali spent two weeks on the stand during Madoff's trial revealing the dirty details of the cover-up the two had engaged in— including the one time when the two had cranked out a stack of falsified records in a back room while SEC investigators were in the building, then stashed them in the refrigerator so the printer heat couldn't be felt on the papers. As CNBC reported in a ten-year anniversary report about the Madoff case, the two men had even tossed the stack of papers around the office in a game of catch to make them look old and worn before handing them over to the investigators on site.

DiPascali's testimony incriminated backroom staff members in the investment advisory arm of the business who also were in on the scheme— the Madoff Five, as they became known: Daniel Bonventre, director of operations; Annette Bongiorno, Madoff's personal secretary since she'd graduated high school who had gone on to become a portfolio manager; Joann Crupi, investment advisor; and George Perez and Jerome O'Hara, the two men who had developed the computer program that was used at the firm to falsify trades.

The tsunami of financial destruction left behind in Madoff's wake continues today, years after his confession. Madoff's assets, once shared with his wife, Ruth, were liquidated and the process of restitution to his wronged clients is still underway. On Dec. 11, 2018, ten years to the day of Madoff's arrest, Irving Picard, a trustee involved in sorting out the mess that once was Madoff's investment advisory firm, made a statement that he had requested the authorization by a bankruptcy court judge of $419 million in distributions on approved claims to 880 accounts.

It's all in a history-making, monumental effort to return all the cash initially invested, which totaled roughly $19 billion. At the time of this writing, the total paid out comes to more than $12 billion. It's nowhere near the $45 billion in fake profits Madoff had claimed to have made on falsified statements, but it's a start.

"Very rarely do you see a case of this magnitude where the victims receive a return like this," said attorney Jerry Reisman, who represented more than 30 victims who lost a total of about $50 million, in an interview with Bloomberg news reporter Erik Larson.

But even now, years later, people are still grappling with the larger questions, like, when did it become a fraud? What was it like for him to manage this colossal charade on a daily basis? How is it that he got away with it for two decades? And could this happen again?

Diana Henriques, business and financial reporter for *The New York Times*, got the exclusive interview with Madoff following his arrest. She eventually went on to author the book about the Madoff affair entitled *The Wizard of Lies: Bernie Madoff and the Death of Trust*. In an interview with PBS's *Frontline* about Madoff, she said:

> One of the most mystifying things about the Madoff mystery, really, is the fact that so many people that you would look to as potential tripwires, alarm bells—people who should have noticed, might have noticed, who could have reported it—invested in it. Now, was that because they thought Bernie had some gimmick that they would detect, profit from and get out in time, or was it because they actually believed it?

The Psychology of Investment Scams

A couple of years ago, I noticed I'd stopped receiving bills from Waste Management. We pay the bills for garbage and recycling pickup on a quarterly basis, so I was used to not seeing many of those. But I realized as I was sitting down to do our household budget that we had been due to pay that Waste Management bill two months prior, and the amount we had been budgeting each month for that bill had not yet been spent. I went through our records and found that indeed we hadn't received a bill for that service in about five months.

Knowing that my not receiving a bill wouldn't hold water as an excuse for not paying the bill, I called the billing number on my last statement and was told our account was current.

"But I haven't mailed a payment," I said, confused. "How can that be?"

But the nice woman insisted that a check totaling the normal amount I usually paid had posted just the previous month to our account. "If I were you, I'd just take it and move on," the representative told me.

And of course it's tempting to do just as she said. So many of us might think, "I'm a law-abiding citizen, always pay my bills on time, act responsibly. Finally, this is the universe's way of rewarding me for that."

But in my line of work, I know things don't work that way. The universe isn't obligated to balance the scales. As Mark Twain said, "The earth was here first. It doesn't owe you anything." I've seen all too often that when something is too good to be true like this, the bubble always bursts. Someone always ends up paying, and it's always more painful down the road. Someone was mistakenly paying our Waste Management bill, and when they discovered the error and wanted their money back, we'd be on the hook for all the back payments.

So I began sending unsolicited payments to Waste Management—that day and for the next two billing cycles, despite the fact that no bill came. And six months later, a bill for the standard amount arrived in our mailbox. The jig was up, but thankfully, we had not been penalized for it.

But we've all had moments like this, where an unexpected windfall—no matter how small—landed in our laps and we wrestled with the choice between taking the money (We deserve it, right?) and refusing it, in response to that nagging little voice in our heads saying, "Don't do it. It's not a good idea."

In this book, I've described a constellation of scams that all have taken advantage of this simple concept, and the reason they've worked—millions of times—is that we usually ignore that little voice and give in to the temptation. Like those people who see no harm in casually putting groceries in a bag without scanning them at the self-checkout lane—because, after all, the store is really making you work to shop there, so the least you should get is a little bit of free groceries—there is a pervasive sense of entitlement. Perhaps it's that American Dream we're all expecting, the idea that just by living here, we are owed something. Perhaps that's why the Ponzis and the Kurniawans and the Madoffs of this world have become as successful as they have.

In his book, *Influence: Science and Practice*, psychology professor Robert Cialdini closely examined the psychology of persuasion and compliance—what makes a person say "yes" to another person's request, whether the request is for something legitimate or a scam. While we'd like to think that most people consider all the available information to guide their decision-making, the fact is that we don't.

What it really boils down to is six principles, or shortcuts, that lead us to make decisions, according to Cialdini:

1. Reciprocity

2. Scarcity

3. Authority

4. Consistency

5. Liking

6. Consensus

Perhaps no one took greater advantage of these shortcuts to scam people better than Bernie Madoff. That he would deign to take their money and invest it was viewed by his clients as a great favor they had been granted, a gift. Because they received such high (manufactured) returns meant that they felt obligated to reciprocate by investing more and more of their money. It was the least they felt they could do, and they wouldn't dare insult him by asking how he would use it and risk being thrown out of his office.

In Cialdini's research, when servers dropped a simple gift—a lowly mint—with the checks at diners' tables, tips increased by 3 percent. Two mints correlated to a 14 percent increase.

Madoff's clients were also convinced to keep investing because he only offered the opportunity to a small, exclusive set of clients, and the opportunity might be withdrawn should they hold off—capitalizing on the principle of scarcity, in which people want more of things they can only have less of.

In scams throughout this book, we've seen the principle of authority abused by scam artists. Con artists who knock on doors wearing uniforms and driving trucks filled with supplies and emblazoned with logos get away with millions in home repair scams. Using technological terminology, fraudsters convince victims by phone that they can do online repairs, all the while hacking their personal information.

Ponzi and Madoff in particular used imprecise, highly technical-sounding jargon to convince others of their knowledge, and their understanding of the markets and the results they achieved served as evidence. After all, how could Madoff, a man who had built a steady, three-decades-long reputation of success and chaired the NASDAQ for three terms, be anything but a knowledgeable, credible expert?

The principle of consistency deals with people's tendency to behave similarly to how they've behaved in the past. Scammers take advantage of this by getting people to commit to small steps that escalate in nature. Vivian Murphy was duped in a Publishers Clearinghouse scam in small steps, with the first ask being only for $890. But each time, the request was for more money. Having already invested some, the rationale became, "Well, I've paid this much, what's a little more?"

A Ponzi scheme only works when small investments grow. The proof of strong returns on a consistent basis convinced Ponzi's and Madoff's victims to invest more, and more, and still more, until there was no more to give.

And people would only have given to these men, and would only willingly hand over money to anyone, if the people asking were likable. Ponzi, Abagnale, Madoff, and other infamous con artists would never have achieved their success without charm and likability. Cialdini says that we like people who are similar to us, who compliment us, and who cooperate with us. We see this play out in all sorts of scams, in which the fraudsters flatter us, who claim they understand us and can relate to us, who want the best for us and our futures. In a study, likability increased the chances that a prospect would agree to a deal by about 35 percent.

The principle of consensus could also be called the bandwagon principle. Remember from earlier in the book that we're often led—like sheep—to agree to things that others are doing, simply out of fear of missing out or being left behind. When prospective customers saw Charles Ponzi handing out large returns to their friends and family members, they didn't want to be left out of the action.

When it comes to investment schemes, all of these principles can and will be exploited to the fullest because of two basic facts: Investments involve large dollar figures, and an investment con artist can only be successful if a mark says yes, then willingly hands that money over.

Investment scams may be the oldest type of scam, dating back to 300 BC, when a Greek merchant named Hegestratos took out a large insurance policy called bottomry, in which case he would borrow money and agree to pay it back with interest when his cargo of corn was delivered. Otherwise, the lender would take possession of the boat and cargo. But Hegestratos had other ideas: He would sink the boat, take the corn to sell, and keep the loan. But before he could get away with it, his crew and passengers saw what he was doing and pursued him, and in his mania to escape he drowned. To the bottomry of the sea.

While the details of scams may differ, when boiled down to their essences, most every investment scam throughout history falls into one of the following categories:

- **The Ponzi Scheme:** By now you should be an expert in the Ponzi scheme, the classic investment scam that made lowly Italian immigrant Charles Ponzi into a household word. In this fraud, the person running the scam, which FINRA calls "the hub," collects money from investors, promising extraordinary returns on their investments. But instead of investing the money, the hub just stashes that money in an account and pays earlier-stage investors with later-stage investors' money. As investors see returns steadily growing, they continue investing more. It can be sustainable for long periods of time, perhaps even decades, as long as there aren't any excessive demands for distributions. But Ponzi schemes require a steady influx of money to stay afloat, which isn't sustainable over the long term, as the well of investors and their cash eventually runs dry and the bubble bursts.

Before Charles Ponzi, there was William "520 Percent" Miller, a bookkeeper living in Brooklyn in the late 1800s. Victimized himself by a pump-and-dump investment scam (more on that later), he searched desperately for a way to make back his money. He told his clients—students from the Bible-study class he taught—that it wasn't fair that so few people (like the Morgans and the Vanderbilts) were making so much money when the rest of them had to go with so little. Fortunately, from his days of hanging around Wall Street, he'd learned a few investment secrets, and if they would trust him (Who wouldn't trust a Bible-school teacher?), he could make them rich to the tune of 10 percent returns—not in a month, but in a *week*. That would amount to 520 percent a year!

The problem was that, of course, such a thing isn't possible. What he was really doing was paying off old investors with money from the new ones, and those returns prompted old investors to become new ones, over and over again. Within eleven months, he'd raked in $480,000.

But Miller wasn't all that smart (remember, he had already fallen for an investment scam once before). In a turnabout-is-fair-play set of circumstances, another banker/con artist named T. Edward Schlesinger, who had lost business to Miller, called his bluff. He knew what Miller was doing, and Miller would get caught unless he paid Schlesinger to help bail him out of the jam. As pressure from legal investigations came bearing down on Miller, he agreed to hand over a share of his revenues to Schlesinger for "safe keeping." But as you might expect, Schlesinger took the $240,000 he'd gotten from Miller, escaped to Germany, and was never heard from again.

Meanwhile, Miller, on the advice of his attorney, fled to Canada, and to get him back into the states, police told him his infant son was sick and that he'd better come quickly. Fortunately, the unscrupulous Miller was also quite stupid. He fell for it and was promptly arrested and sentenced to ten years in prison.

- **The Pyramid Scheme:** Another classic and well-known scam, the pyramid capitalizes on the American Dream of owning your own business to make money. And the pyramid is just what its name suggests. At the top is the scammer, and at the bottom are the nameless rabble of victims. Here's how it works: Unlike your standard business, in which you make money by simply selling products to customers, a pyramid scheme involves selling investments or overpriced, difficult-to-sell products to their own distributors—people who aspire to operate their own businesses. In order to become a distributor, you have to buy a minimum number of products from the company, which in and of itself can cost hundreds, even thousands of dollars. For this example scenario, say you have to spend $100.

Unfortunately, the illusion is soon shattered when the distributors realize these overly hyped products are too difficult to sell and make any of their money back. But there's another way to make money that doesn't involve selling products. The company's owners tell you that if you recruit others to become distributors by buying in, as you've done, you can make that money back, because you now receive a cut of the money they spend on a new starter kit—let's say 10 percent—plus 10 percent of anything they sell. Now you need several recruits in order to make back the money you lost plus make any sort of profit.

This is the point at which these distributors hit up their families and friends to become distributors, just so they can recoup their losses. They'll take advantage of your relationship, perhaps even flatter you by pointing out how great you'd be at it, or what a fabulous opportunity this would be. They may even promise that these products are life-changing and can do extraordinary things, and for a while they may even sincerely believe it. They'll boast about six-figure paychecks and salesperson-of-the-month gifts of cars and exotic trips. And they'll say that if you work hard and stick with it, you, too, can achieve these benefits. These new recruits are promised small royalty payments, which creates the illusion of profits. But they're forgetting that they've already invested huge amounts of money and time into the business, and now they're stuck with useless inventory.

You might also be asked to invest in training seminars, limited-time-only product packages, sales aids, and conference attendance fees, all purported to assist you in growing your business.

Soon, the new recruits realize what you've already learned, only now each of them needs to go out and find a handful of recruits to funnel money up to them, and the base of the pyramid grows until it becomes impossible to continue. Like Ponzi schemes, pyramid schemes need a constant influx of new, aspiring entrepreneurs willing to invest—a strategy that isn't sustainable over the long haul. Think about it: Even in the very best case scenario, every single person in your community would be a distributor, and then what? Who's left to recruit? According to FINRA, by level 10, the pyramid must recruit everyone in the entire United States in order to work, and by level 11, you must surpass the world's population. And the only ones making any real money are the few sitting in that small section at the top of the pyramid, taking their cuts when the distributors below them recruit new blood or sell their merchandise. And because of the insidious nature of a pyramid scheme, the victims of this fraud also become its perpetrators.

And that's with the "best" type of pyramid—where there's actually a product. In what's sometimes called a "naked" pyramid scheme, there's nothing at all being sold except the promise of large profits from an investment. The initial investor recruits a second investor to work under him and requires the second investor to invest a certain amount of money with the initial investor in order to buy in. The second investor is then required to recruit another investor, with each new recruit being required to pay an "investment" to the recruiter above him and recruit new investors. Recruiting others is what helps pay back the recruiter's initial investment and make any sort of profit. But like the example above, it's unsustainable because eventually you run out of potential recruits.

One well-publicized pyramid scheme was that of Fortune Hi-Tech Marketing, founded in 2001 by two Kentucky men named Thomas Mills and Paul Orberson. The company sold a bizarre variety of goods and services, ranging from hair-care products to satellite TV service. Sellers made only a scant .25 to 1 percent on products sold. Where its real profits derived was in recruitment, which ranged from $99 to $299 for initial startup. In 2010, FHTM reported that about 95 percent of its representatives made less than $3,100 a year, and a whopping 29 percent made not one red cent.

The argument rages on about whether such popular businesses as Lularoe, Herbalife, Tupperware, or Mary Kay Cosmetics are pyramid schemes or what's called multilevel marketing (MLM). The key differentiation between the two is that in an MLM there's an actual product worth buying, whereas a pyramid scheme, at heart, offers nothing valuable to consumers. So in a legitimate MLM, there is money to be made simply by selling products—recruiting is just a bonus.

If you're not sure how to tell the difference, consider this checklist:

- Does it promise a large income for working from home?
- Do you have to invest your own money?
- Is recruitment a prominent feature of the business model?
- Is the commission structure complex and difficult to understand?
- Is the sale of product minimized or even nonexistent?
- Does it sound too good to be true?

If you've answered yes to most or all of these questions, you're likely looking at a pyramid scheme.

- **Affinity fraud:** Madoff Securities was also what's called an affinity fraud, which is a type of scam in which the fraudster exploits cultural, ethnic, religious, trade, or other groups' similarities for personal gain. By capitalizing on the trust and friendship that exists within that community, the fraudster convinces the victim to invest.

Madoff devastated his own kind—his victims were almost exclusively wealthy members of the Jewish community, even completely wiping out famed Nazi hunter Elie Wiesel's life savings and stealing $15 million from the Elie Wiesel Foundation for Humanity.

In an affinity fraud, the fraudster tends to promote a Ponzi or pyramid scheme. Take, for example, the case of James Paul Lewis, Jr., who cheated his fellow churchgoers over a period of twenty years. His company, Financial Advisory Consultants, was trusted by more than 5,200 clients, a great many of whom were members of The Church of Jesus Christ of Latter-day Saints. Like Madoff, Lewis reported consistently high—unbelievably high—returns on investments year after year, with some of his investors reputedly taking as much as $250,000 in distributions at one time. Fellow churchgoers clamored to give him their hard-earned money. Prior to Madoff, Lewis held the record for the longest-running Ponzi scheme in history. But when he eventually stopped paying dividends, investors became suspicious, and it all came crashing down. Lewis was arrested in 2004, and in 2006 he was sentenced to thirty years in prison.

In fact, the FBI reported in 2017 that the problem of affinity fraud was especially pronounced in Utah, where members of the LDS church are frequently victimized by scammers claiming to be just like them. *The Economist* calls this ever-growing concern the "hook of Mormon." It has been such a problem that in 2015, the state legislature passed a law that created an online white-collar-crime registry, similar to a sex-offender registry, that publishes names, photos, and criminal details of anyone convicted of financial fraud in the state going back a decade. The Stop Fraud Utah campaign was designed to educate residents about affinity fraud—how to spot it and how to report it.

In her article, "Warning Signs Madoff Investors Ignored," financial writer Lita Epstein warns of the following signs of affinity fraud:

- Steer clear of advisors aggressively shouting from the rooftops how honest and trustworthy and ethical they are. Personally, I always avoid people claiming to be "good Christians". How good you are no matter what your religion has nothing to do with a business relationship or transaction. Over the years, I have learned the hard way that when people claim to be "good Christians" they aren't. When someone says that now, I hold on to my wallet and back out of the room. So should you.

- Avoid those who seem to only be doing business with a particular group of people.

- As always, be wary of anyone promising consistently high returns.

- If you don't understand the investment strategy, don't invest.

- Never allow personal familiarity, community affiliation, or a sense of urgency to stand in for due diligence and written contracts.

- **The Pump-and-Dump:** In this type of fraud, the fraudster manipulates the ebb and flow of market prices by using the principles of scarcity, authority, and consensus. As the SEC explains, this type of scam has two components. First, the scammer buys a bunch of shares of a low-priced stock. Then he tries to inflate the price of the stock by promoting the company with false or misleading statements about how he knows this company is going to be a hot investment, how people need to hurry up and buy it before prices go up. If he does this enough, people believe they're missing out if they don't hurry up and invest. They may even make guarantees on returns or tell the investors that it's a risk-free investment. (There is no such thing). They'll tell investors that they need to hurry up, the clock is ticking, you need to jump on it this very minute or you'll be missing out on the deal of a lifetime. So the company's stock gets falsely inflated, prices go way up, and this creates buyer demand.

Then comes the second part of the scam—he dumps all his shares when the prices are at their highest and vanishes. Between dumping the shares and halting the hype, the price falls, and investors lose their money. Typically, these scams involve little-known microcap stocks, or low-priced stocks issued by very small companies, often those that don't even file financial reports with the SEC, so they're very hard for investors to research, and they tend to be volatile. Without public information, the scammer can easily spread false information to unsuspecting investors and create even more volatility. Of course, when the stock price drops, the scam broker may do the pump and dump again.

- **The Advance Fee Fraud:** You should know by now that anything involving an advance fee can't be good. Like others I've shared in this book, this type of investment scam tries to make investors pay fees up front — before purchasing any stock, receiving any proceeds, or achieving any benefit — in order for an investment deal to go through. They may call this a fee, a tax, a commission, or an incidental expense that will be repaid later. As the SEC explains, the fraudster may target investors who have already purchased low-performing securities or who already have lost money in investment schemes. They offer to sell the securities or recover losses by exchanging worthless stock, and they'll do all this in exchange for advance fees, which they may even tell the investor to wire to an escrow agent or lawyer to lend an air of legitimacy to the conversation. They use official-sounding emails and websites. They may even call it a "finder's fee," to help an investor make financing arrangements, or they will offer things such as bank guarantees, old government or corporate bonds, medium or long-term notes, or other common financial instruments.

In one case, a con artist named Brett A. Cooper lured investors into fictitious "prime bank" or "high-yield" investment contracts by promising extraordinary returns in a matter of weeks, with little or no risk. The investments, he said, involved "standby letters of credit" and "bank guarantees" from major international banks. To invest, they had to pay Cooper a finder's fee, which would help the bank or brokerage firm to accept a "Brazilian bond" for listing and eventual sale. But of course none of the investors received any of these guaranteed returns, and none of it was ever used to buy any of these bank instruments. Still, Cooper took the fees and sent falsified reports from a so-called broker, to help justify the fees to investors. His con earned him $2 million—until the SEC prosecuted him and won the judgment.

And here's one for the books: In one case, the U.S. Department of Justice shut down an international psychic mail fraud scheme in which the clever con artists sent a mass mailing proclaiming they'd had "visions" of great wealth from lottery winnings. All the victims had to do was purchase products and services the psychic had "seen" associated with the winnings, and their good fortunes would come to them. You should be prudently psychic and avoid it all.

So I probably don't need to say this, but just to be certain, no one can "foretell" investment riches. No fee will guarantee you'll get your losses back or see a plummeting stock rise again. No fee will promise returns. Be sure you understand any terminology being bandied about by anyone trying to sell you an investment, and make sure that person is registered with your state securities regulator, and that the investment is registered with the SEC and state securities agency. And anyone who says you must act now isn't for real. If it is a legitimate investment opportunity, it'll still be there tomorrow.

- **Offshore Investment Schemes:** These occur in a lot of different ways, but here's the basic gist: The scammer wants you to send money out of the country, where you can't get to it and they can't be found. These scams are capitalizing on the SEC rule called Regulation S, which exempts U.S. companies from registering securities with the SEC that are sold outside this country to foreign or "offshore" investors. The promoters may be pitching the investment in a seminar, through direct mail or email, by phone, or just by word of mouth. Typically, it's one you've heard of because it's been getting a lot of attention in the media.

The scam may operate over a relatively long period of time, during which the fraudster even sends you some falsified statements or updates about how the company is doing. (Isn't that nice of them to go to all that trouble?) In some cases, they disappear the minute they've got your money, and it's out of the country and thus pretty untraceable.

Sometimes the "offshore" pitch has to do with taxes—you're told to deposit money in an offshore account that you supposedly control, as a way to avoid or lower your tax burden. The scammer will tell you that you're likely to see money flowing in and out, a signal of activity, but really, it's just draining money out of your account. As you might expect, the IRS has no sense of humor here.

- **Boiler Rooms:** FINRA calls these scams boiler rooms because they mostly involved cold callers operating out of boiler rooms. These days, they're mostly conducted by text or spam emails. Perhaps you've seen movies about stock brokers in the early to mid-20th century, in which high-pressure salespeople wearing sweat-stained shirts made cold calls from lists of potential investors (the "sucker list") to peddle little-known, speculative, or even totally fake securities. They'll tell you it's a "can't miss" or "once in a lifetime" opportunity. They'll rush you to make a decision *now*. This helps to skirt the potential that the investor will do his research on the caller or the stock. They'll insist on immediate payment, maybe even getting hostile about it.

  They'll tell you to wire the money to a bank account and that they'll send you stock certificates later. They might even combine this technique with some others, maybe an advance-fee fraud (the "finder's fee," for example, for offering this great opportunity), or a pump-and-dump on a microcap stock. You'll eventually find out the investment and company don't even exist, or, if it does, it's tanked because the salesperson falsely inflated it to begin with. Regardless, say goodbye to your money. Beware of any excessive hype about any investment. The BS Detector should be sounding the alarm on the first call. Because in some cases you'll get twenty calls. The first time you get a call or email about an investment, hang up, push delete, and walk away.

- **Promissory Notes:** Like many frauds, the promissory note scam is typically perpetrated against the elderly, who tend to have a lot of money socked away in savings. A promissory note is a type of debt that companies use to raise money, explains the SEC. It's like a bond. The investors are, essentially, loaning the money to a company. And in return for this loan, like any lender, the investor is promised a fixed amount of periodic income in payments with a high rate of return.

The fraudster (usually someone who is posing as a financial advisor, often someone working on the inside of a reputable company) will tell the victim that this company—usually a well-known company that the mark has heard of—needs capital to grow. It's looking for investors to buy promissory notes that will mature quickly (usually a year or less) and offer guaranteed returns of 10 to 20 percent. It's a fabulous offer, he'll argue, an ideal way for this potential investor to get an added measure of security, for feathering that life savings nest, something substantial to leave behind to their loved ones.

But that promissory note guarantees nothing, as you'd expect, and this is a deal he's constructed all by himself. The victim writes a check—perhaps even cashes in his or her entire savings. The scammer may make some initial payments back to you, just to sustain the ruse and gain your confidence. But eventually you're paid far less than he's promised in return payments or, in a more typical scenario, the payments come erratically and then drop off altogether.

• **Commodity scams:** In this type of scheme, the investment being pitched is something substantial—gold or silver, rare coins, gems, or even soybean, wheat, oil, gas, or something that's increasingly hot, like alternative energy. Typically they are assets traded on organized exchanges like the Chicago Board of Trade, the Chicago Mercantile Exchange, The MidAmerican Commodity Exchange, and others. Because many people know that throughout history investors have made a bundle on gold, oil, gas, and the like, they believe they too can benefit. And what's confusing for victims is that a lot of commodities trading is real—often risky, but real. The scammer, in what may operate as a boiler room pitch, will pitch the tax advantages of investing in something like oil or alternative energy. Or he may suggest that the commodity is a safer way to invest money in a shaky economy. Like in other scams, he'll dangle high, risk-free returns in your face and pressure you to get in now, while the gettin's good.

The FBI reports one case involving Pedro Jaramillo, a self-professed investment expert who used a professional-looking video of himself in a phony office space on Wall Street to pitch other Latin Americans and other immigrants (an affinity fraud, delivered in Spanish language) to invest in commodity futures contracts—agreements to buy or sell raw materials in the future, on a specified date and at a specified price—and that he could guarantee ridiculously high rates of return. But not only was he not licensed to perform any such transaction, he never invested a dime. He merely used the funds—totaling more than $1.2 million—in a Ponzi scheme that lasted almost three years.

Commodity futures present risk, so thoroughly investigate any company you're considering investing with. Ask for written materials detailing the opportunity. Don't be rushed. Don't cave to high-pressure sales tactics or too-good-to-be-true promises.

The Grass is Greener

As always, scammers often exploit new, hot, poorly understood products or industries to lure investors with the promise of astronomical returns. Marijuana, at the time of this writing, has been legalized for recreational use in a number of states and Washington, DC, and in even more states for medical use. It's getting a lot of coverage, with new businesses cropping up on corners and a whole industry waiting to boom.

It's ripe for investment fraud and market manipulation. Unlicensed, unregistered promoters start touting marijuana as an investment, guaranteeing huge returns with little or no risk and falsely manipulating the market. As a result, marijuana stocks have been on fire, says Graham Rapier with *Markets Insider*. Though the industry is still in its infancy, some stocks have already skyrocketed. Canadian cannabis company Tilray, for example, soared by 90 percent in one day on September 19, 2018. But then it abruptly fell, ending the day up just 40 percent. The next day, it fell 19 percent.

The SEC issued an alert shortly after the Tilray debacle, warning consumers of marijuana fraud. By no means are all marijuana companies or investments fraudulent, but in something touted in as a "hot new thing," investors should be exceedingly cautious. Research the company, review its financial statements, check SEC reportings, and research your broker or advisor carefully to be sure this person is knowledgeable and trustworthy.

Lessons for Investors

The lessons to be learned from Bernie Madoff and the investment scams that have run rampant in our society should be clear to you at this point. First, keep good records. Diversify your investments among companies, brokers, and advisors, rather than putting all your eggs in one basket.

Ask a million questions of anyone promoting an investment, and conduct considerable research into any potential investment or strategy, particularly those you don't really understand. Make sure you understand it.

Research anyone selling investments. Look for licensing and registration with FINRA or the SEC on FINRA's BrokerCheck site or find seller licenses with your state's securities regulator. Ask whether the security is registered with the SEC. If it's not, why not?

Avoid pushy salespeople, high-pressure tactics, and rushed deadlines.

And, as always, don't chase phantom riches. Know that there's no way to guarantee an investment is a good one or how much it will be. If it sounds unbelievable, don't believe it. Keep your BS Detector always on.

"There clearly were warnings. And you have to get down into the psychology of a marketplace—the psychology of a mania, popular delusions, the madness of crowds—to really understand why people ignored those warning signs. It's happened before. There were warning signs about the tech stocks. There were warning signs that many of these companies had no business plan, no revenues, no expectation of ever having any revenues and could not possibly be worth what you just paid for them. In that environment, in that context, it looks a little more understandable. It's in hindsight that it becomes incomprehensible." — **Diana Henriques, author of** The Wizard of Lies: Bernie Madoff and the Death of Trust, *in an interview with* **PBS's** **Frontline.**

Chapter Eleven

'Tis the Tax Scam Season

Avoiding tax and insurance fraud

CASE #9: *The Teen Who Took on the Tax Man*

We often think of plots to hoodwink the Department of Revenue as the domain of white-collar businessmen, perpetrated by financially savvy business owners with lots of money trying to play the system by manipulating the numbers. Charles Turner is a 19-year-old who might just make you rethink your presumptions.

The teenager from the Atlanta area was arrested in January 2019—just weeks after turning 19—for running a scam out of his mother's home that nearly stole $25 million from the Georgia Department of Revenue. The teen's walls were decorated with academic awards but he didn't enroll in college or get a legitimate job, as most fresh-out-of-high-school teens do. Rather, he created a fraudulent startup so intricate it's hard to get your mind around.

Turner created two bogus online businesses that purportedly sold electronics. But instead of delivering the goods to customers, he just took their money and stole their bank account and check routing numbers. And those goods the businesses "sold," they were actually just product deals found on Amazon that already existed, which Turner sold for an upcharge.

The businesses were registered as legitimate companies in the state of Georgia, meaning that they had to abide by a tax law stating that they would file certain returns, including a withholding return. This return tells the IRS how much the employer has withheld from employee paychecks and paid to the IRS on behalf of the employees. Ironically, withholding tax is used by the government as a means by which to prevent tax evasion.

Turner used this to his advantage, turning withholding tax against the government. About twenty-five times over the course of a month, Turner drastically overpaid withholding taxes—by about $1 million each time—to the Georgia Department of Revenue in the hopes that he would receive a generous refund.

Turner, an avid online gamer, needed help perpetrating a fraud reliant on having businesses with employees. He began hitting up other teen gamers with offers of jobs.

"One day he was like, 'Yo do you guys want a job?'" recounted Brent Wagster, a 17-year-old from Missouri.

His friend, 18-year-old Clayton Bickmeyer, said Turner explained he only needed to have a certain number of employees on payroll—not for any actual work. "He actually wanted me to recruit some people for his job, and I did," Bickmeyer said.

Turner operated multiple accounts at SunTrust Bank, which actually had filed criminal charges against him the previous month. The bank insisted that Turner had deposited roughly $70,000 in fraudulent checks into one of the bank's branches, just before withdrawing $18,000 out of another location the next day in order to purchase two used cars from separate dealerships.

And just days later, his twenty-five tax overpayments caught the attention of the Georgia Department of Revenue. Meanwhile, Turner's attempts to wire payroll money to his "employees" failed, so he sent checks instead.

"My original pay was $2,000 and then $17,000 in reimbursements somehow, and [Turner] was like, 'Buy yourself a car or something,'" Wagster told Atlanta's WSB-TV Channel 2.

Although a number of these employees decided to take their chances and deposit the checks—resulting in their accounts being shut down as fraudulent—Wagster and Bickmeyer were suspicious and too worried about consequences to try. Turner began emailing employees to tell them he would pay employees any overdue payments through PayPal and that he'd be shutting down one of the businesses to open a vape shop instead. Other emails indicated he had initiated the process to change his name to Matthia Perdue.

With a mounting collection of evidence, investigators raided his home and spoke to his mother, who argued she had no idea what her son had been up to, and that she had been told he was just buying and reselling items on Amazon.

"Did you ever wonder why your 18-year-old son had two almost brand new cars?" investigators asked her.

Her response? "He was telling me he was doing really good and that it was all internet based."

The Georgia Department of Revenue filed charges including felony computer theft and attempted theft of an amount exceeding $13 million.

As the old saying goes, "Nothing is certain but death and taxes."

In our age we can amend that to read, "Nothing is certain but death, taxes and tax scams." Tax-related frauds are responsible for millions of dollars in losses every year—both for the average taxpayer and the IRS. The IRS estimates that each year, businesses don't pay $125 billion in taxes that they should be paying. And taxpayer identity-theft reports number in the hundreds of thousands per year.

In fact, tax scams are so prevalent that each year, the IRS compiles what it calls its "Dirty Dozen" list of aggressive and evolving schemes for that year. Most of them peak during tax-filing season, and they may be as simple as refund inflation or as complex as setting up offshore accounts to avoid taxation. A great many of them involve personal information being exploited for financial gain. Some of them are conducted by tax preparers or other insiders, while others are perpetrated by unscrupulous outsiders trying to evade taxes or use the tax system to defraud the government or innocent individual taxpayers.

Here is a recent year's Dirty Dozen list put forward by the IRS:

1. **Phishing:** Now that you've read this book, this should be well-covered territory for you. Phishing, in which fraudulent emails and websites are created for the sole purpose of extracting money and personal financial information from consumers, is often used in tax fraud scams. As Experian, one of the Big Three credit-reporting agencies, explains, fraudsters send emails to victims that are disguised as coming from the IRS, to frighten or intimidate the recipient into surrendering personal and financial information that can be used in identity theft.

   One phishing scam making the rounds, warns Experian, is the W-2 scam in which cybercriminals tricked payroll personnel, or people who have access to payroll information, into revealing sensitive information about their employees. The scam has targeted large and small companies, from small nonprofits to universities and hospitals. Companies that suspect W-2 data losses should immediately report them to the IRS, which, if alerted quickly enough, may be able to prevent employees from being victimized by thieves who might take the data and file fraudulent returns with them.

   Others may include emails that appear to be from the Taxpayer Advocacy Panel, an actual volunteer organization that advises the IRS on issues regarding taxpayers. The emails claim to be regarding tax refunds, but they aren't, and the information they hope victims will reveal is then used against them in identity theft or straight-up theft.

2. **Phone scams:** We covered this scam pretty thoroughly, but here's a quick refresher: If you get a call—either from a live person or a robot—claiming to be a representative of the IRS and demanding your money, just hang up. The caller may threaten arrest,

deportation, driver's license revocation, liens on your property... it's all bogus. The IRS doesn't call people, and neither does it email people or reach out through social media. You will be notified— probably numerous times—by mail if there is a legitimate problem with your tax return.

3. **Identity theft:** Some criminals will do anything to scam the tax man... including using someone else's Social Security number to file a return that results in them gaining a tax refund. During tax season, when 1099s, W2s, and other tax documents are floating through the mail and correspondence with accountants is rampant, criminals capitalize on the season to do their dirty work. Guard your information vigilantly and ensure that your accountant has the means by which to guard it when it's out of your hands.

   Also, here's a tip from the IRS: File Form 14039, the IRS's Identity Theft Affidavit if you are a victim of identity theft or your Social Security number has been compromised. Section B of the form gives you the option to check the box stating, "I don't know if someone used my information to file taxes but I am a victim of identity theft." This puts the IRS on alert to heavily scrutinize who is supposed to receive your refund.

4. **Return preparer fraud:** Let me say first that the majority of tax preparers are legitimate, knowledgeable, helpful professionals who take your money and your identity very seriously. But like any profession, it suffers from a few bad apples. Some professional tax preparers take advantage of their know-how, your ignorance, and the system to perpetuate return fraud, identity theft, or other scams. Be sure your tax preparer signs your return and has an IRS Preparer Tax Identification Number.

5. **Fake charities:** Because charitable giving is often used as a means by which to reduce tax burdens, the IRS warns that a number of scammers pose as representatives of fake charities, asking for

donations in the hopes you'll be hungry for a tax deduction. In fact, the FTC says this type of scam sometimes comes in ahead of tax preparer fraud for frequency, with roughly 3,700 reports per year.

The names of the charities may sound similar to legitimate charities, but when it comes to donating money, you really have to do your homework. Don't give money on the spot, before you've had time to research the organization. The IRS website offers taxpayers tools and advice for checking out the status of any charitable organization.

6. **Inflated refund claims:** Similar to tax preparer fraud, taxpayers should never participate in any scheme to inflate a tax refund. This may be done by the preparer, who might ask the taxpayer to sign a blank return, promise a big return before looking at a single record, or charge a fee based on a percentage of the refund. There are scammers out there posing as tax preparers who promise large tax refunds in exchange for hefty fees, then they file the returns and have the refunds go right in their own coffers. An individual may never even know the return was filed.

    Also, beware of the fees involved in claims to get you "instant" or "fast" refunds, which may include anticipation loans—loans granted to you in advance of refunds, which involve considerable fees and interest. You can have anticipated refunds automatically deposited into your bank account, usually within just a few weeks, so avoid offers like this.

7. **Excessive claims for business credits:** This fraud may be conducted by a taxpayer who merely wants to take advantage of loopholes—a lot like that banana trick I told you about earlier in the book. It may not be meant as fraud, an outright criminal act, but improperly claiming the fuel tax credit, a credit not available to most taxpayers and usually limited to off-highway business uses like farming, or the research credit, for participation in research activities related to business, are indeed fraud.

8. **Falsely padding deductions on returns:** It's frequently joked about among colleagues and it's tempting to take part in it, but it's important for taxpayers to avoid falsely inflating deductions, such as charitable contributions or business expenses, or improperly claiming credits such as the Earned Income Tax Credit or Child Tax Credit on their tax returns in order to lower their tax burdens or receive larger refunds. Since the tax code changed in 2018, which raised the standard deduction and significantly lowered the number of taxpayers who itemize, it's likely that this particular fraud is sure to happen less frequently, but it nonetheless happens.

9. **Falsifying income to claim credits:** Scammers have been known to convince taxpayers to invent income they never received in order to qualify for credits such as the Earned Income Tax Credit. But ultimately the taxpayer is the one penalized if this is discovered, and the penalties can be heavy, including not only the back taxes but interest and fees. It's a high-risk, low-reward endeavor that often is discovered in the Information Age.

10. **Frivolous tax arguments:** Some fraudsters promote schemes that will provide tax relief to the taxpayer, or they will make outrageous claims about the legality of paying taxes in the first place. They claim, "George Washington didn't pay taxes!" This is true, since the income tax didn't exist until President Lincoln introduced it in 1862 as a way to pay Civil War expenses. Though it went away briefly, with the Supreme Court ruling it was unconstitutional in 1895, it came back with the Sixteenth Amendment in 1913 and has been on the books ever since. Trust me, like 'em or not, taxes are here to stay and certainly are embedded into law. You certainly should take advantage of the Tax Code to minimize your taxes. Tax avoidance is legal. Tax evasion is not. As well, the IRS does not take kindly to people who make these frivolous claims, tying up valuable time and court costs. The penalty for filing a frivolous tax return claim is $5,000 and it may even land you in jail.

11. **Abusive tax shelters:** A lot of fraudulent tax preparers like to promise clients they can help shield them against taxes through complex tax avoidance schemes or shelters. It may sound legit, but it's tax evasion, plain and simple. Are there some structures that limit your tax burden? Certainly, but they're based on specific sets of circumstances and are authorized by law.

    What is the difference between tax avoidance (or using the tax code to your advantage) and tax evasion? Twenty-five years, as in jail time.

12. **Offshore tax evasion:** I mentioned in the last chapter that offshore investments are often used to skirt SEC requirements. It's no different when it comes to the IRS. Fraudsters may hide money and income in offshore accounts or foreign credit cards that they believe can't be traced, and thereby can't be taxed. They may use these cards or accounts to make outrageous purchases without paying taxes. Of course, this is illegal. In other cases, called trust scams, scammers promise that for a fee of a few thousand dollars, they can invest your money in offshore operations to hide it from the tax man. The IRS is onto you. It has increasingly cracked down on abuse of offshore holdings. Failure to report them may be costly—more costly, in fact, than simply paying the taxes would have been to begin with.

The truth is that the IRS simply doesn't pursue as many cases of tax evasion as it used to. In an attempt to change its reputation for picking on the little guy, in 2002 the IRS announced that it would invest most of its time and energy on high-income taxpayers and complex tax avoidance schemes and less of it on auditing the average, middle-class taxpayer. That was compounded in 2011 when Congress began repeatedly cutting the IRS's budget, forcing it to reduce its enforcement staff by about a third, which resulted in fewer audits of everyone. The IRS's reputation in Congress certainly suffered in the wake of the Lois Lerner scandal with the targeting of conservative charities. The IRS suffered further budget cuts as a penalty. The rate at which the agency audits tax returns has gone down 42 percent since all of those budget cuts began.

Nonetheless, when the IRS cracks down, it does so with gusto. A January 2018 report from the Government Accountability Office revealed that in 2016, the IRS blocked at least $10.56 billion of identity-theft tax-return fraud, and it helped to recover $281 million in fraudulent returns that same year. And it drastically increased the amount of six-digit personal identification numbers it gave to taxpayers to authenticate their returns and protect them from fraud. So despite rampant tax fraud, it is comforting to know that fraudsters are simply having less success than they used to, even amid budget cuts.

At a Premium: Insurance Scams

It's official. The National Insurance Crime Bureau says that tax evasion and insurance scams are the white-collar crimes that cost Americans more than any other type of fraud. We pay for them every day in the form of higher taxes, higher costs for goods and services, and higher insurance premiums. The NICB reports that 10 percent or more of property-casualty insurance claims may be fraudulent. What's the cost to you, the average American? Oh, about $400-$700 per year per family in insurance premiums.

In previous chapters I've discussed some types of insurance fraud, including those involving medical, auto, mortgage, and home insurance. Here I'll spend a bit more time on these and other types of insurance fraud that are all too commonplace and have resulted in the rest of us paying the consequences.

Auto insurance scams: Think people only stage car crashes for the insurance money on TV? Think again. This, unfortunately, is a thing. Would-be fraudsters lurk on corners waiting to bilk unsuspecting drivers out of their insurance monies. They may swerve in front of you without warning and slam on their breaks, causing a rear-end collision. They may see you trying to change lanes, then wave you in, only to crash into you and deny the wave, blaming you instead for cutting them off and causing the crash. They may crash into you in a double turning lane. Before you know it, they're making outrageous claims that their neck or back is hurt and they need months of specialized, expensive medical treatment. Sometimes they'll even have someone who appears to be an innocent bystander appear on the scene and insist repeatedly, at the crash site and in calls afterward, that the car repairs, legal assistance, or medical treatment really should be done by a particular service provider – a clever ruse cooked up by a team of scammers to squeeze your wallet and drive up bogus insurance claims.

The insurance companies aren't the only ones paying the price for these maneuvers. Victims' driving records are now blemished, which drives up their insurance premiums or even, in some cases, prohibits them from obtaining or keeping their insurance coverage. They, their passengers, can be seriously injured. The Coalition Against Insurance Fraud (CAIF) reports that in one cited case, an entire family, which included a baby girl, died when their car was hit by a truck when a staged accident went terribly wrong. And even in the best case scenario, a victim's life is turned upside down dealing with car repairs, and endless series of phone calls from insurance adjusters and repair shops, and entanglements with law enforcement officers or even attorneys as he or she tries to become extricated from the problem. And when enough of these scams happen, the insurance industry as a whole must compensate for the outlay of expenses by raising everyone' s premiums.

The NICB says these scams tend to happen more frequently in urban, affluent areas, where there's a higher volume of pricy cars on the road, and the scammers tend to target women and elderly people driving alone, as they're less likely to confront the scammers. And they tend to happen in "no-fault" states, where scammers, who play victims, can make bodily injury claims to their own insurers through Personal Injury Protection, in addition to making a claim to your insurer.

How do you avoid getting taken in such schemes? Do what you can to prevent such accidents from happening in the first place. Avoid tailgating and keep a healthy distance between your car and those in front of you. Make sure you don't become distracted while driving. Distractions such as talking or texting on a cell phone will tell the scammer that you're not likely to recall the details of the accident. And pay special attention to nearby cars in which there are several passengers. Auto accident scams typically involve cars full of three or four people – all of whom file bodily injury claims against your insurance, in addition to the claim for car damage. Finally, be sure to carry paper and a pen in your car to take down important information in case of an accident.

If you are drawn into an accident such as those described above, don't assume it was entirely an accident, particularly if the car has several people in it. First, call the police. Count how many passengers are in the car, says the CAIF, and be sure to take down *all* their names and driver's license numbers – more people may try to file claims than were in the car, so having all their names is a safeguard against this. Write down the car's license plate number as well. Pay attention to the passengers' behavior. For example, do they stand around joking and then start acting injured the minute the police arrive?

Use your phone to take pictures of damage to your own and the other car, and take pictures of the passengers, too. When the police come, be sure you get a report with the officer's name, even if the damage appears minor. If the police report notes only a small dent or scratch, this makes it harder for the scammers to report major injuries later. Finally, if you're a witness, watch for the warning signs of a scam and help the unsuspecting victim if you're able by providing details.

After the accident, remember that you should only do business with medical or legal providers you trust – not someone you're being pressured by witnesses or the "victim" to see. And if this happens, be sure to report it to your state's insurance fraud bureau.

Other types of auto insurance fraud include repair scams, in which an auto repair shop attempts to defraud the car owner and the insurance company by offering verbal estimates and then presenting bills that far exceed the estimates with padded or excessive charges for needless repairs. Or they may use second-rate or flat-out worthless parts that cost them nearly nothing and allow them to pocket your money. And that's if they do the work at all. Many do a shoddy job or don't do it at all, putting you at risk when you're on the road. The CAIF reports the true story of one mechanic who held car parts together with nothing more than bailing wire. It not only wastes your time and money, but it's dangerous, and if your insurer gets involved, it affects premiums.

Even worse, some shops have been known to pull "airbag scams" in which they remove your airbags without your knowledge, replace them with deployed old ones, and then tell you the airbag must have deployed in the accident. They bill insurance for the "replacement" – your old, good airbag – and pocket the money. Or they might just take your airbag, leave you unprotected without one, and sell the bag on the black market. Be sure you receive a written estimate for any car repair before agreeing to it, and only use reputable service shops that are recommended by others and have good records with the Better Business Bureau. And beware of shops offering to "waive your deductible." This may involve using a used or faulty part, billing your insurance, and passing savings along to you. But beware – it's insurance fraud, plain and simple. Keep a close eye on your airbag lights and cover, and be sure to see itemized bills for any suspicious-looking charges.

And this should go without saying, but beware of strangers offering to replace your windshield for free, in exchange for gift cards, cash rebates, or other gifts that will cover your insurance deductible. Believe it or not, many folks have fallen for this scam, in which the con artists claimed the existing windshields had damage they didn't have, made more than one claim for the windshield, and took insurers for hundreds or thousands of dollars. Same goes for tow trucks who just show up, without being called, on the scene of an accident or the minute you step away from your vehicle, then charge you outrageous fees to claim your car or drive it out through the gates of their impound lots.

Medical: Today's health insurance landscape is confusing for even the most avid follower. The rules of Medicare and Medicaid, not to mention the health exchanges inherent in the Affordable Care Act ("Obamacare"), are so hazy and hard to understand that they're territory ripe for scam artists who prey on consumers' ignorance.

Insurance broker Pacific Prime conducted a survey of 2,106 physicians in the U.S. and found that doctors believed that 20.6 percent of all medical care was unnecessary – that includes 22 percent of prescriptions, 24.0 percent of tests, and 11.1 percent of procedures. And although they admitted that fear of malpractice and patient demands drove a large part of this treatment, more than 70 percent of these doctors also admitted that they would perform unnecessary procedures if they would profit from them.

A few bad apples spoil the bunch as they say, and although only a small percentage of medical insurance claims are fraudulent, that small percentage is frequently responsible for driving up costs for the consumer to the tune of *tens of billions of dollars.*

According to the National Health Care Anti-Fraud Association (NHCAA), the most common types of healthcare fraud are:

- Performing medically unnecessary services just to receive insurance payments.

- Accepting kickbacks for patient referrals.

- Falsifying a patient's diagnosis to justify tests, surgeries, or other procedures that aren't medically necessary.

- Billing for medical or dental services that were never provided – either by fabricating entire claims using patient information obtained through identity theft, or by padding claims with charges for services never rendered.

- Manipulating medical billing codes to bill for more expensive services than were actually provided, also known as "upcoding".

- Unbundling, or billing each step of a procedure as if it were a separate procedure.

- Reporting treatments that are not covered by insurance as medically necessary in order to obtain insurance payments (for example, calling a nose job necessary because of a "deviated septum").

- Waiving patient co-pays or deductibles, which is compensated by over-billing the insurance carrier or benefit plan.

- Charging the patient more than his or her copay amount for services that were already prepaid or covered fully by insurance or a benefit plan – which amounts to double dipping.

Another scam prevalent these days is the Obamacare scam, which takes several different faces. It may look like a fake "navigator", someone who appears to be helping you sort out the complex world of insurance coverage by assisting you with the health exchanges, but is really only trying to bilk you out of an unnecessary fee, sign you up for fake coverage, or take your sensitive financial information when you complete enrollment forms. It may also appear in the form of a phone, website or scam email – a phishing scam used to charge unnecessary fees or steal identification information. Or, as we discussed earlier in the book, it may show up through a call claiming to be "verifying" essential information in order for the call recipient to receive a "required new Medicare card" from the federal government – a completely bogus request.

In fact, exploitation over medical insurance confusion has created an entire marketplace of fake insurance policies, stripped-down policies that won't cover essential treatments, or medical discount cards that really do nothing except line scammers' pockets. They not only jeopardize your health but they steal your money and drive up premiums.

The high costs of medical care and health insurance have also created a market for discount cards – and a host of scams associated with them. Though discount cards are a legitimate way for consumers to save money – you pay a monthly fee to pool resources with a group who have access to medical providers, then pay discounted out-of-pocket costs for care – they also have become a method by which scammers take advantage of consumers. They may lie about benefits that don't exist, charge exorbitant associated "fees" for use, or even steal money and sensitive information from users. Be aware that a discount card is NOT insurance and should never be presented as such. At a minimum, victims of discount card scams receive no discounts at all, or they may attempt to use the cards with providers who were put on provider lists, only to find out that the provider never actually consented to participate in that card program. Worse, consumers may lose money through fees or expensive care. And far worse, your physical and financial health may be put at risk when certain treatments are offered that don't exist or aren't covered. If presented with such an offer, be sure you're very clear about what you're signing up for – health insurance or a discount plan. Be wary of such claims as "savings up to 60 percent", "affordable coverage", or "guaranteed benefits". These terms may sound like insurance, but they're murky at best. Ask to have these claims spelled out, as well as all terms. Are there fees? What are they for? What are the costs or discounts for standard treatments? Is credit card or checking account information being collected over the phone or via email? (It shouldn't be). And be sure you know what the refund policy is for cancellation.

Unexpected medical bills are a fact of life. You go to the hospital for surgery, and several weeks later, you receive bills for radiology, anesthesiology, or other services from providers outside your insurance network – it's an unpleasant, though often legal, reality. But a small number of these are fraudulent, involving medical providers who collaborate with or bribe colleagues to be included in medical care, called kickbacks, inflating your medical bill as you lie, unsuspecting, on the gurney. Be sure that before you receive any treatment, you ask about the possibility of seeing all treatments and expected costs in writing. Shop around for providers in your network who provide quality care. And appeal any surprise charges with your insurer; insist that they pick up the tab. Some states even have laws protecting you from surprise medical bills, so seek a state-level consumer advocate to help you navigate the process.

Another emerging medical insurance scam involves long-term care insurance. This type of insurance covers medical services not typically covered by standard private insurance or Medicare/Medicaid – such as hospice, nursing care, or adult day care, or in-home medical equipment. Unfortunately, the folks this type of coverage is designed to help – senior citizens – are the prime targets of scams. The schemes may involve the sales of extra, expensive policies for certain types of care when one policy would suffice; upselling to expensive "replacement" policies promising better coverage that really isn't and may, in fact, be worse; offering lower premiums in exchange for less robust or watered-down policies that don't cover vital treatments; overstating the scope of coverage to imply that it will cover things that it won't; falsifying your personal information on enrollment forms in order to obtain coverage or lower premiums; or flatly selling policies that don't exist. It's crucial that before you sign on the dotted line for long-term-care coverage, you do your research on the provider and the person selling the policy, evaluate whether you actually do need the policy in the first place, shop around and compare policies, thoroughly read the policy to understand what's covered and what's not, fill out applications accurately, never pay cash, make out check payments to the insurance company (never a single person or broker), and take advantage of "free look" periods which allow you to cancel your policy within thirty days and receive a full premium refund if you aren't happy with it.

The murder-for-the-life-insurance-money is another oft-used premise of TV shows and movies, with *Double Indemnity*, written by Raymond Chandler and starring Fred MacMurray, Barbara Stanwyck and Edward G. Robinson, being the best. Art often mimics life. Scam artists have been known to "kill" themselves – faking their own deaths – in order to collect life insurance benefits. Duane Swierczynski writes of one case in which a man called his life insurance carrier shortly after the 9/11 attacks to explain that his wife had been in one of the fallen World Trade Center towers. Her policy carried a $200,000 benefit, which he hoped to put toward his $270,000 mortgage. The man filed the claim, showed officials his wife's appointment book showing that she was at the World Trade Center on the morning of 9/11, applied for Red Cross survivor funds, and even asked for an urn of ashes from the disaster site. The CAIF reported that New York Mayor Rudy Giuliani sent the man a letter of condolence. But the wife wasn't dead. She wasn't even trying to pretend she was dead. The couple continued living and working in their small Georgia town, going about their business and interacting with the community, apparently expecting that the scope of the disaster would mean that the insurer had its hands too full to properly investigate the claim. Unfortunately for them, that wasn't the case. The couple was charged with insurance fraud and sentenced to ten years in prison.

In other cases, murder is much more brutal. In 2018, according to *Insurance Business America,* a 46-year-old Pennsylvania man named Ryan Shover was convicted of first-degree murder for killing Wayne Capelli of Delaware. Capelli was attacked with a baseball bat while walking home from work in February 2013, and his body was discovered in a nearby wooded area days later. An investigation revealed that three of his friends – Michael Kman, David Hess, and Paul Disabatino – had recently talked Capelli into taking out a $360,000 life insurance policy and making Disabatino the beneficiary. Kman recruited Shover to commit the murder, promising him $30,000 from the resulting insurance benefits as payment. But when Kman and Disabatino tried to collect, a criminal investigation into the murder put a halt to the payout. The money instead went to Capelli's child, and the three ringleaders all pled guilty to homicide and insurance fraud.

It's rare, but it happens.

Less known but more common is the life insurance scam in which a phone call informs you that a loved one has taken out a $1 million policy that would ensure you'd be taken care of for life – but the person didn't want you to know about it. There's only one problem, the caller tells you: There's a final premium payment due. It's usually a very specific amount... say, $4,270.89. Without this payment, the policy will lapse. You must pay it now. And boom, just like that, you're out thousands of dollars. As I've said repeatedly in this book, never make urgent payments – ask to see documentation and verify the information. If it's legit, they'll wait.

The rise of health insurance fraud is such a costly problem in the U.S. that the federal government has established strict anti-fraud legislation to combat it, with penalties for basic fraud including up to ten years' imprisonment. But the government can't do all the work. It depends on all of us to remain vigilant. The NHCAA urges consumers to protect their health insurance cards as they would their credit cards. In the wrong hands, they can do a lot of damage, including identity theft. Report the loss of an insurance card immediately.

Report any suspected fraud right away to your insurance company – some carriers even offer the ability to report such incidents on their websites. Stay informed about the health care you receive, read all bills and statements from providers or carriers, and, as always, beware of too good to be true services, tests, coverages, or schemes that could end up costing you your health and money.

Individual: This type of insurance fraud involves individual players – employees, insurance brokers/agents, attorneys, service contractors – scamming the insurance system to obtain payouts.

Many would-be scammers look to profit off workers' compensation insurance, believing it to be a victimless crime. Employers Insurance reports that roughly 1 to 2 percent of all workers' compensation claims are fraudulent. In some cases, employees file bogus claims, collecting payouts and getting time off work while working second jobs on the side, thereby being paid twice. Or they may just be looking for paid vacations. This type of fraud occurs when employees exaggerate their injuries, get hurt off the job and then pretend to injure themselves at work in order to get free medical treatment, claim that prior injuries took place at work, or just stay at home and claim they're still hurting even though they've long since healed.

Still other cases involve employers themselves, trying to get away with lower premiums by falsely claiming that their workplaces are less dangerous than they are or that they have fewer employees than they do. Or they may simply avoid carrying coverage altogether. And in some cases, certain clinics, or medical mills, team up with attorneys to urge employees to undergo treatment that isn't necessary or to file suit against insurers if they won't pay out certain benefits.

These scams cost all of us in the form of lower pay – employers cutting back on payroll in order to compensate for lost money in workers' comp cases; higher prices for goods, services, and coverage; and, yes, higher taxes (workers' comp is, after all, a government-run program). Not to mention the lost productivity when a coworker scams the system and skips out on work. Employers should remain cautious and report suspected cases of workers' comp fraud, offer rewards for workers who provide fraud tips, and alert insurers about suspected fraud cases.

In other cases of individual insurance fraud, people claiming to represent insurance carriers may pocket premiums, sell policies that don't exist, sell you coverage you don't want or need (or slip it in without your knowledge), or misrepresent what is (or isn't) covered.

And of course, we all know there are ambulance chasers out there – attorneys who seek to rip off insurance companies and make money off the backs of individuals who are sick or hurt. While there are certainly legitimate claims to be made involving negligence or malpractice, far too many attorneys manufacture false claims or exaggerate injuries, promising clients they will receive settlements and then pocketing the money themselves. Take, for example, the case of Richard Merritt, a Georgia man convicted of murder who admitted to having earlier pursued numerous malpractice claims for his clients and keeping much of their awards for himself. Among his charges were thirty counts of theft, forgery, and elder abuse. And in 2016, State Representative Ron Reynolds, an attorney in Texas, went to prison for barratry, the illegal solicitation of clients, also known as ambulance chasing.

Some other instances involve attorneys who simply pocket clients' rightfully earned settlement money, or who lowball their insurance settlements so that the attorney quickly collects but the client receives far less than they should. Some attorneys forge their signatures on settlement checks, or have their checks illegally deposited in the attorney's personal accounts.

In cases like these, it pays to do your homework to find a reputable attorney who charges fees that are comparable to the marketplace. Never trust an attorney who promptly approaches you about hiring him/her after a car crash or other catastrophic event. Consider twice the attorney looking for a contingency fee of more than 35 percent of any insurance settlement. Be alert for unreturned calls or emails, and be sure *you*, not the attorney, is managing the settlement. This means insisting that all claim checks be made out to you, regularly contacting the insurer yourself to confirm updates on the claim, and keeping a log of all correspondence and activity associated with the claim and attorney. If the attorney settles for an amount smaller than what sounds right to you, contact your insurer immediately to let them know the settlement was reached without your consent, and report any suspected theft to your insurance company and state insurance department.

When it comes to tax, insurance, or other financial institution frauds, remember these three golden rules: Don't be greedy, don't fall for too-good-to-be-true solicitations, and guard your personal information with your life.

"We don't pay taxes. Only the little people pay taxes."
— Leona Helmsley, the "Queen of Mean," who famously accumulated, with her husband, Harry, a multibillion-dollar real estate portfolio and was convicted on three counts of tax evasion in 1989.

Chapter Twelve

Asset Protection

It's not asset protection if you lose your assets

CASE #10: *Troy Titus, the Legal Eagle*

Plenty of white-collar criminals have tried to justify their actions by claiming their crimes were victimless. Fraud, bribery, Ponzi schemes, embezzlement, insider training, intellectual property infringement, money laundering... these all seem to be the domain of billion-dollar corporations and the filthy rich, involving unseen victims who are often perceived as able to absorb the losses. In truth, the victims of such crimes are often the most vulnerable, those who have sought help and trusted authorities and experts to offer solutions, only to be ripped off in return.

I always suggest consulting with an attorney for help in protecting your assets. These are the people you should be able to trust. You would never think that doing so would actually expose you to greater danger. But in the case of Troy Titus, that's exactly what happened.

Troy Titus of Virginia Beach, Virginia, was a boy genius who graduated high school at age 16, college at 20, and law school at 23. He made his living as an attorney and real estate investor. He was an honors graduate of Liberty University and Regent University Law School, where his father, also an attorney, was the founding Dean. Troy went on to work for 15 years as a practicing attorney, founding Titus Law Group and, later,

Premier Law Group, and at one point he had a dozen lawyers working for him.

Not only that, but he operated a consulting firm, with himself its real estate investment expert, as well as a title insurance company. Titus traveled on the seminar circuit in the Virginia Beach area, and then nationally, putting out DVDs and books that thousands of people were buying. As he explained to audiences on his DVD, "We're going to be talking about an acquisition technique called 'Buying With Cash... With No Cash.'"

As an episode of CNBC's *American Greed* (a show you don't want to be featured on) explains, "Troy Titus preaches the gospel of easy money in real estate. He claims to be all things to all people. If you've got some assets to invest, he promises to make you rich. If you're broke, he can make you whole. But Titus is weaving a tale of deception."

In the first few pre-housing-bubble years of the 2000's, his ideas seemed plausible to many. The real estate seminar and investment business was booming, and flipping properties was commonplace. Everyone believed that the way to get rich quick was to play the real estate market, if only someone would show them how to work the system. Titus was the guy everyone wanted, and he knew it. At his packed seminars, he trolled for clients, posting signup sheets so eager potential clients could schedule one-on-one consultations.

Once alone, he convinced them that the rules for real estate were made to be manipulated. He would then scan their financial pictures and develop customized investment plans that he claimed could help them meet their goals. He knew exactly how to address their fears and promised to take them away with the solutions only he could provide.

In 2005, award-winning record producer and former R&B group Blackstreet star Teddy Riley had accumulated more than $3 million in mortgages and back taxes, and his exclusive, invite-only American Express Black Card had been maxed out. He was completely under water on his new record studio, New Jack Swing Future Records. His creditors had put a lien on Riley's $1.5 million house, and it was headed for foreclosure. Riley turned to Titus, the money magician, for help.

Titus told Riley he could clear the liens from the house with a process he dubbed "controlled foreclosure," a complex procedure he insisted was legal, though shady sounding. Riley, of course, had no reason to question his attorney and even started to believe Titus cared for him and his situation as a friend would.

Titus said if he could just find some investors, Riley would be able to keep his home, his studio, and all his other treasured assets—as long as, at some point, they started paying investors back. Riley thought he was on the road to recovery and left for California for a music project, and Titus starting working to attract investors, luring them with the promise of 15 percent returns on the controlled foreclosure.

"If you choose to use controlled foreclosure as an acquisition technique," Titus boasted in his seminars, "you will find yourself set apart from your competition because you're going to be able to acquire real estate using a technique that the vast majority of real estate investors don't know exists."

They didn't know it existed, of course, because Titus had just made it up. The idea was to buy distressed property for a fraction of its value. In Riley's case, Titus first bought one of the mortgages on Riley's home that was in default. Then, as the mortgage company, he intentionally foreclosed on the property with the intention of buying it back himself. He set up a shadow company, under his control, that would buy the property from the foreclosing entity—Titus himself. Sure, the property would go up for auction and be publicly (though obscurely) listed, but the only person who would show up would be Titus. He told investors he'd buy the property at the new low price, sell it for a huge profit, and give them back huge returns.

If others showed up to bid at the auction, he cautioned in his video, the solution was simple: Cancel the sale and reschedule for another time to be determined. "Eventually," Titus boasts, "people just stop showing up at these sales."

In short, every facet of the sale was to be controlled to ensure the investor got the intended result. And when investors heard this, they enthusiastically hopped on board. In fact, he raised so much money that it amounted to more than three times what Riley's assets were worth, and

Titus then distributed to each investor a deed of trust saying they each held a lien on the property—property that had never been taken out of Riley's name. But Titus never actually legally filed those deeds of trust with the clerk, meaning that the investors never knew the property was severely overleveraged. The city's assessed value on Riley's home was about $440,000, while the debt leveraged against it now totaled roughly $2.4 million.

In other words, even a highly profitable sale could never hope to pay back all the investors—especially because Titus never made the slightest effort to buy the home or studio. He had collected their money, issued meaningless paper in return, and left everyone high and dry, having done nothing. And because the money had all been raised in Riley's name, he was left technically responsible for paying back the investors.

Titus had been perpetrating this scam all over town for years, getting money for investments that didn't go where they were supposed to, backed by collateral that didn't exist. Only the original property owner, the one who sought help from Titus in the first place, was left holding the bag.

After a year or so after soliciting Titus' help, Teddy Riley began receiving calls from investors asking for their money. And then he got another call—from a fellow Blackstreet member explaining that his girlfriend, a realtor, had heard that Riley's house had been auctioned off. Riley called Titus repeatedly looking for answers, but Titus was nowhere to be found and never replied. He was out spending investors' money to maintain his extravagant lifestyle. Eventually, banks foreclosed on the properties, leaving Riley more broke than he'd been before.

Titus' staff and colleagues believed he was just a disorganized genius, a financial guru who was able to gather huge investments but was so busy he often forgot to purchase the properties he promised to buy. How else to explain that he was a real estate expert—a devout Christian and family man with six children—who rarely ever purchased real estate? Now and then, when an investor came calling, he would take money from the pile he'd accumulated from investors and send a token payment. More often than not, though, he'd simply pull a vanishing act.

He was robbing Peter to pay Paul, a classic Ponzi scheme. New investors were essential in order to pay off previous investors. But without the real estate component in the transaction, there was nothing supporting the business.

Titus's good looks, obvious success, high intelligence, and friendly demeanor charmed all who met him—many of them the elderly and vulnerable—and he easily convinced them to invest their hard-earned money with him, promising a whopping 25 percent return that would provide future security. Titus didn't discriminate when it came to defrauding investors. He was no Robin Hood. His victims were the rich *and* the poor. He even stooped so low as to steal needed money for medical and housing expenses from the elderly and incapacitated, with some even being eventually forced out of their homes.

They included Josephine Bodner of Virginia Beach who, in her 70s, turned to Titus in 2001 for help establishing a trust that would pay her $1,500 a month for 27 years. She only received payments for four years before they dried up. Titus stole, in total, more than $300,000 from Bodner.

Another was Gina Katigbak, a San Francisco resident who in 2001 received a colon cancer diagnosis and decided to quit her corporate job and focus on her health. She met Troy Titus in 2005 at one of his seminars and felt so sure of his promises to give her a much-needed income that she withdrew $50,000 from her retirement savings to invest in a distressed property Titus promised would make her money. She never saw a dime.

In 2005, as the housing bubble grew, investors were clamoring for their money and new investments were thinning out. Titus had irked enough people and raised enough suspicions—with bounced checks, questionable investments, and allegations of fraud surfacing in his wake—that the Virginia State Bar revoked his license to practice law, and the FBI began investigating his actions.

A massive three-year investigation turned up a charge of 49 counts of fraud. A one-month trial and four days of jury deliberation returned a verdict of guilty on 33 counts of fraud for a grand total of roughly $8 million (an amount that later was determined to be closer to $12 million).

U.S. Attorney Michael Moore called Titus "an economic sociopath" and "a pathological liar" who "preyed on the weaknesses of other people," reported *The Virginian-Pilot*.

At sentencing, the 44-year-old disgraced attorney wept and blamed excessive pride for his actions. "I wish there was something I could do to explain it," he told the judge. "I guess I got to the point where I completely lost sight of reality."

Meanwhile, Titus' enduring charm had not subsided for many, and more than 20 family members and friends wrote letters on his behalf to the court, pleading for leniency for Titus. One of them, a retired Air Force Lt. Colonel, a friend of Titus' from church, wrote, "He exhibits admirable qualities that few could ever succeed in achieving... I willingly admit that I fail to live up to the benchmark he has set in devotion to noble passions and concern for others."

Nonetheless, Titus was sentenced to 30 years in prison, and his victims will never see their money again.

I never met Troy Titus.

But I know his kind.

Cue the creation of aura.

The guru is supremely confident and certain his is the only way. Others do not have the intelligence and wisdom to know what he knows. He belittles others for their shortcomings, but generously admits not everyone can possess his superior intellect. To become a part of this exclusive club, which not many will ever be allowed to enter, you must always respect his unrivaled brilliance. You must blindly agree with his preeminence. You must ignore any feeling that you are being manipulated to form the opinion that you are working with a superior professional, a true expert, the most renowned. You must know, you must be completely certain, that you are indeed working with the smartest attorney of this or any century if you want to gain admittance to their inner sanctum.

Upon your admittance, you will be able to say that your attorney only takes certain clients and you are one of them. You will learn (or, more accurately, be spoon fed) that the guru's structures are so complicated that the average mortal just wouldn't understand it anyway.

I had such a blinded client come to me. She had come from a seminar and claimed to have set up a structure I probably wouldn't understand. In the face of such guru manipulated nonsense, my response is always: "Then why did you make an appointment to see me?"

This always cuts to the chase. She made the appointment because for all the fancy asset protection talk her guru drizzled on her, she didn't understand the structure.

For some, there is another point of resistance to get past. She will say that her guru was the smartest professional in all of asset protection. She is still blinded by his greatness.

I will then ask what college and law school their guru attended. Upon learning this, without citing or comparing schools, I will say that I went to a similar school and I might understand it. (As a general rule, students from my alma mater don't pop off about getting a degree from the University of California, Berkeley. It is part of the Cal culture. However, as a general rule, our rivals across the Bay always seem to want people to know they graduated from Stanford.)

When the barriers constructed by the guru to keep the uninformed completely uninformed come down – the structure clearly appears as one shining scam.

In this case, Nancy, a woman in her mid-40s from southern California, wanted to invest in a duplex. She had saved $20,000 for a down payment to use for the purchase of a $125,000 property in El Centro. (As you can judge from the pricing, this was several years ago).

Nancy had been told by a friend that a guru giving a Saturday seminar was the smartest person in the world of asset protection. Since she was buying a duplex, she would need asset protection. Nancy listened to her friend and attended, and was immediately taken with the guru. He was handsome and well-spoken and really seemed to connect with her. She set up a consultation with him to see how to best structure her investment.

Nancy said he drew her a chart and I asked to see it. She said it was copyrighted material and she couldn't show it to others. I responded that attorneys can't claim a copyright over client work product. By definition, that material belongs to the client.

Reluctantly, she pulled the structure diagram out of her purse. It was diagrammed as follows:

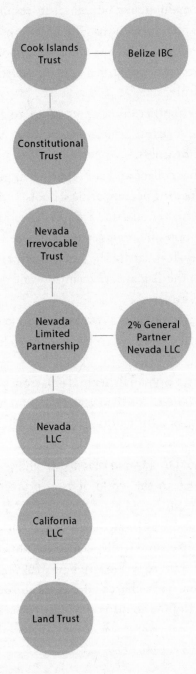

She said the guru called it the Overlord Structure and added that it was probably too confusing for me to understand.

I smiled. "Oh I understand it. I'd call it the Overkill Structure."

Nancy was taken aback. "What do you mean by that?"

"Seven layers is overkill. You don't need all this."

"What do I need?"

"At a minimum, just this," I said pointing to the California LLC. "You are buying a property in California. You will take title to it in a California LLC."

"What about the first layer?" Nancy said, pointing to the Land Trust circle at the bottom. "The attorney said it provided excellent privacy."

"Are you sure he was an attorney?"

"He sure acted like one."

"I have my doubts," I said.

"How?"

"We'll get to it in a minute. What did this promoter say about land trust privacy?"

"That your name is not listed anywhere," Nancy said. "That if a tenant wants to sue you over the property, they can't find you."

"Does that really make sense?"

"Why, yes. That's what the attorney said."

"Okay, we're going to start calling him the promoter. An attorney wouldn't say that."

"Why not?"

"Let's say you were renting an apartment, Nancy, and you got hurt. Who would you contact?"

"The management company."

"Exactly. And they are the agent of the owner, whether it's you individually, an LLC or a privacy misrepresented land trust. The tenant is going to get to the owner."

"But that's supposed to be private."

"Right. Does the management company get in trouble if they don't tell the owner of a claim?"

"I suppose."

"They do. As the owner's agent, the management company is required to notify the owner of the problem. And wouldn't the owner want to know?"

Nancy thought it over and shook her head. "Why?"

"So they can turn the claim over to the insurance company. You're going to be denied coverage if you don't promptly notify them. Without coverage, the owner is personally responsible for the claim. That's not asset protection."

"But," Nancy said with certainty, "they said a land trust offered complete asset protection."

"The land trust cases that go to court deny asset protection. And because these cases end up in court, there's obviously no privacy. Attorneys can find out the true owners."

She lifted her nose a bit. "The lawyer said land trusts offer complete asset protection."

"Okay," said I. "Let's just assume they do. Then why do we need six layers of protection above it? If the land trust really worked as they said, we could just use it all by itself."

"But we need all the other layers because we are such a litigious society." Nancy's eyes brightened, as if a light bulb went off. "How many layers do you use?" she said, with a touch of sarcasm.

I gave her the good lawyer answer. "It depends. Sometimes one. In your case two. We suggest a living trust too. Like a land trust, it offers no asset protection, but it does avoid probate. With a living trust you don't have to go to court to distribute your assets when you pass. The trust does it in place of a judge and probate attorneys at expensive prices. But it provides no asset protection, so we don't consider it a layer."

Nancy was focused on the layers. "So I need two."

"Two. But not seven. I will say the part of the chart I like is for the California LLC to be owned by the Nevada LLC. We'd probably use a Wyoming LLC instead of Nevada since Wyoming is less expensive and offers more privacy."

"So who is on title to the property?" Nancy asked.

"The California LLC. You are collecting rents and doing business in California so you need to be properly set up there. At the county recorder's office, title will be in the name of the California LLC."

Nancy then asked: "So then why is the California LLC owned by a Nevada – or a Wyoming LLC?"

"Because California, like New York, Utah and others, is a weak state." I drew out a chart:

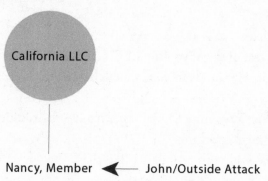

"We have to distinguish between types of attack. When a tenant sues, it is the inside attack. They have a claim against the LLC itself. That's who they rented from and did business with. They can sue the LLC and get what is inside the LLC. If you have ten properties inside the LLC, they can get the equity in all ten. Which is why we don't want to put too many properties into one LLC. But the rules on the inside attack are the same in all 50 states."

"So where does Wyoming come in?"

"For the outside attack. That's where your choice of state becomes important."

"What's an outside attack?"

"Let's say you get in a car wreck with John. John's wreck has nothing to do with the real estate. So he doesn't get a shot at the inside attack. He can't sue the LLC directly. But, if your insurance doesn't cover the claim, he can go after your personal assets, which would include your ownership interest in the California LLC."

"So how do the courts handle that?"

"It depends on the state. California says if John has a claim against you personally, he can force a sale of the California LLC's assets. So your duplex is sold to cover his claim."

"And what does Wyoming say?"

"Well, like Nevada and Delaware, they are much more protective. John can't barge into one of their LLCs and force a sale of the duplex. Instead, John has to apply to a court to get a charging order, which is a lien on distributions."

"What's that?"

"It means that if the Wyoming LLC makes a distribution to you, then John will get it. He stands in your shoes charged to receive whatever you do."

"What if the Wyoming LLC doesn't make a distribution to me?"

"Then John gets nothing."

"Well," she said with a smile. "I like that. They never explained that to me."

"If they did," I said with a laugh, "you'd quickly figure out you didn't need all seven layers. So how many Wyoming LLCs do you need? That's the beauty of it. Just one." I drew another chart.

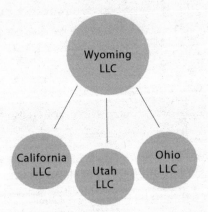

"Let's say you own duplexes in three states. We have an LLC set up in each state to take title. Those three LLCs are owned by one Wyoming LLC. If someone comes after you in the car wreck case, the outside attack, all they are going to get is a charging order against the one Wyoming LLC.

While you actually could have more than one such holding LLC, you really only need one."

"Well, their structure certainly was more expensive."

"I can imagine. But there may be a way-"

"Really? I spent way too much on this."

"What did they tell you about the Constitutional Trust?"

"They said it was based on the US Constitution. Apparently, the Constitution mandates that no state shall impair the obligation of contracts. If you can contract it, you can do it."

"And the Constitutional Trust," said I, "or they're sometimes called a Pure Trust, is a contract that says that taxes don't have to be paid."

"Yes," said Nancy. "That's what they said. They held up an IRS letter saying the trust had no tax requirements."

"And do you know why the IRS issued such a letter?"

"Not really."

"Because the Constitutional Trust doesn't exist. There is no such thing. So of course there's no tax requirement for something that doesn't exist. The person creating this fiction is still liable for the tax."

"They made it sound like the taxes disappeared at the Constitutional Trust level and the money could float tax free up to the Cook Islands level."

"And if that were true, wouldn't everybody do it?"

This time she laughed at herself. "They said only a few really smart people took advantage of this."

I added, "And that you shouldn't tell anyone about it."

She nodded vigorously. "Yes, that's exactly what they said."

"Well, the good thing is that you told me. Now you're not going to jail."

Nancy sat straight up. "Is that what happens?"

"Absolutely. They were encouraging you to commit tax evasion. When taxes aren't paid with a Constitutional Trust, people go to jail. But you just set this up, right?"

Nancy nodded.

"You haven't filed a tax return yet on all this, have you?"

"No," she said.

"Good. We can unwind it before the tax year ends and you'll be fine. But here's why I don't think this was put forth by a lawyer."

"Why's that?"

"Virtually every lawyer who has promoted the Constitutional Trust has gone to jail."

"Really?"

"Con-trust. Convict."

She dejectedly shook her head. "He seemed so nice."HH

"So do most con men. There are still promoters out there doing this under the radar. But here's a bit of good news. In some states, the Attorneys General will go after the bad guys and seek restitution of the money you lost."

"Is that even possible?"

"It is possible. It is a sign of how much the IRS and state authorities despise the Constitutional Trust."

"Alright," said Nancy. "To summarize then, I need two, and not seven layers."

"Yes," said I. "One layer takes title in the state specific LLC. The one or more LLCs in that layer is owned by one Wyoming LLC. Of course everyone's situation is a little different and specific professional advice may be needed for certain cases. But this is the general overview. For certain, I don't want you holding real estate in your individual name whereby you are personally liable. In that case, there is no asset protection."

"I guess it's not asset protection if they can take your assets."

"Very good, Nancy."

Chapter Thirteen

Cyber Bounty Hunters

How can we minimize all the scams?
Incentives usually work.

A bounty hunter is someone who captures criminals for a "bounty," a payment for providing a public service.

In the Old West, local sheriffs were sometimes unable to track down outlaws alone. They couldn't do that and protect their town at the same time. So they put up wanted posters offering rewards for an outlaw's capture, Dead or Alive. Bounty hunters responded, and tracked down the outlaws for the reward. For example, the reward for the capture of Jesse James was $5,000, an enormous amount of money at that time, equal to over $112,000 in today's dollars.

Although the term "bounty hunter" evokes images of vigilantes in the Old West, the term "bounty hunter" was not in use in this context in the 1800s. Rather, the term relating to "one who tracks down and captures outlaws" arose around the 1950s in pulp fiction and Hollywood westerns. In 1954, Elmore Leonard published *The Bounty Hunters*. In the same year, *The Bounty Hunter*, a 1954 western film was released by Warner Brothers. The movie, starring Randolph Scott, was the first film to feature a bounty hunter as its hero. *Have Gun-Will Travel* was an American Western series that was broadcast by CBS on both television and radio from 1957 through 1963. The TV series featured Richard Boone as Paladin, a gentleman gunfighter who typically charged $1,000 per job and traveled around the Old West working as a mercenary for hire. Similarly, *Wanted Dead or Alive* was a CBS bounty hunting Western airing from 1958 through 1961.

Recently, Leonardo DiCaprio played Rick Dalton, the fictional TV star of *Bounty Law* in Quentin Tarantino's *Once Upon a Time...in Hollywood*.

In modern times, bounty hunters generally are known as bail enforcement agents, and they mostly carry out arrests of criminal defendants who have skipped bail and failed to appear at their trials. In some states there is no formal training for bail enforcement agents, and they are unlicensed. In other states, there are varying standards of training and licensing. The state of Nevada has very strict statutory and administrative requirements for bail enforcement agents. The risks can be great.

Local law enforcement agencies also offer rewards in high-profile cases. Funding sometimes comes from outside private donors who provide money to help solve specific crimes. As well, some cities and towns have set up Crime Stopper programs for anonymous tips.

For example, Secret Witness of Northern Nevada currently offers rewards to Secret Witness Tipsters who remain completely anonymous. Reward amounts depend upon the severity of the crime, the number of victims, and the level of violence. Rewards are increased for crimes against the elderly or against law enforcement. If requested, Secret Witness will even administer payment of others' rewards. Generally speaking the Secret Witness rewards schedule is as follows:

Type of Crime	Typical Reward Amount
Murder	$2,500
Attempted Murder	$2,000
Armed Robbery (Gun or Weapon)	$1,500
Armed Robbery (No Gun)	$1,000
Arson	$1,000 - $2,000
Burglary	$250 - $1,000
Narcotics	$100 - $1,000
Rape/Sexual Assault	$1,500
Graffiti/Tagging	$50

Incentives also work in the field of cyber security. Governments and private companies offer "bug bounty" programs where monies are paid to 'white hat hackers' to identify weaknesses within a security or computer system.

A white hat hacker, or ethical hacker, is a good guy. They operate with the system owner's permission to conduct penetration testing, vulnerability assessments and the like. Black hat hackers also harken back to TV Westerns, where the bad guy was easily identifiable by the black hat he wore. Black hatters are motivated by financial gain, anger at the system, the thrill of cybercrime, among other reasons. As we have learned throughout this book, the black hats wreak havoc in every corner of society.

Since not everything in life is just black and white there are also grey hat hackers. As an example of their work, they will search for system vulnerabilities without an owner's permission. If they find an issue, they will ask the owner for a fee to fix it. If the owner won't pay, they sometimes post the vulnerability for the web to see. While not black hat pernicious in their intent their hat is grey since they didn't have the owner's permission to begin with.

White hat hackers can be well compensated. In recent years the Department of Defense has paid out over $500,000 annually to white hatters for uncovering thousands of vulnerabilities under the Hack the Army, Hack the Air Force and Hack the Marine Corps programs. The Department of Homeland Security has established a bug bounty program to minimize internet security problems within their own systems.

Private companies also fund their own bug bounty programs. Apple offers a maximum payout of $1.5 million. In 2019, Google paid out $6.5 million to 461 researchers for their vulnerability assessments.

HackerOne is a founding member of Internet Bug Bounty (IBB), a bug bounty program designed for core internet infrastructure projects. IBB was started by hackers and security providers who were interested in making the internet safer. IBB partners with the global hacker community in order to discover security issues for its customers before these issues can be exploited by cyber criminals.

HackerOne claims to be the number one hacker-powered bug bounty platform in the country. They have launched more federal programs, including Hack the Pentagon, than any other service.

If bounty programs work for tech savvy hackers, why not for sophisticated hunters? Incentives work. The government could certainly expand existing bounty programs to bring in cyber criminals. To be certain there are legal issues to be worked out, but when compared to the lawlessness and impunity with which internet crime is committed, the legal issues seem small.

In fact, the U.S. Constitution allows for bounty hunters. Article 1, Section 8 gives Congress the power in Clause 11 to grant Letters of Marque and Reprisal. At the founding many sovereign nations issued such letters, which allowed private parties (or "privateers") to engage in hostile, for profit acts against state enemies. In many cases, the state and the privateer shared the spoils. The most successful team was Sir Francis Drake, who scored lucrative hits on Spanish shipping, and Queen Elizabeth, who both feigned innocence to other monarchs and gladly took her cut of all the gold and silver. The difference between piracy, a hanging offense, and privateering (or benefitting from private ships of war) was having "letters of marque" sanctioning the bounty.

Article 1, Section 8, Clause 11 is often referred to as the War Powers Clause. It vests in Congress the power to declare war and grant letters of marque and reprisal. So Congress would have to approve the bounties.

But in a new world of extraterritorial threats, including terrorism and cyber havoc, the Constitution clearly allows a mechanism for the country to defend itself using sanctioned private actors. Letters of marque against a broad profile of hostile individuals, organizations and cyber bad actors would save the nation trillions in fighting undeclared wars and occupying countries that don't want to be occupied. Letters of marque would target bad actors wherever they are found, offering great tactical flexibility. The U.S. has plenty of trained individuals to perform the work, privately defending the country and its citizens for a just reward.

Some commentators are adamantly against the idea of cyber bounty hunters. They note that active hacking, or going on the offense, is illegal under the Computer Fraud and Abuse Act. Even if someone in the private sector has been hit by a black hatter, opposing commentators claim there is no legal authority to hack back. As well, they ask who decides what is ethical, just and legally binding? A cyber bounty hunter with a financial incentive to find and accuse could destroy lives of innocents.

These commentators also argue that the government is already engaged in their own shadow form of bounty hunting. A majority of the personnel at the CIA's National Clandestine Service are independents. They claim that 80% of the National Security Agency's budget goes to paying private contractors. Are they privateers?

Governments will not warmly embrace digital vigilantism as they are already engaged in their own covert cyber criminality. A notable example of this, never confirmed, is the American and Israeli use of the Stuxnet computer worm to damage Iran's nuclear program in 2010. While limiting an angry nation's access to atomic capabilities seems worthwhile, it was also technically a violation of international law.

China's military plans do not involve confronting the U.S. military directly. Instead, in what they call 'systems destruction warfare,' they will undermine American operations. At this point, no one will be arguing about technical violations of international law.

Christian Brose is the author of *The Kill Chain: Defending America in the Future of High-Tech Warfare.* In the May 23, 2020 edition of the Wall Street Journal, Mr. Brose wrote:

> We must...redefine our objectives. If China continues to grow in wealth, technology and power, it will become a peer competitor to the U.S. Recovering our global military primacy is no longer a practical goal. We must instead pursue a more limited and achievable goal: denying military dominance to China. The U.S. military will have to focus less on projecting power and controlling territory than on preventing China (and other competitors) from projecting power themselves and committing acts of aggression beyond their borders. We must create defense without dominance.

This will require us to think differently about modernizing the U.S. military. The goal cannot be to accumulate more and better versions of traditional platforms in expensive pursuit of a 355-ship Navy or a 386-squadron Air Force. We must focus instead on developing networks of systems that enable U.S. commanders to understand the battle-space, make decisions and act – the process that our military calls "the kill chain" – and to do so better, faster and more dynamically than our adversaries. This battle network, not platforms alone, creates real military advantage.

Similarly, the Wall Street Journal reported in their June 2, 2020 edition:

The International Committee of the Red Cross in a letter last week signed by international political and business leaders called for governments to take "immediate and decisive action" to punish cyber attackers.

"There are more and more cyberattacks...on the healthcare sector and unless there are really strong measures taken, they will continue," said Cordula Droege, chief legal officer at ICRC. "What we're seeing at the moment are still indications of how devastating it could be."

The next war or triggered economic collapse will involve taking out critical infrastructure, as well as military capabilities. The electric grid, telecommunications, healthcare, transportation, finance, water and waste water treatment, among other key resources are targets that will be attacked and must be defended. Having a corps of certified and licensed defenders may provide a crucial edge toward military advantage. They may also provide an immediate advantage to every American now suffering from the financial and emotional onslaught of scams.

The scamster in some small country who believes they are free to disrupt and ruin the lives of millions without consequence must see that other cyber criminals are being caught in the act, extradited to the United States, prosecuted and sent to jail for a very long time. When boastful

American scamsters learn their friends not only dislike their criminality but like being paid for a tip off or learn that lesser confederates are now more likely to turn on them, a positive disrupting factor is introduced. These criminals must know that the new sheriff is willing to pay millions to trained, sophisticated hunters to bring order and justice to the Wild West of the internet. When criminals have to think twice about their criminality, when they witness other bad actors going to jail, crime does go down.

But the question remains: How can a government act against cyber bad actors when they also engage in cyber bad acts?

Other questions will arise. What if a cyber bounty hunter tries to collect on a government? And what if a government, in failing to pay, turns a white hat to black hat perdition? (Hopefully that last one is just an action adventure movie). To be certain, the issues will be complicated. But they pale in comparison to the billions in losses and social risks of not addressing widespread deception. Failing to act now only allows the monster to grow. Citizens will accept the cognitive dissonance that protecting the country *with* cyber criminality is different than protecting citizens *from* cyber criminality. Helping individuals to scam proof their assets is not inconsistent with collectively scam proofing the country. You can do both at the same time.

So either governments admit (as sheriffs in the Wild West did) that they can't do the job and let the bounty hunters in. Or they step it up and actively protect their citizens from cyber criminality. Whatever course the people's representatives choose it must be acted upon immediately. The threat to our country is great. The damage being inflicted upon millions of innocent Americans every day hollows out our core.

Cyber bounty hunters (either in house or contracted) will be utilized by all government in the future. Their citizens will demand it. The only question is what will come first: The real thing, or the TV show.

Chapter Fourteen

To Scam Proof Your Assets

If the contents of this book have you concerned, good. You should be. By now you've seen the prevalence of scams of all sorts and witnessed the destruction they've caused to millions in lost money, lost reputations, lost homes, and even lost freedom and spiritual depression. The number of victims are increasing by the day.

As discussed, the justice system and the cybersecurity industry have not decreased the onslaught. In their halfhearted attempt at "Whack-a-Mole," the more they stop one scam, an even craftier one pops up.

While there's no way to guarantee it won't happen to you, you have, hopefully, deduced by now from reading this book that many scams have common traits. The scams evolve and change but the patterns remain constant. Applying those patterns to your critical thinking skills and knowing you have the freedom to call BS on it all will go a long way toward protecting you from becoming a victim.

Unfortunately, we do not live in a society that does a great job of teaching critical thinking. Far too much time is spent asking students to memorize facts, while not enough time is spent instructing students from an early age in how to make reasoned judgments, based on a set of quality information and without the influence of personal feelings or biases. As you've seen on the previous pages, a great many people have become victims because they rushed into poor decisions without performing due diligence or because they were motivated by fear, greed, loneliness, low self-esteem, or a sense of urgency.

How can we engage in critical thinking? How can we best utilize our BS Detector? First of all, recognize that you have always had these skills. They're hard wired into all of us. Like our ancestors, a thoughtful observation of the details of your surroundings and objectivity when making an analysis are skills to be accentuated and used often. A clear understanding of bias (your own and those of any manipulators in your midst) and the ability to both detect it and get past it are important.

While you can't prevent others from trying to maneuver your emotions and decision-making capabilities to steal your identity, money or assets, you can take steps to sharpen your critical thinking skills and build your resilience to their devious tactics. Decide what is true, and what you should do.

A key step is to gain emotional distance. The vast majority of scam victims were selected precisely because they were susceptible to emotional manipulation. Whether they were overly confident, felt rushed, had a fear of missing out, suffered from loneliness, craved validation and flattery or were simply too trusting or optimistic, their decisions were impaired by their emotions. The greed-fear setup is the most common, because it works. The con artist preys on your greed and then uses fear – of authority, of missing out, of financial loss, of isolation – to seal the deal. But emotion is what gets us to stop using our heads, and scammers know this. As any emotions rush forward, your BS Detector should hold them back.

As Professor Steven Novella, an academic neurologist at Yale School of Medicine, wrote in his book, *Your Deceptive Mind: A Scientific Guide to Critical Thinking Skills*, "Our brains are belief machines. We are motivated to believe, especially those things that we want to believe...The default mode of human psychology is to arrive at beliefs for largely emotional reasons and then to employ our reason-more to justify those beliefs than to modify or arrive at those beliefs in the first place. Therefore, in many ways, we are slaves to our own emotions if we let ourselves be."

So when presented with any deal that looks unbelievably good, any email or call asking for your personal information, any situation that involves strangers and from the outset could either be legitimate or not and provokes a strong emotion in you, your first step should be to take a step back. Do nothing. Pause. Take a moment to identify your emotional response. Are you feeling worried about money? Are you indulging in wishful thinking, a fantasy? Are you feeling peer pressure, afraid you're the only one who's missing out? Identify the emotions you're feeling and realize that they might affect your decision-making abilities. Try to label the feeling(s) you're experiencing. Taking this simple action will help prevent you from reacting impulsively and give you time to think through how to respond.

This is the first step in a technique called "Label to Disable," which is described by Tara Susman-Pena, Mehri Druckman, and Nino Oduro in a course guidebook titled *Fighting Misinformation: Digital Media Literacy*, one installment in The Great Courses personal development series.

"The ability to handle your reactions to emotionally charged material and experiences is an extremely powerful skill," the authors write. "It enables you to buffer yourself against the force of information manipulation. The key idea is to defuse your own immediate emotional response so that you can engage your critical thinking skills."

Next, conduct your due diligence. Adopt a mindset of mistrust of every offer or deal or request. Don't trust. Just verify.

But, you ask, don't great, legitimate opportunities come along now and then? Absolutely. But they're rare, and if they're legitimate, they can stand up to scrutiny. Your financial, emotional, and physical wellbeing are worth whatever time you need to invest in performing due diligence. Investigate who's offering the deal, how it's being offered, what you're expected to offer up, how secure that transaction is, and what you could potentially lose if the person isn't actually on the up and up.

When it comes to the source of the offer, remember that we humans have a natural tendency to want to believe experts. We naturally put trust in authorities, or those whom we perceive as authorities, in matters that we don't fully understand ourselves. As Novella points out in his book, "A common mistake that many people make is to consider someone who is an expert in one thing to be an expert in all things-as if they can have general expertise. Sometimes experts make this mistake themselves and stray from their true area of expertise."

As we've seen countless times in this book, with Charles Ponzi, Bernie Madoff, Troy Titus, and scores of others, the perception of expertise triggered unwarranted trust in their authority as well as their own belief in their infallibility, even in the face of mounting evidence to the contrary. Remember that no one is above due diligence. Everyone must pass your BS Detector test. Read reviews, get information in writing, and research as if everything you own is at stake. Because it could be.

Cyber Insurance

One way to protect yourself is to obtain cyber insurance. In this era, when almost every business operation uses online efficiencies, companies of any size or industry type must consider cyber insurance. The consequences of an attack can lead to enormous out of pocket costs and even bankruptcy. Insurance can mitigate such risks.

There are several different policies to consider, so be sure to work with a knowledgeable insurance broker to obtain the right mix of coverages for your specific situation and the kinds of threats you may face.

As an overview, some of the coverages which may overlap include:

- First-Party Liability

First party refers to the company's costs from a cyber-attack. These include:

1. Attorney's fees for defense and advice on regulatory requirements.

2. Forensic investigations into the attack.

3. Notifying victims and paying for their credit monitoring.

4. Loss of income due to the attack (or Network Business Interruption).

5. Public relations efforts to rehabilitate the company's image.

- Third-Party Liability

This coverage protects the business when a breach occurs on a third party's network. Any party that worked on a compromised system as a contractor is usually sued. Cost resulting from plaintiff's attorneys and regulators can be covered, including:

1. Settlements and damages from the incident.

2. Legal defense bills.

3. Dealing with formal inquiries and regulatory mandates.

4. Paying fines and fees to regulators.

- Network Security

This important coverage protects companies from data destruction and breaches, malware, cyber extortion and ransomware, viruses and business email compromise. It is necessary to know what is and isn't covered to avoid gaps in coverage.

- Privacy

Customer and employee information can be sensitive and costly if compromised. Privacy coverage protects against the loss of physical records and for the costs of securing information with privacy risks.

- Media Liability

When electronic media is improperly used or intellectual property is infringed (which happens frequently and often innocently) this coverage is useful. Slander and libel may also be covered with these policies.

- Errors and Omissions

This coverage relates to negligent performance issues with a professional service or product. Accidental cyber incidents are still technical mistakes for which this overlooked coverage can be useful.

As is evident, there are a number of coverage issues. Given that each business will have different risks and potential threats, a one size fits all policy of cyber insurance will not be advantageous. Work with your insurance broker to know what types of cyber risks are covered by your basic business liability policies and what other coverages are needed to fill the gaps.

As well, learn the exclusions within each policy. If they are not to your satisfaction negotiate with the provider or seek out another option. Know that attorneys in this field state that insurers routinely decline cyber coverage claims. (Isn't that a scam: Collecting insurance premiums and denying all claims?) Be prepared to go to your state's Insurance Commission to demand coverage.

Another way to protect your business is with strategic contracting. Work with your attorney to draft contracts that minimize the company's liability. Provisions to limit the types of damage and the dollar amount for which you are responsible along with limits on product or service warranties can be very useful in narrowing the claims window.

Test Your Scam Radar:

- If it sounds too good to be true, it is. It was strategically designed to convince you that you can't possibly lose.

- We humans have a tendency to overestimate our own competence in areas about which we know just a little bit or have some interest, also known as the overconfidence effect. And we tend to underestimate our own potential for deception. Both can lead us into trouble.

- Remember that no one dresses too well, is too educated, or is too nice to fool you and commit a crime. Don't give anyone a pass because they're charming or likable. Charles Ponzi, Bernie Madoff, Frank Abagnale and Troy Titus, some of the world's most notorious, were renowned for being likable, charming and smart.

- Even knowledgeable, wealthy, kind people, including business owners, counselors, advisors, church and community leaders, heads of large and prominent families, your next-door neighbor, or your friend from church, can and do commit crimes.

- Anyone can be a mark. Even the folks you'd least expect to fall prey to con artists. Doctors, teachers, financial experts, even psychotherapists can be susceptible to scams. Even you.

- Statistically speaking, those who have been victimized by scams are actually more likely, not less, to fall prey again.

- Don't fall for flattery. Compliments are offered to derail you. Just because someone compliments you doesn't make them more worthy of your trust. See it for what it is – hokum.

- The elderly are a prime target for scams. Their children and relatives must be on guard. Everyone must retain a higher level of caution when it comes to queries, offers, and attempted transactions.

- Scammers use the bandwagon technique, so don't be too quick to hop on board. It only seems like everyone's doing it because that's a carefully crafted illusion. But it's likely not the reality.

- Don't make big decisions based on the fear of missing out. If it's actually a good deal, it will be there tomorrow, and it will pass your efforts at scrutiny.

- Don't let fear of losing a deal force you into making a rash decision on the fly. Creating a sense of urgency is a scammer's go-to tool. When someone is pushing you to give answers right away or act quickly, run the other direction.

- If you've lost a loved one, gone through a divorce, been laid off from a job, or had some other life trauma recently, your chance of being scammed more than doubles. Avoid making big decisions when you don't have the mental and emotional bandwidth to make good ones. Take a step back and heal so you can come back stronger.

- Don't get tricked into keeping secrets. If someone's telling you it's your little secret, that the deal is just between the two of you, it's a scam. Legitimate offers would never come with such a proviso. A legitimate business wants you to spread the good word to new customers.

- Any "professional" who says other professionals wouldn't understand their program or strategy is manipulating you. Your BS Detector has to ring loud in such cases.

- Remember that photos are easily manipulated. Don't always take photos at face value. A simple internet search might reveal a fake.

- Be aware of your cravings for a good deal and counteract it with due diligence and time for decision making. Discuss it with an advisor. And, as you already know, spouses are usually very good at seeing through the hype.

- Humans are optimistic by nature. We *want* that amazing deal, that cool product, that huge cash prize to be real. It's in our DNA to find justifications that it is. Don't be too trusting or optimistic. Healthy skepticism and caution are a good thing. Anyone making an authentic offer would expect and welcome the opportunity to have the authenticity reviewed and proven.

- Remember that no one from the government will initiate contact with you by phone and ask for money. Also remember that the government does very little to stop widespread deception. You are on your own here for now.

- Groundbreaking cures, scientific discoveries, hot investments and other such "opportunities" should be corroborated. If they were real, more than one person would know about them. They would be endorsed by doctors, the FDA, the Better Business Bureau, banks, or by other authoritative bodies. Before accepting such information as true, make the attempt to verify it.

- You should never have to pay to obtain a prize or receive money that's owed to you.

- You don't have to give your personal information to just anyone who asks for it. You should be sure it's really needed and know how that information will be protected.

- Legitimate businesses don't need your gift cards, and they won't insist that you wire them money. These are untraceable transfers of money that can't be verified or refunded, which is why they're being asked of you.

My hope is that the information in this book will keep you from being targeted by scammers in the first place. To help arm yourself against this pervasive criminality, please consult this checklist of simple actions you can take in all your dealings with others to ward off scammers looking for vulnerabilities.

And now, let's conclude with an important scam-prevention checklist:

I. Safeguarding Personal Information

As we learned from the master of identity theft, Frank Abagnale, anyone can steal your identity with just your name, date of birth, and Social Security number. You should be absolutely vigilant about safeguarding this information. Remember that identity theft is often an inside job, committed by friends, family, employers, and coworkers. Don't take for granted that they will keep your information safe, and take measures to prevent abuse of this access.

The following tips, provided by cybersecurity companies Palo Alto Networks and Norton LifeLock, as well as the Association of International Certified Professional Accountants, will help you to safeguard your, and others', personal data, whether it's stored on paper or electronically:

- Use a locking mailbox or mail slot so thieves can't steal your mail.

- Lock doors to restrict access to paper and electronic files.

- Shred papers such as receipts, bank or credit card statements, or anything containing personal information before discarding it.

- Require password access to computer files.

- Encrypt electronically stored personal data.

- Keep backups of electronic data, for recovery purposes.

- Don't email unencrypted, sensitive personal information.

- Don't store usernames, passwords, Social Security numbers, credit card information, or other personal information on note-taking apps. These are not encrypted and are easily hacked.

- Only use secure Internet connections that are password-protected. Remember that public Wi Fi connections often are open, and scammers can easily hijack personal information you share while surfing on them. Also, make sure you change your home wireless router's default username and password.

- Make sure your devices with Internet connectivity are not set to share access to files or let them be seen on public networks.

- Create strong, unique passwords for all your online accounts. Sensitive passwords should have at least 20 characters.

- To keep track of all your passwords and ensure their security, consider using a password manager, which is a type of downloadable software that generates and stores passwords for you automatically. Many browsers have them built in, or you can use a tool such as LastPass, Dashlane, or I Password that work across multiple browsers.

- Set up two-factor authentication (2FA), which ensures that anyone trying to access your account has to verify their identity twice, which offers an extra layer of protection. Usually, this means that in addition to entering a password, you would be sent a text with a code that you would need to input to verify your identity. This is especially important on accounts that provide access to financial information. You can verify which major sites in a wide range of categories have this option at TwoFactorAuth.org, which also provides links directly to those pages.

- Check your credit report at least once a year and carefully review it for errors. About 20 percent of them include errors, which may or may not be due to fraud. If you catch any, correct them. If something doesn't look right, it could be a sign you've been targeted for identity theft.

- Set up a fraud alert with any one of the Big Three credit unions-TransUnion, Equifax, or Experian. If you place a fraud alert on one, they are required to notify the other two. So you only need to contact one of the bureaus. If you only *suspect* fraudulent activity, you will be given a one year fraud alert for free. However, if you are a proven victim of identity theft you are eligible for a free extended fraud alert which lasts for seven years. Fraud alerts require creditors to contact you at the number you give (when setting up the alert) before opening any account. Make sure you use your cell phone number for this so that when you are attempting to get credit in person (buying a car, for example) you will have your phone with you and be able to answer the call. If you are not available to answer the call and verify your identity your credit application will be held up.

- If you do not want to deal with the hassle of a fraud alert, there are many free credit monitoring apps with which you can set up notifications. Any time something changes on your credit report you will be notified by email or text message. Most of the apps are bureau specific. For example, one app may pull from TransUnion and another app may pull from Experian. Take a look at this when you are creating an account. You will probably need to use a couple different apps to make sure you are getting alerts from all three credit bureaus.

- If you believe you are the victim of fraudulent activity, insist that it be notated on any collections account, and ask to be directed to the company's fraud department or, if no fraud department exists, ask for a manager. Don't hesitate to escalate your situation to the next level. If you cannot get results from customer service or a manager, perform a google search to find contact information for the executive offices. If you can find their contact information and send them an email or give a phone call it can usually be taken care of quickly. In some cases, such as utility fraud, you may not know about it until the situation is in an advanced state, so you can't afford to wait. Be your own advocate.

II. Avoid Being Targeted

Safeguarding your personal information is crucial to ensuring scammers won't steal your information. But that won't stop the telephone calls, scam texts, and phishing emails from coming. Here are some steps you can take to keep yourself from being victimized.

Phone:

- Add your number to the Do Not Call List, and never answer calls from unfamiliar numbers.

- Beware of calls from the IRS, courts, collection agencies, or government entities, particularly those asking for money. Typically, they will not contact you by phone. You would first have received correspondence by mail. And even if you do actually owe the money, it should never be a surprise.

- Caller ID is useful, but not guaranteed effective. Know that scammers often cloak their numbers in local or familiar-looking numbers.

- Don't take someone's word that they're an expert. Make sure it's verifiable. Check for licensing in his/her profession, training, experience, references, and reviews from others, particularly if you are hiring them to work in your home or have access to your money or assets. If you can't find information, take that as a red flag.

- Verify fundraising efforts before donating to anyone. Be sure the organization is legitimate and that the contact and payment information you find matches what the person soliciting the donation gave you.

- Don't respond to urgent requests for money or information with short deadlines, and don't work with anyone who insists on keeping a transaction secret.

- Legitimate businesses will have no problem sending you more information by mail to help you make up your mind. But scammers will.

- Never buy, rent, or invest in anything sight unseen.

Email:

- Don't follow links in emails, and don't open attachments. Hackers often use these tactics to access your device, gather personal information from you, or access your financial records or accounts.

- Disregard emails with suspicious or misspelled sender names, email addresses, domains, or links. Other red flags include messages from foreign countries or odd-sounding English.

- Exercise extreme caution with any requests to change vendor payment instructions. Never respond to a request for login and password information.

- If you suspect something is wrong with your computer, don't click links or call numbers that show up in pop-up ads. Call the tech support number associated with your computer or service plan. Tech support doesn't contact you. You must be proactive.

- If you're a business owner or manager, ensure your staff know how to avoid ransomware and phishing attempts.

Internet:

- Make sure your device operating system and software are frequently updated. Old software can contain security bugs that leak personal data. Set your devices to update automatically.

- Install up-to-date antivirus and security software.

Final Thoughts

We live in a society in which research, scientific and technological advancement is evolving more rapidly than was ever believed possible. Yet it's an unfortunate fact that some of the early adopters of such advances will use that knowledge for ill purposes. The more we use email, social media, smartphones, and the Internet, the more bad actors will use these supposed betterments to rip us off.

As we have seen, the impacts can range from minor - a bounced check, a late fee, the loss of a few hundred buck to the severe, resulting in such disastrous effects as loss of identity, skyrocketing legal fees, loss of good financial and credit standing, homelessness, untenable amounts of debt, total bankruptcy, and even imprisonment. Not to mention the emotional devastation, the shame, the anxiety and depression, which in some cases have led to suicide. The wreckage is wide and saddening.

I've written this book to give you the education you need to be empowered to protect yourself. Being aware of the tricks used against you just might make you hesitate to answer that unfamiliar phone number, to hold off on clicking that link or replying to that email. If you're reminded of Charles Ponzi the next time someone asks you to invest in a new opportunity, or if you remember the heartbreaking tales of folks who lost their life savings the next time you enter into a major financial transaction, I've done my job, because that small moment of pause may mean the difference between losing just a few minutes of your time and losing everything you have.

Finally, if you have been the victim of a scam, while you may regret the memory, there is no shame in admitting it. Tell your elected officials that you want something done about it! Every time you are scammed or attempted to be scammed, email your Congress person and Senator and demand that it be stopped. Please consult the next page, Fight Back! for appropriate contact information.

Scammers are becoming more sophisticated every day. If left unchecked they will use their skills to bring down power grids and other sophisticated systems. The black hats will engage in systems destruction warfare and direct the kill chain against us. To be certain, they are already using technological tricks and mind-manipulation tactics that fool the experts. Even Warren Buffet's company, one of the best investment houses of all time, has been scammed.

In the time it took you to read this book, thousands of people have been victimized – people of all ages, education levels, incomes, genders, and professional backgrounds. Being preyed upon doesn't make you stupid. It makes you human. You're part of a large and growing club of angry victims. Anger at the scamsters is appropriate, as is anger at law enforcement for doing nothing. But know that it's not too late for us to gain the upper hand. Fight back on the next page.

You've taken an important step toward fighting back by reading this book. Pass along what you've learned here to others, and by all means share your own story. The more all of us tell these stories, the more we bring scammers out of the shadows and make it harder for them to strike again.

Good luck.

Appendix A

Fight Back!

Cyber criminality must end.

We must fight back to end it.

Every time an attempt is made on you or your family—whether successful or not—you must report it.

1. Start with Congress. Tell your Senators and Representatives to take action. Now. Demand that this crime wave end. You can find their contact information here:

    - Senators: Senate.gov – On the very top of the page, there is a drop down menu that says "Find Your Senators". Use the drop down to choose your state. You will then be given contact information for your senators.

    - House Representative: House.gov – On the very top of the page, there is a box that says "Find Your Representative" that asks for your zip code. Enter your zip code and the contact information for your representative will be given.

2. Report Cyber Crimes to IC3. They report how many cases occur each year. Their numbers do not provide the complete picture because too many people don't report. Please report! You will be helping everyone.

You can submit a report at: IC3.gov

The Internet Crime Complaint Center (IC3) will thoroughly review and evaluate your complaint and refer it to the appropriate federal, state, local or international law enforcement or regulatory agency that has jurisdiction over the matter. IC3 is a partnership between the Federal Bureau of Investigation and the National White Collar Crime Center (funded, in part, by the Department of Justice's Bureau of Justice Assistance).

3. Report to the Federal Trade Commission (FTC) at IdentityTheft. gov. Don't google this name. Some links take you to the wrong place. If you want to keep a copy of your report print it straight away as online availability is limited.

4. File with your State Authorities.

- To find your Attorney General: naag.org, click "Who's my Attorney General" at the top of the page. They are then listed alphabetically by state.

- To find your state's consumer protection office: usa.gov/state-consumer – Use the drop down menu to find your state's contact information.

5. For utility fraud: Contact your state utility commission at: naruc. org/about-naruc/regulatory-commissions. You can also contact the National Consumer Telecom & Utilities Exchange at nctue.com to get a copy of your disclosure report. This is sort of a utilities credit report. You can check to see if accounts that are not yours have been reported in your name.

6. File a local police report. Most areas have an online reporting option. Please let us know if your local police department does anything.

7. Report unwanted calls or texts, including illegal and spoofed robocalls, at ConsumerComplaints.fcc.gov.

It is imperative that you report every problem or attempted scam to Congress and the IC3. Demand that action be taken. Demand that criminals be prosecuted for your future personal security and our country's security.

Appendix B

Suicide and Cyber Criminality

By Ted Sutton and Will Boyden

The shame and embarrassment from scams and stolen identities is not fully understood. Citizens lose billions of dollars to cyber criminals. But money is not the only troubling benchmark.

The true immorality of these crimes - the number of resulting suicides - is not measured.

There is only anecdotal evidence pointing to the ultimate in human suffering.

Albert Poland Jr., a man who suffered from Alzheimer's and dementia, was constantly targeted by Jamaican telephone scammers. "At age 81, his mind was faltering," reported Wayne Drash in a 2015 CNN article. The scammers used this to their advantage, telling Poland that he had won the jackpot in a lottery, worth millions of dollars. But first, he would have to pay the $1,500 he owed to the IRS. Poland did so. Of course, the money went to the scammers. The calls continued, sometimes reaching 50 a day. Some days his mind was better than others and he would catch their tricks. Other days, forgetful of what happened in the past, Poland would send over more money. Over the course of this devious scam, Poland forwarded over $5,000 to the Jamaican scammers. Then one spring morning, as his wife was getting ready for church, Poland decided to stay home. "He walked to the basement of the family home. He carried with him a snub-nose .38 revolver," wrote Drash. Poland left a suicide note for his family hoping that his $2 million prize would come and prove to his family members that he had done the right thing. The money never came.

The Identity Theft Resource Center (ITRC) conducts research on people who have had their identity stolen. Their study, "Identity Theft: The

Aftermath 2017," reveals disturbing statistics on the emotional impacts from scams. After respondents had their identity stolen, 67% had anxiety, 53% felt a sense of powerlessness or helplessness, and 31% experienced overwhelming sadness. Importantly, the ITRC's study revealed that 7% of respondents felt suicidal. How many actually committed suicide is not reported.

Adam Levin, founder of CyberScout and co-founder of Credit.com, gave his insight on this widening problem. "People have to pause and realize," said Levin, "that you are one click away from becoming a statistic." That statistic may involve suicide.

Army veteran Jared Johns killed himself after being scammed. Two inmates at Lee Correctional Institution pretended to be parents of a 17 year old girl and claimed she had sent illicit photos to Johns. The inmates tried to get $1,189 out of Johns so they would stay quiet about this event. "Jared Johns, 24, suffered from post-traumatic stress disorder after serving in Afghanistan, and the condition left him unable to cope with the threats that he received in the moments leading to his suicide," wrote Kirk Brown in a 2019 USA Today article. Scammers will exploit their victims to death. After the suicide, Johns' father said of the criminals, "I feel like they're the ones who shot him."

In July of 2019, the U.S. Senate Special Committee on Aging reported another scam resulting in a suicide. Marjorie Jones, an 82 year old woman, fell for the same trick as Albert Poland. Jones was told over the phone that she had won a major cash prize. All she had to do was pay some taxes and fees. Frantically, she tried to gather $6,000 from her family. When she eventually got the money, Jones handed it over to the scammers, and never heard back from them. One week later, Jones killed herself. When her family looked into this, they realized that Jones had given away not only the $6,000, but also all of her life savings.

In her testimony before the Senate Aging Committee, the grand-daughter of Marjorie Jones stated, "We also discovered, not only did they drain her of all the money it took her a lifetime to save, but that she had taken out a reverse mortgage on her home and she cashed out all of her life insurance. She died with $69 in her bank account." During the hearing,

Senator Susan Collins noted that Americans received over 48 billion unwanted robocalls in 2018. Sadly, Jones was one of these Americans. "It is clear to us that the circumstances that led to her death were caused by these criminals. She was robbed in every sense," the granddaughter added.

While there is no accurate estimate of how many people kill themselves after being scammed, it is clear that identity theft, fraud, and scams are emotionally devastating to many victims. The best way to prepare for these events is to understand what they look like.

Scammers gain your trust, use your fear of missing out and make you feel as if you must act quickly, all in an effort to take advantage of you. Dr. Stacey Wood, a professor of psychology at Scripps College, states, "What research has shown on this issue is that humans are better liars than lie-detectors." It is clear then why so many fall for scams. At the same time, some people tend to be more easily tricked. Once someone falls for a scam, they have a mark on their back to be targeted again in the future. "Once you are on the hook," said Wood, "it's really difficult to disentangle yourself."

The only way out for some is the most extreme exit. People are losing their lives because they cannot live with the pain of being scammed. This horror is silently spreading across the United States. As mentioned, the ITRC reports that 7% of the surveyed people feel suicidal after having their identity stolen. And so it must be asked again: How many victims actually kill themselves?

We don't know. We should know.

Scams and identity theft have more than a financial impact. The emotional impact can be far worse. A national database would shed more light on this important data point.

What can you do right now?

Be on the lookout for changes in the most vulnerable. Elderly parents and friends, for example, are most frequently targeted. Talk to them. Scammers tell them to keep everything a secret. You may have to draw it out.

According to Adam Levin, after death and taxes, being scammed is the third guarantee in life. In the face of this inevitability, your helping hand may be a matter of life or death.

Ted Sutton attends the University of Wyoming College of Law. Will Boyden studies business at Gonzaga University.

Index

About the Author

Garrett Sutton, Esq., is the bestselling author of *Start Your Own Corporation, Run Your Own Corporation, The ABC's of Getting Out of Debt, Writing Winning Business Plans, Buying and Selling a Business* and *The Loopholes of Real Estate* in Robert Kiyosaki's Rich Dad's Advisors series. Garrett has over thirty years' experience in assisting individuals and businesses to determine their appropriate corporate structure, limit their liability,  protect their assets and advance their financial, personal and credit success goals.

Garrett and his law firm, Sutton Law Center, have offices in Reno, Nevada, and Jackson Hole, Wyoming. The firm represents many corporations, limited liability companies, limited partnerships and individuals in their real estate and business-related law matters, including incorporations, contracts, and ongoing business-related legal advice. The firm continues to accept new clients.

Garrett is also the owner of Corporate Direct, which since 1988 has provided affordable asset protection and corporate formation services. He is the author of *How to Use Limited Liability Companies and Limited Partnerships*, which further educates readers on the proper use of entities. Along with credit expert Gerri Detweiler, Garrett co-authored *Finance Your Own Business* and also assists entrepreneurs build business credit. Please see CorporateDirect.com for more information.

Garrett attended Colorado College and the University of California at Berkeley, where he received a B.S. in Business Administration in 1975. He graduated with a J.D. in 1978 from Hastings College of Law, the University of California's law school in San Francisco. He practiced law in San Francisco and Washington, D.C. before moving to Reno and the proximity of Lake Tahoe.

Garrett is a member of the State Bar of Nevada, the State Bar of California, and the American Bar Association. He has written numerous professional articles and has served on the Publication Committee of the State Bar of Nevada. He has appeared in the *Wall Street Journal, The New York Times* and other publications.

Garrett enjoys speaking with entrepreneurs and real estate investors on the advantages of forming business entities. He is a frequent lecturer for small business groups as well as the Rich Dad's Advisors series.

Garrett serves on the boards of the American Baseball Foundation, located in Birmingham, Alabama, and the Sierra Kids Foundation and Nevada Museum of Art, both based in Reno.

For more information on Garrett Sutton and Sutton Law Center, please visit his Web sites at www.CorporateDirect.com and www.Sutlaw.com.

Best-Selling Books in the
Rich Dad Advisors Series

BY BLAIR SINGER

Sales Dogs
You Don't Have to Be an Attack Dog to Explode Your Income

Team Code of Honor
The Secrets of Champions in Business and in Life

Summit Leadership
Taking Your Team to the Top

BY GARRETT SUTTON, ESQ.

Start Your Own Corporation
Why the Rich Own their Own Companies and Everyone Else Works for Them

Writing Winning Business Plans
How to Prepare a Business Plan that Investors will Want to Read and Invest In

Buying and Selling a Business
How You Can Win in the Business Quadrant

The ABCs of Getting Out of Debt
Turn Bad Debt into Good Debt and Bad Credit into Good Credit

Run Your Own Corporation
How to Legally Operate and Properly Maintain Your Company into the Future

The Loopholes of Real Estate
Secrets of Successful Real Estate Investing

Scam-Proof Your Assets
Guarding Against Widespread Deception

Piercing the Veil
When LLCs and Corporations Fail

BY KEN MCELROY

The ABCs of Real Estate Investing
The Secrets of Finding Hidden Profits Most Investors Miss

The ABCs of Property Management
What You Need to Know to Maximize Your Money Now

The Advanced Guide to Real Estate Investing
How to Identify the Hottest Markets and Secure the Best Deals

ABCs of Buying Rental Property
How You Can Achieve Financial Freedom in Five Years